DIOSCORUS OF APHRODITO

The Transformation of the Classical Heritage

Peter Brown, General Editor

I   *Art and Ceremony in Late Antiquity*, by Sabine G. MacCormack

II   *Synesius of Cyrene: Philosopher-Bishop*, by Jay Alan Bregman

III   *Theodosian Empresses: Women and Imperial Dominion in Late Antiquity*, by Kenneth G. Holum

IV   *John Chrysostom and the Jews: Rhetoric and Reality in the Late Fourth Century*, by Robert L. Wilken

V   *Biography in Late Antiquity: The Quest for the Holy Man*, by Patricia Cox

VI   *Pachomius: The Making of a Community in Fourth-Century Egypt*, by Philip Rousseau

VII   *Change in Byzantine Culture in the Eleventh and Twelfth Centuries*, by A. P. Kazhdan and Ann Wharton Epstein

VIII   *Leadership and Community: The Transformation of Late Antique Gaul*, by Raymond Van Dam

IX   *Homer the Theologian: Neoplatonist Allegorical Reading and the Growth of the Epic Tradition*, by Robert Lamberton

X   *Procopius and the Sixth Century*, by Averil Cameron

XI   *Guardians of Language: The Grammarian and Society in Late Antiquity*, by Robert A. Kaster

XII   *Civic Coins and Civic Politics in the Roman East, 180–275 A.D.*, by Kenneth W. Harl

XIII   *Holy Women of the Syrian Orient*, Introduced and Translated by Sebastian P. Brock and Susan Ashbrook Harvey

XIV   *Gregory the Great: Perfection in Imperfection*, by Carole E. Straw

XV   Apex Omnium: *Religion in the* Res gestae *of Ammianus*, by R. L. Rike

XVI   *Dioscorus of Aphrodito: His Work and His World*, by Leslie S. B. MacCoull

LESLIE S. B. MAC COULL

DIOSCORUS
OF APHRODITO

HIS WORK AND HIS WORLD

UNIVERSITY OF CALIFORNIA PRESS
Berkeley • Los Angeles • London

University of California Press
Berkeley and Los Angeles, California
University of California Press, Ltd.
London, England
© 1988 by
The Regents of the University of California
Printed in the United States of America
1 2 3 4 5 6 7 8 9

Library of Congress Cataloging-in-Publication Data
MacCoull, Leslie S. B.
　　Dioscorus of Aphrodito.
　　(The Transformation of the classical heritage ; 16)
　　Bibliography: p.
　　Includes index.
　　1. Dioscorus, of Aphrodito. 2. Poets, Greek—Egypt—
Biography. 3. Lawyers—Egypt—Biography. 4. Manuscripts,
Greek (Papyri). 5. Manuscripts, Coptic (Papyri).
6. Aphroditopolis (Ancient city)—Antiquities.
7. Egypt—Antiquities. I. Title. II. Series.
PA3968.D62Z78　1988　　884'.01 [B]　　87-30135

ACLS Humanities E-Book edition 2013
ISBN: 978-1-59740-978-0
HEB08397.0001.001

FOR MIRRIT

Dir gewidmet ist mein Leben:
deine Liebe sei mein Lohn.

Haydn, *The Creation*, No. 32

CONTENTS

List of Plates   ix

Acknowledgments   xi

Abbreviations   xiii

Preface   xv

I · SOURCES AND LIFE   1

The Papyri   2

The Place   5

The Career   9

II · THE GREEK AND COPTIC DOCUMENTS   16

Major Works Preserved in Coptic   36

From Antinoë Back to Aphrodito, 570–573 and After   47

III · THE GREEK POEMS   57

IV · THE CULTURE OF DIOSCORUS   147

Appendix: Chronology   161

Bibliography   163

Index of Sources   169

General Index   173

Plates   175

PLATES

following page 174

1. The region of Aphrodito
2. Aphrodito (Kom Ishgaw) in 1980
3. Canal outside Aphrodito
4. The Coptic church at Kom Ishgaw
5. *P. Cair. Masp.* II 67177
6. *P. Cair. Masp.* I 67097, top
7. *P. Cair. Masp.* I 67120
8. *P. Cair. Masp.* I 67097, below
9. *P. Cair. Masp.* II 67182
10. Detail of *P. Cair. Masp.* III 67353r (Coptic)
11. *P. Cair. Masp.* III 67315

Plates 2–4: photographs by the author
Plates 1, 5–11: photographs courtesy of the Egyptian Museum, Cairo

ϯⲉⲟⲟⲩ

ACKNOWLEDGMENTS

I should like to express my thanks to the following institutions and people who have helped me during the nineteen years of work that went into this book: The American Research Center in Egypt; the American School of Classical Studies at Athens; the Beinecke Rare Book and Manuscript Library, Yale University; the British Library; the British School at Athens; the Institute of Christian Oriental Research and the Department of Semitic and Egyptian Languages and Literatures, Catholic University; Collège de la Sainte Famille (Pères Jésuites), Cairo; Columbia University; the Coptic Museum; the Deutsches Archäologisches Institut, Cairo; Duke University (Perkins Library and the Divinity School Library); the Dumbarton Oaks Center for Byzantine Studies, where I began my research and where much of the writing was done; the Egyptian Museum; the Franciscan Center for Christian Oriental Studies, Cairo; the French and Italian Archaeological Institutes at Athens; the Griffith Institute, Oxford; the Institut français d'Archéologie orientale, Cairo; the Library of Congress; the Österreichische Nationalbibliothek (Papyrussammlung); the Papyrussammlung, Staatliche Museen, Berlin (DDR); the Pierpont Morgan Library; the Pontifical Institute of Oriental Studies at Rome; the Society for Coptic Archaeology; and Trinity College, University of Toronto.

Levon Avdoyan, Roger Bagnall, Robert Bagnall, the late Paulinus Bellet, Monica Blanchard, Sebastian Brock, Francis Campbell, Florence Friedman, Jean Gascou, Francis Gignac, Sidney Griffith, Peter Grossmann, Ann Hanson and the late Arthur Hanson, Deborah Hobson, Susan Finan Ikenberry, Patrick Jacobson, James Keenan, Craig Korr, Enrico Livrea, Helene Loebenstein, Cyril Mango and Marlia Mundell Mango, Robert Markus, Elizabeth McVey, Kathleen McVey, Stephen Morse, Robert

Murray, John Oates, Lucia Papini, Thomas Pattie, the late Bernard Peebles, Lee Perkins, Rosario Pintaudi, Günter Poethke, Linda Collins Reilly, Kent Rigsby, Georgina Robinson, Cornelia Römer, P. J. Sijpesteijn, Emanuel Silver, the late Msgr. Patrick Skehan, Kenneth Snipes, Robert Taft, Janet Timbie, Claudia Vess, Gary Vikan, Guy Wagner, Claude Wehrli, the late Hans-Julius Wolff, and Klaas Worp.

I am grateful to the Göttingen Academy of Sciences, and to Professor Dr. Ernst Heitsch, now of Regensburg, for permission to reproduce the Greek texts in E. Heitsch, *Die griechischen Dichterfragmente der römischen Kaiserzeit* I–II (Abh.d.Akad.d.Wiss. in Göttingen, phil.-hist. Kl., 3.Folge, Nr. 49 & 58) (Göttingen 1961–1964).

I should like also to honor the memory of the late David Crawford, my predecessor in Cairene papyrology, who was martyred in 1952.

This book belongs in a special way to four people: Elliott Chapin, Maxwell Vos, Peter Brown, and Mirrit Boutros Ghali. "Work is love made visible." By now it will be clear to the person to whom this book is dedicated *(do ut des)* that it is scholarship and not money, kinship, or power that assures the perpetuation of a people's heritage. Where his treasure is, there will his heart be also. It is time for him to come home.

Washington & Cairo
May 1988

ABBREVIATIONS

Abbreviations for papyri follow the forms established in J. F. Oates, R. S. Bagnall, W. H. Willis, and K. A. Worp, *Checklist of editions of Greek papyri and ostraca*, 3rd ed. (Greek papyri) and A. A. Schiller, "Checklist of Coptic documents and letters," *Bulletin of the American Society of Papyrologists* 13 (1976) 99–123 (Coptic papyri). Other abbreviations used in this work are given below.

ACO	*Acta Conciliorum Oecumenicorum*
AKM	*Abhandlungen zur Kunde des Morgenlandes*
ARCE	*American Research Center in Egypt*
ASAE	*Annales du Service des Antiquités d'Egypte*
ASP	*American Studies in Papyrology*
BES	*Bulletin of the Egyptological Seminar*
BIFAO	*Bulletin de l'Institut français d'archéologie orientale*
BKT	*Berliner Klassikertexte*
BSC	*Byzantine Studies Conference*
Byz Sorb	*Byzantina Sorbonensia*
CAG	*Commentaria in Aristotelem Graeca*
CSBE	R. S. Bagnall and K. A. Worp, *The Chronological Systems of Byzantine Egypt* (Zutphen 1978)
CSCO	*Corpus Scriptorum Christianorum Orientalium*
DACL	*Dictionnaire d'archéologie chrétienne et de liturgie*
GLECS	*Groupe linguistique des études chamito-sémitiques*
NHS	*Nag Hammadi Studies*

Abbreviations

OLP	*Orientalia Lovaniensia Periodica*
Pap.Brux.	*Papyrologica Bruxellensia*
Pap.Castr.	*Papyrologica Castroctaviana*
PG	*Patrologia Graeca*
PLRE	*Prosopography of the Later Roman Empire*
PO	*Patrologia Orientalis*
SC	*Sources chrétiennes*
Stud Hell	*Studia Hellenistica*
SH	*Subsidia Hagiographica*
SOCC	*Studia Orientalia Christiana Collectanea*
ZDMG	*Zeitschrift der Deutschen Morgenländischen Gesellschaft*
ZSS	*Zeitschrift der Savigny-Stiftung für Rechtsgeschichte*

PREFACE

On n'écrit un livre
qu'avec la joie.
Fernand Braudel

It is just over a hundred years since Huysmans's des Esseintes led readers of the "decadence" on what would now be called a trip through the sensibility of Late Antiquity. And it is sixty years since Helen Waddell's singing prose made people begin to be aware that the classics did not come to an end with the age of the Antonines. I am lucky to have come of age as a scholar just at the time when the period after A.D. 284 began to come into its own.

During the past fifteen to twenty years there has been what may well be termed a paradigm shift in scholarly perception of the period A.D. 300–700. "Late Antique" people now have a "local habitation and a name," in Coptic a *ma-n-shōpe*, a 'place to be'. This was not the case in the early days of papyrology. As E. Wipszycka has written, "Quant aux textes byzantins, avec leur écriture de type déjà médiéval et truffée d'abréviations, avec leurs innovations linguistiques et leur orthographe souvent fantaisiste, ils éveillaient en eux [les premières générations de papyrologues] une répugnance instinctive."[1] I have been struck by the persistence of these older judgments since I began working on Dioscorus nineteen years ago.

The pioneers, Jean Maspero and Sir Harold Idris Bell, the first ever to read Dioscorus's papers, were repelled by what they were working on, and

---

1. E. Wipszycka, "Le degré d'alphabétisation en Egypte byzantine," *Rev.Et.Aug.* 30 (1984) 282.

their distaste shudders from the pages of their editions. Bell wrote: "his personality, as revealed in the documents he has left us, certainly does not inspire respect, and his verses indubitably merit damnation; . . . his verses, if infamous as literature, are at least of interest as illustrating the morass of absurdity into which the great river of Greek poetry emptied itself."[2] Maspero wrote: "Le style est flou, les expressions inadéquates à l'idée, la construction grammaticale souvent insaisissable. . . . Les idées y sont nulles, l'invention en est tout à fait absente. . . . Les concetti de mauvais goût, les jeux de mots de bel esprit provincial. . . . Ce jargon grotesque . . . avec ses platitudes boursouflées et ses bizarreries de décadent."[3] Even J. G. Milne wrote: "At no moment has he any real control of thought, diction, grammar, metre, or meaning."[4] It is time to go back and read, with the resources of contemporary Late Antique scholarship, what actually stands on the surface of the papyri, instead of repeating the textbook caricatures of another age.

This task is begun. My teacher, and the teacher of so many of North America's papyrologists, the late C. Bradford Welles of Yale University, impressed upon all of his students the necessity of assessing the ancient world on its own terms by using primary sources.[5] Thanks to the work of Roger Bagnall, Klaas Worp, Jean Gascou, and James Keenan, among others, we are seeing the start of a rebirth of "Byzantine" (i.e., post-A.D. 300) papyrology. Without the help and *amicitia papyrologorum* of these colleagues, I would have worked in fruitless isolation. Instead, cooperative research in many disciplines has begun to create a sound basis for understanding the society of Byzantine-Coptic Egypt.

In an era in which one's very subject matter can be proclaimed subversive, in which it is no longer politically permitted to make discoveries in certain fields on their native turf, it is urgent that whatever remains of the culture of Christian Egypt be studied while it still exists. The change from forty or fifty years ago, when Bradford Welles and Pierre Jouguet did their work and then chatted about it in Groppi's, when the tables of contents of periodicals were filled with new Coptic finds, is frightening and sad. Lefebvre's boxes of Coptic papyri have been allowed to disappear. We must call attention to the threatened state of our field. To quote the late Benedict Nicolson, "tact and urbanity are the enemies of scholarship."

---

2. H. I. Bell and W. E. Crum, "A Greek-Coptic glossary," *Aegyptus* 6 (1925) 177.

3. J. Maspero, "Un dernier poète grec de l'Egypte, Dioscore, fils d'Apollos," *REG* 24 (1911) 427, 469, 470, 472. The number of times in *P.Cair.Masp.* he cannot resist putting the word "poète" into inverted commas is disconcerting.

4. In *P.Lit.Lond.* (1927) 68.

5. Compare A. E. Samuel's preface to his *From Athens to Alexandria* (Louvain 1983).

The work and the world of Dioscorus present their own coherence, the coherence of a world that loved life and that died an inexplicable death. Dioscorus wrote, in prose and verse, of a world of visible hierarchy and celebration: of Sirius rising to bring the inundation, of pageant and symbolic action, of Dionysos and his train in the fields, of the Parousia of Christ and of the finger of God writing on the imperishable tablets the name of the poet's friend. Working as he did at the meeting place of law and poetry, he knew that

> einzig das Lied überm Land
> heiligt und feiert.

· I ·

SOURCES AND LIFE

*Dioscorus does not always
make sense to us moderns.*
C. Bradford Welles

On a July day in 551, a leading citizen of Aphrodito, a city of Middle Egypt, stood in the office of Palladius, the count of the sacred consistory, in Constantinople. With him were three officers of his civic delegation, including a representative acting for one Shenoute, sometimes identified as his brother. Dioscorus, former *protocometes* or headman of Aphrodito and descendant of its leading family, was following in the footsteps of his father Apollos, who ten years before had come to the capital to defend Aphrodito's right of independent tax collection *(autopragia)*. Conditions at home had since become worse, and it lay with Dioscorus and his fellow *syntelestai* (contributors) to put them right.

What in fact brought these people, townsmen of a provincial town, to a capital where their countrymen, the Apions, had already spectacularly made their mark? The right of citizens to appeal to the emperor; the awareness that the complexities of culture and faith that preoccupied them were unavoidably bound up with what happened in New Rome; a basic problem of both livelihood and status that needed to be resolved.

Concentrating on an individual, rather than a collectivity or a problem, is perhaps unfashionable; however, the accident of physical survival has preserved for us the personal papers of this individual, Dioscorus of Aphrodito, with a completeness unparalleled in the ancient world. We know the scope of his interests, literary and financial; what he noticed in

his surroundings; the shape of his mind.[1] We can even read his immediate
thoughts in the form of the rough drafts of his poetry, written on the backs
of legal documents from his office. He is uniquely representative of that
Late Antique culture flourishing in Egypt from ca. 400 to 641 and after—a
figure in a coherent cultural landscape.[2] The history of that culture is not
yet written, but Dioscorus's life provides a door into that world.

THE PAPYRI

In 1901, during the reign of Khedive Abbas Hilmy and the proconsular
administration of Lord Cromer, some villagers in Kom Ishgaw were digging a well. Their Upper Egyptian village lay on the left (west) bank of the
Nile, four hundred miles south of Alexandria, south of the sizable and half-
Christian city of Assiut, north of what had been Shenoute's White Monastery at Sohag. As so often happens in Egypt when digging is done, they
found not water but antiquities: in this case papyri, masses of them, the
bundled tax archives of a city. Someone called the police, but before
anyone in authority could arrive, many of the papyri had been burned by
villagers anxious not to be caught with the goods.[3] The surviving papyri
were dispersed through middlemen and dealers, most to find their way to
the British Museum and the University of Heidelberg. The science of
papyrology was young then, and no scholar had ever seen anything like
these voluminous tax codices written in thin, elegant, almost minuscule
hands. Bell[4] in England and Becker[5] in Germany identified them as the
records kept by Greek and Coptic scribes under the eighth-century Arab
administration of a town called Aphrodito.[6]

1. The earlier surveys of Dioscoriana, unsympathetic to say the least, by J. Maspero,
"Un dernier poète grec de l'Egypte, Dioscore, fils d'Apollos," *REG* 24 (1911) 426–482 and H.
I. Bell, "An Egyptian village in the age of Justinian," *JHS* 64 (1944) 21–36, have been
superseded. For general treatments, see now J. G. Keenan, "The Aphrodite papyri and
village life in Byzantine Egypt," *BSAC* 26 (1984) 51–63; and L. S. B. MacCoull, "Dioscorus
and the dukes: aspects of Coptic Hellenism in the sixth century," *BS/EB* 14 (1988).
2. The words are those of A. Grafton, *Joseph Scaliger* (Oxford 1983) 229.
3. J. Quibell, "Kom Ishgaw," *ASAE* (1902) 85–88; Keenan, "The Aphrodite papyri," pp.
51–63. On how the "pipeline" has always worked, cf. J. M. Robinson, "The discovering and
marketing of Coptic manuscripts," in *The roots of Egyptian Christianity*, ed. B. Pearson and J.
Goehring (Philadelphia 1986) 2–25.
4. H. I. Bell, "The Aphrodito papyri," *JHS* 28 (1908) 97–120.
5. C. H. Becker, "Arabische Papyri des Aphroditofundes," *Z.Assyriol.* 20 (1906) 68–104;
cf. idem, "Historische Studien über das Londoner Aphroditowerk," *Der Islam* 2 (1911) 359–
371.
6. The major publications are *P.Lond.* IV (1910) and *P.Schott-Reinhardt* (1906).

Four years later, in 1905, matters repeated themselves, again by sheer chance. During house-building operations in Kom Ishgaw, the mudbrick wall of an old house collapsed, revealing deep foundations that had covered over yet another massed find of papyri. The local grapevine alerted Gustave Lefebvre, the inspector of antiquities, who hurried to the spot.[7] A few acts of destruction similar to the earlier burning had taken place, but this time most of the papyri were dispersed to dealers, and thence worldwide from Imperial Russia to the American Midwest,[8] to libraries eager to participate in the new rebirth of Greek literature made possible by papyri. Among the papyri there was indeed a text of Menander;[9] but the body of the find consisted of the private and public papers of the sixth-century owner of that text, the lawyer and poet who would become known as Dioscorus of Aphrodito.[10]

The papyri that Lefebvre managed to keep from middlemen and traffickers he brought to the Museum at Cairo (then at Boulaq). He went back to Kom Ishgaw twice more, in 1906 and 1907, and succeeded in finding more sixth-century papyri on the site of the original find. A few had been bought by a M. Beaugé, of the railway inspectorate at Assiut. These documents also were brought safely to Cairo, and the whole lot was assigned to the editorship of Jean Maspero, a young classical scholar and son of the head of the Antiquities Service, Gaston Maspero. Before his death in battle in 1915, Jean Maspero managed to produce the three pioneering volumes of *Papyrus grecs d'époque byzantine*, of which the first was published in 1911. Together with Bell's 1917 edition of the sixth-century Aphrodito

7. J. Maspero, "Etudes sur les papyrus d'Aphrodité," *BIFAO* 6 (1908) 75–120, 7 (1909) 47–102, 8 (1910) 97–152; cf. his preface to *P.Cair.Masp.* I (1911). Because the eighth-century papyri were the first from the site to become known, the form found in those later documents, "Aphrodito," with a Greek omega, first found its way into the scholarly literature. As the sixth-century documents from the second find began to be read, the form "Aphroditēs komē" from the earlier period came to be known. But although the form Aphrodito is, strictly speaking, a retro-usage from the Arab period, it is more common in writings about the site, and Dioscorus is universally known as "Dioscorus of Aphrodito." In one way it would be more accurate always to refer to the sixth-century city as Aphrodite, as some scholars do at present. But in this work I have kept the old familiar form.

8. See G. Malz, "Papyri of Dioscorus: publications and emendations," *Studi Calderini-Paribeni* 2 (Milan 1957) 345–356; add Hamburg, Vienna, the Vatican, and Ann Arbor to her list.

9. Photoreproduction, L. Koenen et al., *The Cairo codex of Menander* (London 1978).

10. The find made earlier (in 1902) thus contained material of later date (eighth century, as above, n. 7); the later find (in 1905, 1906, and 1907) contained material of earlier date (sixth century), namely, the Dioscorus papers. It is the material from the second Aphrodito find with which this book deals. No oldest inhabitant of Kom Ishgaw in the 1980s remembers from childhood anything his parents or grandparents might have related about the original findspots of the papyri; I was unable to trace either one.

papyri that had been acquired by the British Museum (*P.Lond.* V), and Vitelli's 1915 edition of those bought by the University of Florence (*P.Flor.* III), these texts constitute the bulk of what we know as the Dioscorus archive of sixth-century Aphrodito, the city that lay under Kom Ishgaw.

Our evidence for the life, work, and world of Dioscorus thus comes from one find (over time) from one place, in preservation widely dispersed, yet in intention forming a unity. The papers kept during a single human lifetime that spanned much of the sixth century reveal the background, activities, and interests of the person who chose to keep them. Numerous discoveries of Byzantine Egyptian remains at sites all along the Nile Valley, from the Fayum to Syene (Aswan), provide a perspective on the period broader than could be obtained from the archives of just one individual in one city. Most of these discoveries were made in the late nineteenth century and the first half of the twentieth century, when the political climate still allowed exploration in the field of what was once Christian Egypt. Dioscorus can thus be placed in the wider context of his land and his times, on the basis of evidence that, though for the most part long known,[11] remains underutilized. Because we meet him firsthand in his own words, the single figure of Dioscorus of Aphrodito as seen in and through his archive remains the most accessible introduction to the *moeurs* and the *mentalités* of sixth-century Egypt.

The paperwork surviving from Byzantine Aphrodito falls into numerous categories, both public and private. Of the public documents we have petitions, depositions before officials, proclamations and edicts ($\pi\rho o\sigma\tau\acute{a}\gamma$-$\mu\alpha\tau\alpha$, $\kappa\epsilon\lambda\epsilon\acute{u}\sigma\epsilon\iota\varsigma$), and records of proceedings; land cadasters and orders for their remaking; fiscal receipts, orders for payment, accounts, and documents of surety. From the private sphere there are accounts, inventories, sales, cessions, donations, heritable leases; leases of land, buildings, and movable goods; pledges, loans, acknowledgments of debt, and sales on delivery; receipts; marriages, divorces, wills, settlements, dispositions of estates; and letters, both public and private. (This classification is taken from Jean Gascou's ongoing project for a guide to the Aphrodito archives.) Such a totality and richness of material is unknown to historians of other provinces of the later Roman Empire, where climate has not preserved these witnesses to the day-to-day workings of society. Thanks to the papyri, the society of Aphrodito and the life of its leading citizen can be

11. Papyri from clandestine native diggings at Kom Ishgaw in the late 1930s are just beginning to be known: see L. S. B. MacCoull, "Missing pieces of the Dioscorus archive," *Eleventh BSC Abstracts* (Toronto 1985) 30.

observed directly and in illuminating detail. At intervals over a period of six years, the present writer has worked at first hand with all of the Dioscorus papyri in Cairo.[12] After struggling with the difficult conditions, bad state of preservation, and frustrating logistics of this *depot*, one sees the realities of Dioscorus's world in an even sharper light.

THE PLACE

Aphrodito stands on a hill.[13] Unusual among Egyptian sites, which more often lie below the present ground level, the modern village of Kom Ishgaw perches atop a tell that must conceal remains of the Byzantine and Umayyad city (see Figure 2). Aphrodito has never been scientifically explored.[14] The papyrus finds were made by accident, and Quibell and Lefebvre simply looked around the papyrus findspots to gather what they could in the way of artifacts—only a few carvings of wood and bone; the late period was of little interest at the beginning of this century. We do not know what Dioscorus's house or the Apa Apollos monastery looked like. Until, in some better future, field archaeologists have found the physical remains of the Byzantine/Coptic environment, we can try to reconstruct the city of Dioscorus from the documents, and view it in its own landscape.

Kom Ishgaw lies amid a network of irrigation canals in the wide cultivated belt west of the Nile's edge (see Figure 3). South of Assiut, the road toward Kom Ishgaw[15] goes by Sidfa with its Uniat school; Tima, largely Christian even today; the Uniat bishopric of Tahta; and Shotep, the ancient Hypselis, where the late sixth-century Coptic exegete Rufus wrote his extensive biblical commentaries.[16] This is a Christian heartland of great antiquity. Some 45 miles to the south is Shenoute's town, Sohag; across the

12. Only now are some of *P.Cair.Masp.* becoming accessible to the outside world through photographs made by the International Photographic Archive of Papyri (IPAP). A reedition, projected by Professor J. G. Keenan, would be most desirable. With the other collections one is more fortunate. Firsthand work in London is uncomplicated, and reproductions from nearly all collections are obtainable to facilitate research on Dioscorus papyri beyond the level of the (often early and unsatisfactory) *editiones principes*.

13. I am grateful to the pastor of St. George's Coptic Orthodox Church at Kom Ishgaw and the staff of the Lillian Trasher Orphanage at Assiut for help in visiting the site in 1980–1981.

14. A survey is planned by Professor J. G. Keenan of Loyola University, Chicago (cf. *ARCE Newsletter*, April 1986).

15. For an amusing older account, see Bell, "An Egyptian village," p. 21.

16. The fragments are now being collected and edited by Dr. Mark Sheridan, O.S.B.

river from that lies the Panopolis (Akhmim) that was the target of Shenoute's attacks on paganism and gnosticism.[17] East of these twin cities, up the river's bend, is the Pachomian headquarters of Pbow (near Chenoboskion), where the monastic library once included Homer, the Bible, Menander, and the *Vision of Dorotheos*;[18] in the same vicinity were deposited the texts that have become famous in our own time as the Nag Hammadi Codices. To the north, some 110 miles by river, lie the chief twin cities of Upper Egypt: Hermopolis on the west bank, and Antinoopolis (Antinoë), seat of the Duke of the Thebaid, directly across the Nile on the east. Around Aphrodito itself are the well-documented monastic sites of Bawit, Der Bala'izah, and Wadi Sarga. Dioscorus, the proud son of an elite family, was at home in a landscape of deeply rooted classical and Christian culture. This is the land of the wandering poets and of the founding fathers of the Coptic church.

Dioscorus was, as well, a citizen of no mean city. If buildings and amenities help to define a city, Aphrodito had its share. Its name in Egyptian, (ⲧ-) ⲝⲕⲱⲟⲩ, comes apparently from ⲝⲕⲟ 'to sell' and means Emporium, the area market for the strategically located Antaeopolite nome.[19] Facilities for river traffic that distinguished the town included the wharf where grain for shipment to Constantinople in the *embole* was loaded, and the jetties for the trans-Nile ferries and ordinary riverboats.[20] In town stood the "house of the old man Psimanobet, the ancestor," which may have been the townhouse of the Psimanobet–Dioscorus family, who, true to pattern, divided their time between their country properties and their old headquarters in the town. There were two potteries, and an olive-oil works on Isis Street. Outside the city were a fortified house with a tower, a solar (ἡλιαστήριον), and storerooms; country houses (χωρήματα); a *castrum*; and at least two hospitals (*xenodocheia*), including the one of Dioscorus's family monastery, that of Apa Apollos (*P.Cair.Masp.* I 67096.29). And forming a network round about the city were the lifelines of its food supply, the dikes

17. Dioscorus's kinsman by marriage, Fl. Phoebammon son of Triadelphus, leased land in the nearby area of Phthla that belonged to Shenoute's monastery (*P.Ross.-Georg.* III 48; cf. J. G. Keenan, "Aurelius Phoebammon, son of Triadelphus, a Byzantine Egyptian land entrepreneur," *BASP* 17 [1980] 145–154).

18. J. M. Robinson, "Reconstructing the first Christian monastic library," Smithsonian Institution Libraries lecture, 15 September 1986.

19. Originally the nome town was Antaeopolis (ⲧⲕⲱⲟⲩ), directly across the river. Though the rise of Aphrodito is difficult to document in the papyri (see L. S. B. MacCoull, "The first appearance of Aphrodito in the papyri," *ZPE* 62 [1986] 54), it had left Antaeopolis far behind in importance by the latter part of the reign of Justinian.

20. For the structures and streets of Aphrodito, see A. Calderini, *Dizionario dei nomi geografici e topografici dell'Egitto greco-romano* I.2 (Madrid 1966) 323–325.

and canals; they seem to have changed little, except for Ottoman-period dilapidation and modern metal waterwheels, since Dioscorus's lifetime. Above all, Aphrodito and its surrounding area boasted over thirty churches and nearly forty monasteries, as well as dozens of farmsteads whose names recall original religious or monastic owners or settlers.[21] None remain standing; but in the sixth century this one Byzantine Egyptian city must have gleamed with white limestone and the columns and arches of basilicas along every vista. Religious building was an index of excellence,[22] and Aphrodito was a city of churches (see Figure 4).

Greater Aphrodito was a sizable settlement. Despite the many difficulties of method that beset attempts to estimate its population, from the indices of personal names recorded in published papyri it might be reasonable to posit, for the sixth century, some three thousand tax-paying male heads of household. This would give a population of about fifteen thousand. Its landholdings in the Antaeopolite managed to balance marginality with fertility. Despite difficulties with the weather and the rapacity (attempted or successful) of officials, we know, for example, that for just one assessment of the first quarter of the sixth century there were nearly four thousand arouras (about eleven million square meters) planted in wheat, seventy-two in barley (for beer), and nine in vineyards (*P.Freer* 2 III 26). With yields from tenfold to twentyfold (on sowings of one artaba, thirty to forty liters, per aroura), we would be dealing with a global production of sixty thousand artabas, or four artabas (four hundred pounds) of basic grain foodstuff per person per year. (This, of course, is reckoned for after the *embole* or grain for Constantinople was collected and skimmed

21. Evidence collected in S. Timm, *Das christlich-koptische Ägypten in arabischer Zeit* III (Wiesbaden 1985) 1438–1461, s.v. 'Kom Išqaw.'

22. Cf. M. M. Mango, "Patterns of public and private construction in the cities of the eastern provinces, 4th to 7th century," *XVII intl. Byzantine congress abstracts* (Washington, D.C. 1986) 210 (dealing with Syria for the most part, but a good comparison). Somewhat confusingly, Aphrodito had a "holy catholic church" (i.e., the principal church: cf. W. E. Crum, "A use of the term 'Catholic church,'" *PSBA* 27 [1905] 166–172), a "holy catholic new church," a "holy catholic south church," and "holy catholic churches" of Apa Mousaios and of Apa Romanos, all attested as existing at about the same time. Did these buildings correspond to confessional divisions (i.e., monophysite and dyophysite), though all were styled καθολική, or to parochial divisions by place (the south of the town being separated off)? Indeed, of the dedications of Aphrodito's churches and monasteries, can a sorting into Chalcedonian and non-Chalcedonian be made? Most church dedications are simply typical of Egyptian piety (SS. Menas, Victor, Colluthus, Mark); most monasteries are called after the local founder, except for Our Lady, the Pachomian Sourous, and the Shenoutean Zenobios. It is interesting that, for a period that later historians construe as one in which the confessional lines were so painfully sharply drawn, evidence for this situation does not appear in the documentary sources.

off.) Over and above this quite adequate subsistence level, supplemented by meat from the herds of sheep and honey from the beekeepers, the landlords and *syntelestai* (contributors, or members of the landowners' *koinon*) dealt in surpluses that enabled them, as local *dynatoi*, to support the cultural flowering that distinguishes this period of Egypt's history.

The canal system had only a short distance to lift water from the river, which brought luxury goods and human skills. Even the less productive land was put to work as pasture, looked after by often unruly shepherds[23] who were conscripted as field guards. Although Dioscorus on occasion pleaded poverty, for rhetorical effect, his world was a prosperous one. It seems to have suffered hardly any effects from the sixth-century plague.[24] Trades, professions, the civil service, the military, and the church are abundantly represented.[25] Dioscorus's learning—poetic, rhetorical, legal, and biblical—was undergirded by a thriving material culture; his personal landscape was far from being one of deprivation. And the events of his life can be traced through transactions that reflect every aspect of this rich environment.

Dioscorus was a Coptic *dynatos*,[26] a member of his society's most prominent and privileged group, Alexandria educated,[27] widely traveled, and living halfway between the two districts of the Hermopolite and the Panopolite that were headquarters of classical learning in Egypt. As such, he was far from being the lowbrow Copt too often caricatured by historiography.[28] Rather, he exemplified the kind of local *propriétaire* who supported and made possible the high creativity of Coptic culture. In Alexandria he became familiar with the best of Monophysite and Aristotelian thought (and the anti-Nestorian and the beginnings of anti-Chalcedonian controversies of the period that sparked such work), and had become

23. J. G. Keenan, "Village shepherds and social tension in Byzantine Egypt," *YCS* 28 (1985) 245–259.

24. Cf. G. Casanova, "La peste nella documentazione greca d'Egitto," *Atti XVII congr.intl.papirol.* (Naples 1984) 949–956, esp. 954. Dioscorus's reference in *P.Cair.Masp.* III 67283.9 (of A.D. 547/8) is figurative, not literal.

25. See L. S. B. MacCoull, "Notes on the social structure of late antique Aphrodito," *BSAC* 26 (1984) 65–77.

26. Cf. F. Winckelmann, "Ägypten und Byzanz vor der arabischen Eroberung," *Byzantinoslavica* 40 (1979) 161–182, and idem, "Die Stellung Ägyptens im oströmisch-byzantinischen Reich," in *Graeco-Coptica*, ed. P. Nagel (Halle 1984) 11–35.

27. See L. S. B. MacCoull, "Dioscorus of Aphrodito and John Philoponus," *Studia Patristica* 18 (Kalamazoo 1987) I.163–168.

28. Still repeated in D. W. Johnson, "Anti-Chalcedonian polemics in Coptic texts, 451–641," in Pearson and Goehring, *Egyptian Christianity*, 230–233. There is no evidence whatever for a Roman/Byzantine plot to keep the Copts an "underclass."

acquainted with the new *Digest* and *Codex* of Justinian in his student days. He had in his youth lived through the forcible replacement of Patriarch Theodosius by Paul of Tabennisi (from the nearby Pachomian headquarters); for most of his lifetime he would live through a period of vacancy of the non-Chalcedonian patriarchal see, until the accession of Damian in 578. The period of his youth (especially from 531 to 538) witnessed the development of the Monophysite church of Egypt; he would have been aware of the death in Egyptian exile, in 538, of Severus of Antioch, already a culture hero, and of Jacob Baradaeus's journeys in support of non-Chalcedonian clergy. In the imperial capital he visited, Justinian's theological activity would have been evident. And Dioscorus's pride in and indebtedness to his fifth-century predecessors in the craft of poetry are apparent.[29] Present to his mind were the language of Homer and Nonnus, and of Shenoute, the Pachomian corpus, the Apophthegmata, and the Bible with its extensions in liturgy and hagiography. In tracing the events of Dioscorus's life, we are not to lose awareness of the wider world within which that life unfolded.

THE CAREER

We can infer, from the dates in the archive, that Dioscorus was born about A.D. 520. His father was the former *protocometes* (village headman) Apollos, later to become a monk; his grandfather another Dioscorus; his great-grandfather Psimanobet (Coptic for 'the man from the place of geese').[30] From his writings it is obvious that he received the best education in the classics and the law that was available, most probably at Alexandria.[31] True to the Mediterranean paramount value of family, he married and fathered children. And he embarked upon the sort of legal and administrative career only to be expected of the scion of Aphrodito's first family.

29. As is his combining this craft with the life of a public man of affairs. If the epithalamium in *P.Ryl.* I 17 dates to the fourth century (Hermopolite), its technique foreshadows that of Dioscorus in his own wedding poems; if the address to the Nile in *PSI* VII 845 dates to the sixth century (provenance unknown), it would be interesting to know its *Sitz im Leben* (is the anti-women tone the result of some particular local social problem?). Could the encomium in *P.Flor.* II (Heitsch 36), with its Heracles figure that was to be so familiar to Dioscorus, be by Pamprepius of Panopolis (see Chapter 3)?

30. Or "the gooseherd."

31. Cf. the discussion of his educational background in MacCoull, 'Dioscorus of Aphrodito and John Philoponus," pp. 163–168.

The first dated document from Dioscorus's archive, *P.Cair.Masp.* I 67087 of 28.xii.543, shows him involved in a case at law concerning damage to a field, before one Colluthus, *boethos* of the court at Antaeopolis, the former nome capital.[32] Dioscorus was successful in getting the *defensor* to fill out a deposition. His title is already Flavius (the higher rank), as was that of his father (who had formerly been an Aurelius, the lower rank).[33] In the following year Aurelius Apollos, son of Hermauos, sold him wool for one-third solidus, payable on delivery (*P.Cair.Masp.* II 67127). In 546 he made a loan to two Aphroditan farmers (P.Eg.Mus.inv.S.R. 3733 A6r). In 547 he leased land to a priest and his brother (*P.Cair.Masp.* I 67108), and cosigned the transfer of land tax in a document in which the priest Jeremiah son of Psates ceded land to him (just under two arouras of sown land, plus reed-growing land and wooded land: *P.Cair.Masp.* I 67118 of October 547). On 27 August of the same year, as *protocometes*, he leased one aroura to the deacon Psais, son of Besios and Tasais (*P.Cair.Masp.* II 67128). Altogether the usual sort of activity for the young squire-jurist.[34]

The year of 547/8, an eleventh indiction (cf. poem H6 in Chapter 3), was a troubled year for Aphrodito. The inhabitants petitioned Justinian (*P.Cair.Masp.* I 67109v) and Theodora (*P.Cair.Masp.* III 67283) for protection of their right of *autopragia,* independent tax collection, against the rapacity of the pagarch of Antaeopolis. Dioscorus's tenant Aur. Psaios was remitted part of the rent he owed (ten artabas of grain) for the coming twelfth indiction (*P.Cair.Masp.* I 67095, 1.iv.548), while Dioscorus leased one aroura to the weaver Victor for flax planting (*P.Cair.Masp.* I 67116). Again in 549 (14.viii) he leased three arouras of land to the same deacon Psais (*P.Cair. Masp.* II 67129), and he lent money (one solidus less three keratia) to the priest Jakubis son of Abraham (*P.Cair.Masp.* III 67251, 18.x). His landholdings increased in 550, with a cession to him of land by Psates, reader in the principal church of Aphrodito (*P.Cair.Masp.* I 67108), in conjunction with a dowry dispute.

The following year found Dioscorus in Constantinople, having audience, together with his colleagues, Callinicus son of Victor, Cyrus son of Victor (representing, probably, Dioscorus's brother Senouthios), and Apollos son of John, with Fl. Palladios, count of the sacred consistory (*P.Cair.*

32. See the remarks of Keenan, "Village shepherds."

33. Cf. *P.Cair.Masp.* I 67064.13–14, a letter to Apollos complimenting his son the lawyer. On Apollos's upward social mobility, cf. J. G. Keenan, "Aurelius Apollos and the Aphrodite village elite," *Atti XVII congr.intl.papirol.* (Naples 1984) 957–963.

34. On this sort of career, among Dioscorus's contemporaries and connections, cf. Keenan, "Aurelius Phoibammon," pp. 145–154. For Dioscorus's own career, cf. H. Comfort, "Dioscorus of Aphrodito as a lawyer," *TAPA* 65 (1934) xxxvii.

Masp. I 67032). They obtained an imperial rescript ordering the duke of the Thebaid to undertake an official inquiry into Aphrodito's right of *auto-pragia* (*P.Cair.Masp.* I 67024–67025).[35] (Soon after this, perhaps in July or August 551, Dioscorus wrote his isopsephistic poem on S. Senas, perhaps in thanksgiving for the outcome of his journey.[36]) Dioscorus also obtained help in the capital with problems concerning his inheritance (*P.Cair.Masp.* I 67026–67027–67028), which are mentioned later in his encomiastic poetry. The documentation that has survived from this visit gives telling glimpses of the bureaucratic mind at work: the Constantinopolitan officials are eager to settle the matter before it reaches the ears of the emperor.

In connection with Dioscorus's return from the capital,[37] there appear his first efforts at encomiastic poetry (H6 and H8: see Chapter 3), written in hexameters and seasoned with autobiographical allusions. In the same year, 553, he of course continued working: he rented out a wagon (cf. P.Vat.CoptiDoresse 1)[38] for harvest transport to a group of farmers headed by Aur. Menas (*P.Cair.Masp.* III 67303, 27.iv.553). Still *protocometes* in this year (*P.Cair.Masp.* III 67332), he wrote a tax agreement addressed to the pagarchs Julian and Menas (*P.Lond.* V 1661, 24.vii).[39] In 555 (3.v) he leased pastureland to George son of Psaios, a shepherd from Psinabla in the Panopolite (*P.Lond.* V 1692), and in 557 he made a loan to the deacon Mousaios son of Callinicus (*P.Cair.Masp.* II 67130, 25.ii). For the last years of the reign of Justinian, we have no further dated transactions from his archive.[40]

The accession of Justin II in November 565 saw Dioscorus having

35. Cf. V. Martin, "A letter from Constantinople," *JEA* 15 (1929) 69–102; R. G. Salomon, "A papyrus from Constantinople," *JEA* 34 (1948) 98–108. And see G. Geraci, "Dioskoros e l'autopragia di Aphrodito," *Actes XVe congr.intl.papyrol.* 4 (Brussels 1979) 195–205; G. Poethke, "Metrocomiae und Autopragie in Ägypten," in Nagel, *Graeco-Coptica*, pp. 37–44.

36. See my commentary in "The isopsephistic poem on St. Senas by Dioscorus of Aphrodito," *ZPE* 62 (1986) 51–53.

37. Dated by Maspero ("Un dernier poète grec de l'Egypte, Dioscore, fils d'Apollos," *REG* 24 [1911] 460–466) to 553. I have refined the chronology somewhat.

38. See L. Papini, "Annotazioni sul formulario giuridico di documenti copti del VI secolo," *Atti XVII congr.intl.papirol.* (Naples 1984) 767–776; eadem, "Notes on the formulary of some Coptic documentary papyri from Middle Egypt," *BSAC* 25 (1983) 83–89. She dates these papyri to either 520–522+ or 535–537+ (the latter seems more likely).

39. Compare the texts in *BIFAO Bulletin du Centenaire* (Cairo 1981) 427–435.

40. However, *P.Lond.* V 1686 and *P.Cair.Masp.* II 67170–67171 have been redated to 564/5: R. S. Bagnall and K. A. Worp, "Chronological notes on Byzantine documents, V," *BASP* 17 (1980) 19–22. The thirteenth indiction in P.Berol. 11349.37 might, however, be 564, as the document describes Dioscorus's problems with a negligent tenant. (But 579 is also possible.)

moved from Aphrodito (cf. *P.Cair.Masp.* III 67319) to Antinoë, seat of the
Duke of the Thebaid, where he sought to reestablish himself as a jurist
through exercise of his talent as an occasional poet.[41] (In Byzantine Egyptian society, a well-turned verse could serve as a self-advertisement and a
job application.) He wrote a hexameter encomium to the image of the
emperor,[42] and an iambic poem addressed to Victor the *hegemon (praeses)*
asking to serve in the city as *notarios* (see Chapter 3). In this year he sold
land to the monastery of Sminos (Zminos) in the Panopolite (*P.Lond.* V
1686, 7.xi), and wrote a lease of a *pomarion* or plot of gardenland together
with its trees and plants, irrigation machinery, and a mudbrick shed, on
behalf of the same house (*P.Cair.Masp.* II 67170–67171). He also leased land
in the north property of Pka(u)met to Aur. Psempnouthios, a *mechanarius*
(*P.Cair.Masp.* I 67109, 18.vii).

These were busy years for Dioscorus, the lawyer and poet. In 566
(28.ix) he was retained by Aur. Athanasia in a case at law to claim an
inheritance from her father (*P.Cair.Masp.* II 67161); and he drew up the
division of an inheritance among a widow and her five sons (*P.Cair.Masp.*
III 67314). He paid off a debt owed by his late father Apollos and his
brother Senouthes (*P.Hamb.* III 231, 22.ii; cf. *P.Mich.* XIII 669). Also from
this year or the year or two following come his arbitration of an inheritance
for Phoebammon the *stippourgos* (flax worker), *P.Lond.* V 1708, and the
poem fragment *P.Lit.Lond.* 101 (cf. *P.Cair.Masp.* 67055 and 67179), on the
verso of *P.Lond.* V 1710, a piece of an encomium. (For the chronology of
Dioscorus's complete poems, see Chapter 3.)

In 568 Dioscorus drew up a contract (28.iv) for Aur. Psois and Aur.
Josephis son of Pekysis, carpenters (*P.Cair.Masp.* II 67158), and executed a
loan contract wherein John, deacon of the monastery of S. Victor at
Pindaros in the Antinoite, lent Fl. Christopher of Antinoë two solidi without interest for two months (*P.Cair.Masp.* II 67162, 22.v). He also wrote the
document in which Aur. Colluthus, poulterer, paid a debt of two solidi to
Aur. Martin of Antinoë, a dependent of the noble house of Duke Athana-
sius (*P.Cair.Masp.* II 67166, 15.iv). In 569 he had even more to do: when Fl.
John son of Acacius, *logisterius* of Lycopolis, borrowed fifteen solidi from
Aur. Maria, daughter of Cyriac the *scholasticus* (lawyer) and granddaugh-
ter of the late *illustris* Theodosius (*P.Cair.Masp.* III 67309, March), it was
Dioscorus who drew up the contract. He acted similarly when Fl. Victor,

41. On some elements of the unrest leading to his move, see Keenan, "Village
shepherds," 245–259. Cf. *P.Hamb.* III 230.

42. See L. S. B. MacCoull, "The panegyric on Justin II by Dioscorus of Aphrodito,"
Byzantion 54.2 (1984) 575–585.

son of the late *scholasticus* Phoebammon[43] and grandson of the late Count Thomas of Antinoë sold one aroura of land to Aur. Melios (*P.Cair.Masp.* II 67169 and 67169bis, 11.ii). (It would seem that the lawyer class was sticking together to help one another.) Dioscorus also wrote the loan contract in which Aur. Colluthus son of Lilous, vegetable seller at Antinoë, lent nine and one-half keratia to Aur. Colluthus son of George, butcher in the city (*P.Cair.Masp.* II 67164, 2.x), a transaction involving people of more modest class.

Dioscorus executed two transactions in this year recorded and preserved in Coptic: the land cession, *P.Cair.Masp.* II 67176r+P. Alex.inv.689 (dated 28.x.569),[44] and the arbitration, *P.Cair.Masp.* III 67353r. In the first document, we meet the principals, two half-brothers, Julius son of Sarapammon and Anoup son of Apollo, who reappear in the second papyrus. Julius and Anoup were making arrangements for their property before entering the monastic life (see Chapter 2). Also likely to be dated to 569 or shortly thereafter is Dioscorus's other Coptic arbitration, *P.Lond.* V 1709, which begins with the same formulary phrases as does 67353r. The London document deals with the affairs of another family, that of Phoebammon and Victorine and their half-sister Philadelphia, children of the late deacon John, another dependent of Duke Athanasius's house. These Coptic proceedings afford precious evidence for the conduct of cases and the development of Coptic private law before the Arab conquest.

In 570, Dioscorus, still in Antinoë, drew up the will of Fl. Phoebammon, the chief physician of the city (*P.Cair.Masp.* II 67151–67152, 15.xi). He also produced a contract of divorce (*P.Cair.Masp.* III 67311) and drafted a request to the new Duke of the Thebaid, Callinicus, passing on a complaint by one Apollos of Poukhis against the *topoteretes* (tax warden) of Antaeopolis (*P.Cair.Masp.* III 67279). From these years come poems addressed to Duke Callinicus himself: while still with the rank of count he had been the recipient of Dioscorus's epithalamium H21, on the occasion of his wedding to Theophile, and his accession to the dukedom is celebrated in the hexameter encomium H5 (see Chapter 3). Most of Dioscorus's occasional poetry

43. Cf. *P.Cair.Masp.* III 67312, 31.iii.567, the will of his brother, Fl. Theodore; and *P.Cair.Masp.* III 67299, a land lease.

44. I am grateful to Professor K. A. Worp of Amsterdam for accurately reading the dating clause. Text and commentary appear in L. S. B. MacCoull, "A Coptic cession of land by Dioscorus of Aphrodito," *II intl.congr.copt.stud.* (Rome 1985) 159–166. See L. S. B. MacCoull, "The Coptic archive of Dioscorus of Aphrodito," *Cd'E* 56 (1981) 185–193; eadem, "Additions to the prosopography of Aphrodito from the Coptic documents," *BSAC* 25 (1983) 91–94. The antiquated prosopography of V. Girgis, *Prosopografia e Aphroditopolis* (Berlin 1938), needs to be replaced; a guide to the Aphrodito archives is in progress.

and his variations on his own favorite themes are dated in this Antinoë period.

By 573 Dioscorus had returned to Aphrodito. His work in the ducal capital was done, and pressing business involving his family holdings recalled him—again the classic life pattern of the Mediterranean landed gentry. Acting as agent for the monastery of Apa Apollos, which his father had founded, he drew up the contract in which a monk of the house, Psates, donated a building site and two solidi to found a *xenodocheion* (*P.Cair.Masp.* I 67096).[45] Dioscorus appears to have been less active as a lawyer after his return to Aphrodito, but from this period (573–576) comes his most ambitious poetic effort, the pair of encomia on Duke John (H2 and H3; see Chapter 3). In these elaborate productions, blending elements of earlier styles of work, he included elegant, almost baroque self-references to leading themes of present and past years, and even a quick glance at the Tritheist controversy.[46]

The latest datable document from Dioscorus's archive is a leaf from the eight-page account book *P.Cair.Masp.* III 67325, IV^r 5 bearing the date 5.iv.585 (Pharmouthi 3, third regnal year of Maurice, third indiction). The accounts, in Dioscorus's hand, seem to come from a few years earlier—the eighth indiction of I^v 14 must be 574, not 589. His account keeping continues serenely in the expected vein of concern for the local landlord: receipts and disbursements of grain, seed grain, amounts of chickpeas and of mud for bricks; payments for a camel driver and a builder; many ecclesiastical tenants, including "Apa John my in-law." There is even a local field that has come to be known by the name ΠΙΑ ΔΙΟϹΚΟΡΟΥ, 'Dioscorus's Valley.'[47] And so, nearing seventy, he fades from history.

So sketched, outlined from a list of documents, the bare bones of a life seem like the record of days of a Japanese minor court poet or a Chinese official, doing his job and producing polite literary effusions on festive occasions. Too, the culture of Byzantine Egypt was one in which literary cultivation was the sine qua non, the way to office and advancement. But this province was, above all, the place and the time, where all the traditions

45. Cf. *ZPE* 26 (1977) 279.

46. See L. S. B. MacCoull, "A Trinitarian formula in Dioscorus of Aphrodito," *BSAC* 24 (1982) 103–110 and "μονοειδής in Dioscorus of Aphrodito: an addendum," *BSAC* 25 (1983) 61–64; MacCoull, "Dioscorus of Aphrodito and John Philoponus"; A. van Roey, "Les fragments trithéites de Jean Philopon," *OLP* 11 (1980) 135–163.

47. "Valley" in Middle Egyptian topography—and ΠΙΑ is an extremely common formation element in place names—really means a level irrigated space. From the present-day site of Kom Ishgaw one can still look out over a Dioscorian landscape (see Figure 1).

met and cross-fertilized, and this process is what we see at work in Dioscorus's life and productions. His abundant papers embody in every phrase his society's characteristic presuppositions about the world—the total ease in which Christianity and the pagan learning were interwoven without a second thought, the visual opulence, the varying weights of value given to different areas of learning, the uniqueness of what was local and familiar.[48]

The glimpse we get of the values and the morale of Dioscorus's class gives a new and fresh twist to Rostovtzeff's preoccupation with the possibility of attenuating the forms and the matter of a culture. This local aristocracy was deeply rooted in its own heartland, its own landscape; cosmopolitan bearers of Hellenic culture though they may have been, they never forgot the textures and flavors of their home province. Their classicism, like their Christianity, was worn with a local flair.

We might also, parenthetically and for comparison, consider the role of the Apions, the Psimanobets' grander neighbors, people who had held the highest offices and married near-royalty. To what extent were they Egyptians and to what extent Constantinopolitans, if the question can be asked at all? They were Egyptians who had moved out and up; but compare the remarks of Alan Cameron.[49] He draws a picture of their boredom (or that of their spouses) on the obligatory visits to Oxyrhynchus (a phenomenon not unknown among their twentieth-century counterparts). Dioscorus never sat in the imperial cabinet, but he functioned, as decade succeeded decade, as one of the people who held the society together. Though not an officeholder in the capital, he embodied the best qualities of local loyalty and of what a traveled and experienced person could bring to local culture.

In Dioscorus's contracts and poems, the phrases create their own universe. We shall watch this happening in detail in the poetry and the prose. Perhaps, after all, this vision is the real gift of Late Antique Egypt, not just the monastic movement or the other facile suggestions: the ability to take a Homeric tag or an Aristotelian truism learned at school and transmute it into a koan, a counterintuitive paradox, seeming not to make sense, yet that shakes our foundations, making us rethink our assumptions. Dioscorus's world gave birth to its own riddles, and its own solutions.

48. "A common-sense quest for local solutions to the urgent problem of maintaining a traditional way of life, on the part of an aristocracy whose horizons had always been at least partially local." P. Wormald, review of *Western aristocracies and imperial court* by J. F. Matthews, *JRS* 66 (1976) 222.

49. Alan Cameron, "The house of Anastasius," *GRBS* 19 (1978) 268–269.

· II ·

THE GREEK AND COPTIC DOCUMENTS

I fought the law, and
the law won.

Bobby Fuller

To be a jurist in the mid-sixth century was to be at the leading edge of learning. The careers of such men as Agathias[1] and Tribonian[2] stand out against a background of the unknown thousands of provincial lawyers who kept the empire running. The phenomenon of the jurist as a man of letters, far from unknown in the English-speaking world and on the Continent, was also notable in Late Antiquity. The prose writings of Dioscorus of Aphrodito come from a literary background in which skill in classical learning stamped the local writer as a recognizable member of the shared culture.

The growing rhetoricization of legal acts[3] reflected a combination of

---

1. Averil Cameron, *Agathias* (Oxford 1970) 1–11.

2. A. M. Honoré, *Tribonian* (London 1978) xvi–xvii, 30–69—p. 39: "At this point professional tradition unites with the Christian spirit of renewal and the Greek bent for rational ordering." And n. 386: Dioscorus too was a τῆς ἀρχαίας πολυμαθείας ἐραστής.

3. There is abundant literature on the process of rhetoricization of the law, a process that had been going on since the heyday of the Second Sophistic. The broad theories of J. Stroux, *Römische Rechtswissenschaft und Rhetorik* (Potsdam 1944) are no longer accepted (cf. L. Wenger, *Die Quellen des röm. Rechts* [Vienna 1953]); see A. A. Schiller, *Roman law* (The Hague 1978) 569–571, 582–584. But compare F. Schulz, *Roman legal science* (Oxford 1946) 262–277, 295–299 (cf. 328–329). When the Florence concordance to the Greek Novels is finished, much work will be facilitated (cf. Honoré, *Tribonian*, chaps. 3 and 4). Much of the legal literature of this period still lurks in the adespota of Roger A. Pack, *The Greek and Latin literary texts from Greco-Roman Egypt*[2] (Ann Arbor 1965). We might think also of the

the classical training required by society and the permeation of language by scriptural and patristic echoes. A legal document as it came from Dioscorus's pen was far from a dull, flat-footed, matter-of-fact record of a transaction. But it was also not simply a verbose exercise in the sound of one's own voice or the freakishly antiquarian hunt for obscure words.[4] Even more so than a poem, a legal document was a mirror of his world, inasmuch as it was a working reality that actually effected something.[5] One could not be too careful in the face of the law[6] (especially as it had come to be understood by the 560s). The legal act and procedure were intimately bound up with their social context.[7] As a practicing member of the Egyptian bureaucratic elite,[8] Dioscorus consciously tried to do full justice (in every sense) to the problems that came his way. His travels, as well as his family background of philosophical learning,[9] high status, and involvement with monasticism, added to his competence as a professional.[10] In the Greek and Coptic documents that compose the body of his work, we can

---

juristic fragments from the binding of Nag Hammadi Codex VIII (see *NHS* 16, Leiden 1981). The rhetoric of the law is seen even more in the praxis of the documents than in the prescriptions of jurists.

4. See H. Zilliacus, *Zur Abundanz d.spätgriech. Gebrauchssprache* (Helsinki 1967), esp. 20–25 (cf. 10), 62–68. R. MacMullen, "Roman bureaucratese," *Traditio* 18 (1962) 364–378, is overfull of unhelpful jargon. We are in the presence of matters other than the "leere Floskeln" beloved of classical critics (e.g., W. Spiegelberg and F. Rabel, "Ein koptischer Vertrag," *Abh. Göttingen, phil.-hist. Kl.*, n.F. 16.3 [1916–17] 75–84). Cf. L. S. B. MacCoull, "Child donations and child saints in Coptic Egypt," *EEQ* 13 (1979) 409.

5. Cf. Marc Bloch, *The historian's craft* (New York 1953) 168: "the vocabulary of documents is, in its way, only another form of evidence. . . . Each significant term, each characteristic turn of style becomes a true component of knowledge—but not until it has been placed in its context, related to the usage of the epoch, of the society or of the author." Also A. E. Samuel, *From Athens to Alexandria* (Louvain 1983) 9: "Because economic behavior is so indicative of over-all social attitudes, we can use the evidence of economic theory and activity to reveal those tacit assumptions about man and society which underlay the construction of social and cultural institutions." Even the act of making up a valid transaction reveals a world. A document was a dispositive thing: H.-J. Wolff, *Das Recht der griechischen Papyri Ägyptens* (*Hdbuch d.Altertumswiss.* 10.5.2) (Munich 1978) 141–144.

6. Cf. L. S. B. MacCoull, "Child donations," pp. 409–415.

7. R. V. Colman, "Reason and unreason in early medieval law," *J.Interdisc.Hist.* 4 (1974) 571–591, esp. 571–579—a brilliant study.

8. See T. F. Carney, *Bureaucracy in traditional society: Romano-Byzantine bureaucracies viewed from within* (Lawrence, Kansas, 1971) II.117–122, 176–187 (cf. 78–83). Unlike John Lydus, Dioscorus does not voice open disillusionment with his job or with "the system."

9. It is Dioscorus's papers that have preserved the Horapollon letters: J. Maspero, "Horapollon et la fin du paganisme égyptien," *BIFAO* 11 (1914) 163–195.

10. Cf. F. S. Pedersen, "On professional qualifications for public posts in late antiquity," *Class.etMed.* 31 (1975) 161–213. As one might expect, though, breeding and connections counted. Dioscorus had both status as local gentry and educational attainment.

see how the functions of recording and of decision became fused.[11] In this process lay the seeds of the future of Coptic law.[12]

The documentary production of Dioscorus offers the penultimate stage of development—before the evolution that took place after the Arab conquest—in which to observe the perennial interpenetration of *Reichsrecht* and *Volksrecht*[13] in a late Roman province. And more: the polarities observable in the praxis of Aphrodito and Antinoë are not only those of the imperial legislation of Old and New Rome[14] vis-à-vis the inherited custom of the country.[15] The tensions also appear as an interaction between two modes of perceiving the role of the human intellect, one profoundly positive and one profoundly negative—an ambiguity that has continued to affect Coptic culture to the present day. The actions and transactions of Dioscorus and his fellow citizens show forth their definitions of truth, their mechanisms for finding out truth, and their underlying assumptions about how truth operates in human life.[16]

The style, in Greek and Coptic, in which these transactions are couched reflects the network of interlocking responsibilities[17] so characteristic of the Late Antique city (particularly in Egypt with its uniquely inescapable landscape).[18] Dioscorus's personal documentary style, as seen in its own time,[19] bears the imprint of several major influences. Besides the technical language he had learned and used as a working tool,[20] he every-

11. Cf. B. Stock, *The implications of literacy* (Princeton 1983) 41–42; cf. 58–59.

12. The position taken by A. A. Schiller in "The courts are no more," *Studi E. Volterra* (Milan 1969) 469–502, is rather extreme: he asserts that the non-Chalcedonian Copts' loathing for the "official" justice of the Chalcedonian government was so intense as to bring about the development of a whole system of private, personal, arbitration-based justice for the community. The actual situation surely did not draw such hard-and-fast lines before the conquest. (Afterwards became a different matter.) Cf. Colman, "Reason and unreason," pp. 573–575.

13. So formulated after the title of Mitteis's classic work, *Reichsrecht und Volksrecht in den östlichen Provinzen d. röm. Kaiserreich* (Leipzig 1891).

14. Cf. A. A. Schiller, "The fate of imperial legislation in late Byzantine Egypt," in *Legal thought in the USA under contemporary pressures*, ed. J. N. Hazard and W. J. Wagner (Brussels 1970) 41–60.

15. For an earlier period, cf. E. Seidl, *Rechtsgeschichte Ägyptens als römischer Provinz* (Sankt Augustin 1973).

16. The divisions in Late Antique Egyptian society are usually discussed as being those of center vs. periphery, of "classical" vs. "anticlassical" elements, along linguistic and confessional lines. (Cf. Chapter 3, n. 58.) These analyses do not work any more than does a simple *Reichsrecht/Volksrecht* methodology.

17. Cf. Colman, "Reason and unreason," 573–575.

18. P. R. L. Brown, *The making of late antiquity* (Cambridge, Mass. 1978) 3–4, 81–85.

19. Zilliacus, *Abundanz*, pp. 6–8, 43–47, for examples.

20. Ibid., 63.

where echoes the Scriptures and the liturgy. His Greek style appears modeled to a perceptible extent on the rhetoric of Cyril of Alexandria,[21] and his vocabulary shares elements with the philosophical usage of John Philoponus.[22] Of course, beneath the surface of his Greek lies Coptic syntax: the parataxis, the effective asyndeton, the aesthetic implied in an analytic language of particular verbal systems and word orders.[23] His Coptic style itself combines businesslike straightforwardness, vividness in narration, and imaginative embellishment. The tendencies visible in Dioscorus's prose can be seen taken further in such sixth- to seventh-century pieces as the Greek ecclesiastical letters in *P.Grenf.* II 112[24] and *BKT* VI 10677, and the Coptic synodal letter of Patriarch Damian in *Epiphanius* II 149–152. (Recognizable stylistic elements are still alive nearly three hundred years later, in the documents of the Hermopolite monastery of Apa Apollo.[25]) Dioscorus's documentary work stands nearly midway in the history of that Late Antique *Geschäftsprosa*, which was itself an art form.

Dioscorus was a bilingual man functioning in a bilingual society. As Roger Bagnall has stated, "the Coptic papyri of the archive need editing, for without them any synthetic study of the world of Dioskoros would be a

21. See A. Vaccari, "La grecità di S. Cirillo d'Alessandria," *Studi P. Ubaldi* (Milan 1937) 27–40; cf. L. R. Wickham, *Cyril of Alexandria: select letters* (Oxford 1983) xiv, for a decidedly negative opinion of Cyril's style. See also C. Datema, "Classical quotations in the works of Cyril of Alexandria," *Studia Patristica* 17 (Oxford 1982) 422–425.

22. See L. S. B. MacCoull, "μονοειδής in Dioscorus of Aphrodito: an addendum," *BSAC* 25 (1983) 61–64; and eadem, "Dioscorus of Aphrodito and John Philoponus," *Studia Patristica* 18 (Kalamazoo 1987) I.163–168.

23. Cf. I. M. Diakonoff, *Hamito-Semitic languages* (Moscow 1965) 38–41. Coptic does not form certain kinds of compounds, and places weight in the noun more than the verb; this explains much. Zilliacus, *Abundanz*, p. 10, is surely wrong in not seeing many signs of Coptic interference in sixth-century Greek documentary style (from Egypt). (Cf. F. T. Gignac, *Grammar of the Greek papyri of the Roman and Byzantine periods* I [Milan 1976] 46–48.) Dioscorus's prose, however, is not to be dismissed as the bumblings of a babu who had never properly learned to think in or to employ the language of the high culture (cf. H. I. Bell, "An Egyptian village in the time of Justinian," *JHS* 64 [1944] 27–31, one of the milder condemnations of his style). Its charm lies in sharply rendered perceptions and unexpectedly happy juxtapositions. (For this sort of *poikilia* and variation as Late Antique stylistic traits, cf. the remarks of M. Roberts, "The *Mosella* of Ausonius," *TAPA* 114 [1984] 344 with nn. 8–10, 353.)

24. Now redated to A.D. 557 by S. Bernardinello, "Nuove prospettive sulla cronologia del Pap.Grenf. II 112," *Scriptorium* 34 (1980) 239–240; cf. "Cronologia della maiuscola greca di tipo alessandrino," *Scriptorium* 32 (1978) 251–255.

25. See M. Krause, "Das Apa-Apollon-Kloster zu Bawit" (Diss., Leipzig 1953), now finally to appear in printed form. The MSS are British Library Or. 6202, 6203, 6204, 6206; their oath formulas can be integrated with those collected by K. A. Worp, "Byzantine imperial titulature in the Greek documentary papyri: the oath formulas," *ZPE* 45 (1982) 199–223. My initial study of them will appear in *BASP* 24.

farce."[26] Unfortunately, our knowledge of the Coptic portion of Dioscorus's papers is not yet complete;[27] and, given conditions in Egypt, substantive results cannot be expected in any foreseeable future. In searching the Coptic documentary papyri in collections known to contain Greek items by Dioscorus, I have not found anything either in his hand or mentioning his name. Did the process by which the Dioscorus archive came to be scattered among numerous libraries affect only the Greek papyri? In any case, such Coptic documents as I have found to exist will be fully incorporated into the present treatment.

What little information we have of the circumstances of the second Kom Ishgaw find in 1905 or the clandestine diggings in 1937 and 1938, followed by over forty years of total lack of interest, does not even now enable the researcher to track down Dioscorus's Coptic pieces. Three boxes of Coptic material from the site were given by Lefebvre to the Cairo Museum;[28] however, because Jean Maspero could not read Coptic, they were put aside, and the fate of their contents is still unknown. Those sixth-century Coptic Aphrodito documents that have come to rest in the Vatican library, having been removed to safety at the time of the transfer of material to the then-new Coptic Museum, are not in Dioscorus's hand. We may assume, however, that he had kept them among his working papers. Perhaps they were inherited from his father, although the Vatican papyri contain few clues as to dating. Numbers 5 and 1 probably come from 535/6 and 536/7,[29] during Apollos's floruit and Dioscorus's youth. Their phraseology displays the characteristic fullness of Greek usage and legal idiom[30] we are later to find noticeable in Dioscorus's own work at the Aphrodito and Antinoë chanceries. But, apart from the normal "squirearchical" documentation (in Greek) outlined in Chapter 1, we do not hear Dioscorus's own voice in either language until 547/8, when he had become the heir to his estates and assumed the role of spokesman for his community.

The earliest preserved monument, the first extended piece of Dios-

26. R. Bagnall, review of *I papiri Vaticani di Aphrodito* by R. Pintaudi, *BASP* 18 (1981) 177.

27. See my overview, "The Coptic archive of Dioscorus of Aphrodito," *Cd'E* 56 (1981) 185–193. Further pieces, it seems, lurk in the Cairo Museum among the material numbered S.R. 3733; I am still in process of preparing texts. Two are in the Ismaila Museum.

28. *P.Cair.Masp.* III, preface; L. S. B. MacCoull, "Additions to the prosopography of Aphrodito from the Coptic documents," *BSAC* 25 (1983) 91.

29. See L. Papini, "Notes on the formulary of some Coptic documentary papyri from Middle Egypt," *BSAC* 25 (1983) 83–89, and "Annotazioni sul formulario giuridico di documenti copti del VI secolo," *Atti XVII congr.intl.papirol.* (Naples 1984) 767–776.

30. L. Papini, ibid. *(utraque).*

corus's prose writing, is the petition to the empress Theodora of 547/8, *P.Cair.Masp.* II 67283, written just at the end of the empress's life. This production dates from the eve of Dioscorus's journey to the capital, before he began (as far as we know) the composition of poetry. In this, his first work, we can see some of the elements that went into the formation of his mind: familiarity with his family's papers, reminiscences (perhaps) of Apollos's trip to Constantinople, knowledge of the workings of the chancery and, of course, the classics and the scriptures. In it we can already see many of the elements that are to be characteristic of his developed prose style: ornamental and emotionally expressive nouns, declamatory flourishes, biblical and classical reminiscences effectively interwoven. It builds in a crescendo from a simple opening identifying the petition's author and recipient to an elaborate rhetorical close that depicts the empress's healing hand protecting the land from evil.

The opening of the text is addressed by the Aphroditans to a deacon, Victor, and a body of officials (with the title $\theta\alpha\nu\mu\alpha\sigma\iota\acute{\omega}\tau\alpha\tau\iota$, *admirandissimi*) whose function is lost. A *clarissimus* called Julian has overstepped his powers by threatening to bring them, the petitioners, before the pagarch of Antaeopolis in the matter of the yearly assessment, although the proper authorities in their case are the Duke of the Thebaid and the imperial house. (In other words, the Antaeopolitan pagarch had no right to collect from an autopract town.) Next comes a rhetorical tugging at the heartstrings, almost a pastoral, a depiction of the community's striving to live the quiet life ($\mu\epsilon\tau\rho\acute{\iota}\omega\varsigma$), the good life ($\epsilon\grave{\upsilon}\zeta\omega\acute{\iota}\alpha$), in the wake of barbarian raids and the pagarch's greedy entourage. Then, in arguing his case, Dioscorus begins to pull out his classical and biblical stops: "God alone knows," he says, "all the illegalities perpetrated by them, and the murders of the plague ($\lambda o\iota\mu\acute{o}\varsigma$) that struck and brought total outrage ($\acute{o}\lambda o\lambda\acute{\upsilon}\gamma\mu\alpha\tau\alpha$, a coinage of Dioscorus's own)." This deliberate allusion refers simultaneously to the Thucydidean plague (compare the use of $\sigma\nu\mu\beta\alpha\acute{\iota}\nu\epsilon\iota\nu$ in Thuc. 2.47) and to the plagues of Egypt in Exodus (here, of course, stood on their head). And after a recital of "confiscations, injustices, despoilings . . . more than this papyrus has space for" (he will reuse that phrase in *P.Cair.Masp.* I 67002, in 567), he again brings in the telling power of classical myth. As in Pandora's box, "the one, only, sole thing we have left is hope" (line 12). And should that hope come true, should the empress and the bishop of Antaeopolis curb the pagarch, *soteria* will come to Aphrodito, and the people will return to their Good Life (and regular taxpaying). Above all, they will have been healed ($\acute{\upsilon}\gamma\iota o\hat{\upsilon}\sigma\theta\alpha\iota$) by the hand of the Lady Empress and of the ecclesiastical authority ($\acute{\eta}$ $\acute{\upsilon}\mu\acute{\epsilon}\tau\epsilon\rho\alpha$ $\epsilon\grave{\upsilon}\kappa\lambda\epsilon\acute{\iota}\alpha$), by which (both together) "evildoers are punished, dwellings are made splendid, and the possessions of your native people are kept safe from being undermined or razed" (presumably by tax collectors illegally looking for that last keration).

In this splendid rhetorical closing, with the image of the healing hand adorning Egyptian civic life and enabling the good life to be led (an image resembling Hestia Polyolbos), Dioscorus has given, at the beginning of his career, a classic statement of Late Roman civic values. Could Apollos have seen Theodora, in 541, and come home full of tales? Perhaps. In any case, Dioscorus's striking image of the healing hand and the civic benefits it enacts both vividly recalls visual depictions of the Hand of God in Late Antique art and boldly states an ideal. The ideal was one of simultaneous visible splendor in the city's material structure and shining justice for its inhabitants. However imperfectly realized, still the ideal was there, and it is a merit of Coptic society to have clothed it in such all-enfolding and luminous imagery.

By the last years of the reign of Justinian, financial and social tensions at Aphrodito were an old story, and one familiar to the former young squire who had been to the capital of the empire and was no stranger to responsibility. The events that led to and prompted Dioscorus's career move from Aphrodito to the ducal court at Antinoë have already been sketched.[31] From 564 (probably) we have, in Coptic, the record of an arbitration[32] in a case at law that illustrates the sort of last-straw frustrations he had to endure in the business of estate management. Some eighteen months later he will have transferred to the Antinoë chancery, now jurist and poet rather than homebound landlord.

P.Berol. 11349,[33] drafted by another notary but with a small annotation in Dioscorus's hand, begins with the technical operative verb of arbitration, ⲁⲓⲥⲱⲧⲙ 'I have heard'. The arbiter states in the first person that he has heard the case (ϩⲱⲃ = *rem*) of the two parties, Dioscorus and Joseph son of Hermauos, and that the dispute has been about a field owned by Dioscorus and leased by Joseph. The latter party is accused of negligence.

In the first part of the narrative, Dioscorus speaks in the first person. He contends that Joseph, his tenant, has so imperfectly worked the land he has leased from Dioscorus that the field has not yielded its quota of tax

31. Cf. MacCoull, "Dioscorus and the dukes," *BS/EB* 1987.

32. Noticed by A. A. Schiller in his introduction to the second edition of KRU (Leipzig 1971).

33. I am grateful to Dr. G. Poethke of the Staatliche Museen zu Berlin (DDR) for photographs of the papyrus. It is not, except for an annotation, in Dioscorus's own hand, but it yields a coherent text.

(*demosion* and *phoros*), and that therefore Dioscorus is unjustly stranded with the tax liability. At harvest time (Pachons and Payni), Dioscorus himself secretly checked the accounting and was so shocked at the outcome that he lodged a complaint against Joseph; thus, if the arbiter finds Joseph guilty, it is he who will (rightly) have to pay the tax. It seems that Joseph has also compounded his negligence by allowing animals with their herders to trespass across the field,[34] thus making the land even less able to yield its needed quota. Dioscorus concludes his accusation by alleging that Joseph has even acted in collusion with the (unnamed) *boethos* to cover up what he has done. Next, the arbiter records Joseph's flat denial of any negligence; then, switching into the first person, he states that he attributes the wrongdoing to Joseph the tenant, not to the owner who has brought the complaint, but that Joseph may not have known that his actions constituted negligence.

Unfortunately, no absolute date has been preserved in this document; however, the thirteenth indiction mentioned in line 37 would suggest the year 564, when Dioscorus was still at Aphrodito and being bedeviled by the Menas affair (see later discussion), rather than 579, when he was back home in what seem to have been comparatively peaceful days. At the end of the document it is recorded that Dioscorus takes his oath on the amounts of money involved and that, for his part, Joseph goes surety for the amount, presumably, of the tax. The end of the papyrus is lost, so we cannot know what judgment the arbiter formally pronounced.

Even in a bare narration like this, a plea at law that aims to tell simply the facts, we can discern features of Dioscorian style, this time in Coptic (and being filtered through the offices of a notary). "He made my portion into rust and blight," he says; he paints a picture of chicanery and deception undermining the fundamental ties of a society in which ancient custom (ⲛⲛⲓ̈ⲱⲧ) interacted with statute law to ensure that the land and its irrigation (cf. line 22, ⲡⲃⲉⲕⲉ ⲛ̄ⲧⲙⲏⲭⲁⲛⲏ) kept everyone alive. Dioscorus senses that the weight of every word contributes to the workings of the law.

During 565, the last year of Justinian's reign, Dioscorus pursued his career of land entrepreneurship and estate management, framing documents of sale in normal legal style as he had done in the previous fifteen years and more (e.g., *P.Cair.Masp.* II 67170–67171 and *P.Lond.* V 1686, recording his dealings with the Panopolite monastery of Zminos and refer-

---

34. Compare J. G. Keenan, "Village shepherds and social tension in Byzantine Egypt," *YCS* 28 (1985) 245–259.

ring to his troubles with the Phthla shepherds). But it is when he is newly arrived in Antinoë the next year, filled with indignation at the behavior of Menas, the encroaching pagarch of Antaeopolis, that we see his next documentary productions in the high style.

By the autumn of 566[35] Dioscorus had moved to Antinoë. Personally and professionally it was a step up. As a *nomikos* probably on the ducal *taxis*, he would command the respect and the fees that were owed to a learned jurist with his experience; as resident in the first city of the Thebaid, he had the opportunity to increase his skill as a man of letters; and as a representative of his heritage, he would become still more deeply involved in the defense of Aphrodito against the perennial inroads of the Antaeopolitan pagarchy. Aphrodito's rights and his responsibility for them had brought him to the capital of the empire, and they would continue to claim him here at the seat of the duke. The wicked pagarch comes to be the central figure of his rhetoric—a plague out of the Old Testament, a raiding barbarian, almost an antichrist. (To what extent an annual tax requirement based on the pagarchy, rather than *autopragia*, was felt by contemporaries to be an irremediable flaw in the system is unknown.[36]) In his first year at Antinoë, Dioscorus composed two of his grandest pieces of prose centering round this theme, *P.Lond.* V 1677 and *P.Cair.Masp.* I 67002. The *didaskalia* to Theodora has become grand-opera eloquence. Right at the beginning of his Antinoë period, Dioscorus pulls out all the stops.

P.Lond. V 1677, a petition to a *magister*, is a document written out of burning personal outrage. The affair of Menas, pagarch of Antaeopolis, is the very last straw that has driven Dioscorus to become a suppliant (and job seeker, as we have seen from his early poetry) at the ducal court. Menas has used his office in collusion with the unruly shepherds of Phthla—we have not heard the last of them—to damage Dioscorus's family holdings. To expose this wrong, he brings to bear every rhetorical figure and liturgical and scriptural echo he can orchestrate.

Dioscorus begins with a dative, in *cheirographon* style: "To my truly good master and philanthropic benefactor (φιλανθρωπενεργέτῃ, a compound he has coined)," he writes, "the *clarissimus* and *spectabilis magister*, a request and petition from your poor inhabitant, Dioscorus," centering his name between crosses on the page. (He does not name the *magister*, but could it be the *magister* Dorotheos of *P.Cair.Masp.* I 67003 [see later discus-

35. *P.Cair.Masp.* II 67161; Bell's introduction to *P.Lond.* V 1674, p. 56. On the social and cultural attractions of the ducal capital, see MacCoull, "Dioscorus and the dukes."

36. A question not raised in W. Liebeschuetz, "The origin of the office of the pagarch," *BZ* 66 (1973) 38–46.

sion], and also the Dorotheos of his poetry?) Next, his *captatio benevolentiae* is a decorative and elaborate period that centers on the word εὐεργεσία (picking up the earlier title) and radiates forward and backward with the qualities, both passive and active, of that faculty. "Your loving and good (φιλοκαγαθός), bright benefaction is spoken well of and is far famed everywhere by everyone, and it always seeks all that is advantageous and profitable to the soul (ψυχωφελῆ, a Cyrillian word)." So, because this official is already known to be someone who has the physical and spiritual welfare of the citizens at heart, Dioscorus will lay at his feet what has happened to him at the hands of Menas, whose titles he recites with a touch of sarcasm. The events are illustrated by one of his favorite devices, an ascending series of three epithets: in this case harm, destruction, and στενοχωρία 'being in a tight place'. In addition to the problems with the shepherds in Phthla,[37] and δυσφήμεια, Menas has been φρεναπατής, a cheat at heart (Dioscorus is possibly thinking of ways in which -ⲚϨⲎⲦ can combine in Coptic). Again, Menas's wrongs come in a triple wave: not just appropriations of money and foodstuffs, but actual violence (φονίους). The family estates have been subjected to ". . . and pillage and falling-apart (σάθρωσις)."

In this state, "worse than the aftermath of a barbarian raid" (a topos Dioscorus will use several times), what can be done? Man is left ἀπερίστατος, without his safely enclosing boundaries, unguarded and open to attack on both sides. And so Dioscorus invokes the *soteria* of the eternal God and calls to witness the *magister*'s whole family, that his exalted *exousia* may, with God's help, avail to redress the wrongs described in the document.

Dioscorus's word order and vocabulary reflect his deepest values. His most complex period here begins with εὐφημεῖται καὶ διαβεβοῆται ἡ . . . ὑμῶν . . . εὐεργεσία. It is not enough just to have the faculty of benefaction—one must be seen and known and talked about as having it. Dioscorus combines positive concepts into rare compound coinages, setting them like jewels to adorn the high points of his prose. His contrasted epithets—another favorite method of procedure—and his triple crescendos are used with force and deliberate point.

Close reading of a text like this rewards the historian with a wealth of meaning. When the documents of this period have been read at all, other than purely as sources of fact, they have been held up as laughable. How could these writers, using ten synonyms where a bare word would do,

37. Keenan, "Village shepherds," 245–259.

inflate their petty troubles to sound like the end of the world? How could they have turned the skills of the free orator to such base ends? But this mode of criticism has been found wanting. We must listen from the inside. Dioscorus's feelings as a member of his society emerge nakedly from the texts he writes for specific cases. Egyptians especially, rooted in their landscape, were painfully aware of how fragile were the boundaries marking off their lives: green from dry, nurturing from barren and threatening. They also knew how shaky could be the fences between themselves and barbarism, physical and cultural. And they were clear about the priorities within their own world. To see justice and order and the saving splendor of hierarchy manifest in one human official[38] (addressed, too, by a resoundingly abstract title) was to feel that the earth was still under their feet. At his conclusion, Dioscorus repeats the concepts of *soteria* and *diamone:* above and below, a sureness in things.

In the small world of this one petition, Dioscorus is treating two of the most serious problems of his time: illegal tax encroachment by pagarchs, and the transfer of sown land to shepherds. He invokes both theological and civic values (reading βουλευτικά in line 44) in his efforts to right these wrongs.

At the end of the indiction year 566/7, Dioscorus directly addressed the Duke of the Thebaid himself, Athanasius, both on his own behalf and in concert with the property owners *(syntelestai)* of Aphrodito. His second petition recounting the Menas affair, *P.Cair.Masp.* I 67002, also begins by calling itself a δέησις and ἰκεσία, a supplication. But then his prose takes wing, depicting a poignant vision of the Christian consummation of all things, the saving dispensation, working itself out in the circumstances of Egyptian society.

"All justice and right dealing," he begins, "ever brighten the progress of your exalted authority, which is preeminently best; and we have long since received it [i.e., your authority] the way those in the netherworld once waited for the *parousia* of Christ, the eternal God." This striking figure was noticed even by Bell.[39] We have already seen how justice is a central theme in Dioscorus's poetry. Here he couples δικαιοσύνη with the Aristotelian δικαιοπραγία 'just dealing'. In the real world of the bureaucracy, one did not always entail the other. The duke's welcomed πρόοδος 'progress', his *adventus* really (cf. below *P.Cair.Masp.* I 67003.10, συνέλευσις), is rendered by the

---

38. Compare the vision of the policeman's uplifted hand in Charles Williams's *The greater trumps* (London: Faber and Faber, 1954).

39. Bell, "An Egyptian village," p. 33.

Plotinian word for emanations. The coming of the duke is a kind of emanation of Justice itself. In the previous document, Dioscorus began with sound; here he begins with light, with the beams of justice lighting up the duke's advent the way Christ's Harrowing of Hell struck a beam of light upon the dazzled shades. The balanced endings of his clauses, with their metrical value as *clausulae*, meaningfully play one against the other; *exousia, parousia*. It is a beautiful picture (and one not found, it seems, in the iconography of the Coptic visual arts)—that of all the patriarchs and prophets and human forebears, and even the "good pagans," having their longings fulfilled at last. Just so are the Aphroditans' longings for justice to be fulfilled.

"For," he goes on, "after God, our Lord and Savior, the true helper and benefactor who loves humankind, we hold your Highness with all hope of salvation, who are everywhere praised and proclaimed and reported to us in all necessities, that you will extend a way out of our wrongs and deliver us from the unspeakable things, too many for this papyrus to contain, which have happened at the hands of Menas." Dioscorus constructs a doubly balanced sentence: first he pairs God and the duke, and then, branching off, he uses a pair of verbs to describe how the latter will καί . . . ἀποσπάσασθαι καὶ ῥύσασθαι. He contrasts the eternal aspect of divine aid with the Thucydidean συμβεβηκότα. He concludes his preamble by praising the duke's σύνειδος, his faculty of conscientious discrimination, with a typical triplet, calling it πάνσοφον (compare the poetry), εὐκλεέστατον (a standard epithet for a duke), and, all important in the scale of values, φιλάγαθον. These qualities of the duke's mind, coupled with the complementary φρόνησις (reason) and νουεχία (common sense), will enable him to grasp the situation, comprehend everything clearly, and work a peripety (line 8).

In the rest of this petition, Dioscorus's rhetorical style takes a scriptural turn. He describes his young children as "hardly knowing their right hand from their left" (I.12), which Gelzer noted as an echo of the last verse of Jonah.[40] The dishonest Menas, classically ἄσπλαγχνος (a word used by the sixth-century Alexandrian deacon Olympiodorus and in the Greek life of Pachomius), acts in league with those Phthla shepherds (again) "like the hosts of Midian" wrecking the Israelites' food supply (I.19). Finally Dioscorus proclaims himself—in words reminiscent of those of Ecclesiastes (4:1)—ἀνεκδίκητος, a man without an *ekdikos*, a *defensor*, whence he asks for the duke's *ekdikia*.

40. *Archiv* 5 (1913) 189 (footnoted by Maspero in his edition).

After a narrative of the pagarch's wrongs—imprisonments, confiscations—Dioscorus reminds the duke that the Aphroditans are his men "and men of the imperial house" (II.14–15). He returns to the opening theme: "And it is for us a work of prayer [a Copticism: ϩⲱⲃ ⲛ̄ϣⲗⲏⲗ] day and night [cf. e.g., Ps. 1:2] to be worthy of the grace of your *parousia*, so we may come to be under your justice, in *apolausis*." I am reminded of the gracious personification of Apolausis at Dumbarton Oaks—another paramount Late Roman value.

We have not heard the last of this pagarch's misdeeds. In another crescendo, Dioscorus recounts how Menas interferes (counterproductively, one would think) with the irrigation system, the lifeline of the Egyptian countryside, for his own short-term ends. After the responsible *syntelestai* had strengthened the canal at the time of the Nile flood, "for access and irrigation" (a sort of cross between a hendiadys and a zeugma), the pagarch impeded their work, acting μετὰ πολλῆς ληστρικῆς τε καὶ παναγικῆς καὶ στρατιωτικῆς βοηθείας, a phrase combining triple epithets in a descending order of forcefulness with a periphrasis employing an abstract noun ("soldierly help," i.e., help consisting of soldiers, who behaved like unprofessionals and robbers). Then, having set fire to "the splendid houses (λαμπρά 'shining') of the former great landowners" (the stately homes of Aphrodito) (II.24), Menas and his men committed the final horror. They did violence to the nuns (παρθένους and ἀσκητρίας) living in the area.[41] Dioscorus expresses his revulsion in words once again reminiscent of Ecclesiastes (4:2–3), saying that those of old were better off. (Again, we have the awareness of ancestral usage brooding over the Egyptian landscape.)

In the last twenty lines, Dioscorus once again describes the fury[42] of Menas and the shepherds, even to the pitch of hyperbole: "human blood ran like water over the land," he says. (In local mythology, a few stones thrown can be a massacre.) At the end, he recalls again the duke's *parousia*: "We clasp the knees of your Highness, whom we behold like those who see God" (III.21). The pagarch is "like a ramping and a roaring lion" (θυμολεοντόφθορον; 1 Pet. 5:8), but he and his works will be uprooted. In a pair of parallel final clauses, the Aphroditans will again live the good life, and will make perpetual intercession (expressed in a chiasmus, ἐνδελεχῆ αἰωνίως

---

41. The houses of women religious at Aphrodito/Antaeopolis are listed in the survey of P. Barison, "Ricerche sui monasteri dell' Egitto bizantino ed arabo," *Aegyptus* 18 (1938) 121–122, 98. (Compare below, comments on *P.Lond.* V 1674.)

42. Possibly also a scriptural echo; there are overtones of the descriptions of fierce destroyers in Isaiah and Jeremiah.

εὐχὴν καὶ πρεσβείαν) for the great men in *exousia:* "the all-glorious commanders, the most excellent consuls, the most famous patricians, the most perfect dukes, the thoroughbred augustal, ever lords of the eparchy." Thus, Dioscorus closes with a magnificent picture of the assembled grandees of the Thebaid and all Egypt—rank on rank, crescendo, their hierarchy reflecting the order and degree of heaven.[43] Having begun with a *proskynesis* of humility, he closes with a triumphant celebration of visible glory.

At about the same time as he wrote the previous document (566/7), Dioscorus was retained by the Antinoite monastery of the Apostles at Pharoou to compose another petition to the same duke (*P.Cair.Masp.* I 67003). While at Antinoë, he was to have more than one transaction with this religious house, comparatively distant though it was (see the comments on *P.Cair.Masp.* II 67176+P.Alex.inv. 689). Its full title was that of the "Christ-bearing Apostles." Could it have been the same place as the Φαρατοπος attested in *P.Michael.* 40.9? (I owe this idea to K. A. Worp.) And can the name derive from ϩⲣⲟⲟⲩ 'voice'? The monks refer to themselves as ἐρημῖται, probably implying the sort of more idiorrhythmic, less Pachomian arrangement in which the monks lived in separate dwellings (like Kellia).

In fact, Dioscorus had the closest possible family connection with this monastery, for it had been founded by his father, Apollos. We know that Apollos had entered the monastic life, although whether he joined before or after his journey to Constantinople is uncertain.[44] He subsequently spent the rest of his life in the monastery in the Antaeopolite nome that he founded, named Apa Apollos after himself (with the dedication to the Christ-bearing Apostles [*P.Cair.Masp.* I 67096, 573/4]), and for which he named Dioscorus *curator.* Apollos was dead by 546/7, twenty years before the present Greek document was written. But the identification is assured by the conclusion of P.Alex.inv. 689, written in Coptic in Dioscorus's hand and dated 28 October 569. It is addressed "to the pious superior of the monastery of Pharoou and its whole village, from Dioscorus, the most humble son of Apa Apollo of Pharoou" (lines 26–29). We can thus conclude that the house of the Christ-bearing Apostles of Pharoou and that of Apa Apollos of the Christ-bearing Apostles were one and the same.

43. Wilcken suggested (noted by Maspero in his edition) that this passage sounds like an acclamation. Compare the excellent overview by C. Roueché, "Acclamations in the later Roman Empire: New evidence from Aphrodisias," *JRS* 74 (1984) 181–199. The site of Aphrodito did not yield inscriptions. Could Dioscorus have been echoing local acclamations he had heard at Antinoë, both in his poetry and in his prose?

44. J. G. Keenan, "Aurelius Apollos and the Aphrodite village elite," *Atti XVII congr.intl.papirol.* III (Naples 1984) 957–963.

Dioscorus thus continued to discharge his office as estate manager of his family foundation while he resided at Antinoë and made available to the monks' cause the best of his professional legal and rhetorical skills.

Dioscorus's opening is a variation on that of the previous piece: in this, too, δικαιοσύνη and δικαιοπραγία brighten the progress of the duke, here titled "Your Excellency" (ὑπερφυΐα). "And," continues Dioscorus, "all the pure monasteries and the most holy churches [oratories] of God rejoice under your auspicious good government, by which every injustice, which is to be shunned and averted, is driven away from them, (especially) injustice committed by those who are used to meddle and interfere with their property in greedy and tyrannical fashion." Εὐαγές is the standard epithet for μοναστήριον in these texts (cf., e.g., the subsequent discussion of *P.Lond.* V 1674.74). It can be thought of as bearing simultaneously a neutral/middle and an active sense: the presence of monasteries, live centers of holiness, purifies and hallows the land (cf. also Nonnus *Paraphr.* 18.97). Also, Dioscorus invents a number of locutions for the concept of church: πανσεπτὸς οἶκος (of God or a saint, *P.Lond.* V 1708.165–166), ἅγιος οἶκος Θεοῦ (*P.Lond.* V 1708.244, 258). Hence, εὐκτήρια here does not have to mean only oratories or chapels (as against, e.g., the technical designations in *P.Freer* 1–2 IV.2, 3, III.13, V.26, 32). It is natural that a religious house, in commissioning the framing of a petition, should seek to adorn with decorative terminology the role of religious institutions within society.

The monasteries, then, of the Thebaid are as glad of the advent of good ducal government as are the lay landowners. They look to the duke's authority as having the power to prevent that deep and painful wrong, the attempted alienation of church *temporalia*. This offense Dioscorus characterizes with the harsh infinitives φιλοπραγμονῆσαι καὶ πλεονεκτῆσαι. In a sixth-century Mediterranean society, the actions of people who cannot keep their hands to themselves, to the point of preying on ecclesiastical goods,[45] deserve to be branded τυραννικῶς. Dioscorus ends his sentence with an adverb like a slap in the face.

The religious and all who live in the face of the duke's συνέλευσις (*adventus*, 1, 10) pray, the preamble goes on, "that supplications and intercessions be perpetually and incessantly made to God the παμβασιλεύς [a

---

45. On the inviolability and inalienability of ecclesiastical property in sixth-century Egypt, see Nov. Justin VII.11 (15.iv.535) (cf. Nov. Justin II. 5): A. Knecht, *System des justinianischen Kirchenvermögensrechtes* (Stuttgart 1905, reprint Amsterdam 1963); A. Steinwenter, "Die Rechtsstellung der Kirchen und Klöster," *ZSS* 50 (1930) 1–50; idem, "Aus dem kirchlichen Vermögensrechte der Papyri," *ZSS* 75 (1958) 1–34; M. Kaplan, *Les propriétés de la Couronne et de l'Eglise dans l'empire byzantin (vᵉ–viᵉ s.)* [ByzSorb 2] (Paris 1976).

word we find in Dioscorus's poetry] for all those in authority in the whole eparchy, for two things: pity on us, and burning zeal [note the sound-play: οἰκτόν . . . καὶ οἰστρόν] for every good work that is offered to God and greatly pleases Him." First, therefore, the Egyptian landscape is pictured as dotted with these powerhouses of prayer, raising a chorus of perpetual intercession. Then, the point is clearly made that the defense of ecclesiastical property is, theologically, an ἀγαθὸν ἔργον, a good work that avails for the soul. In helping the monastery, the duke cannot lose.

Dioscorus's prose here progresses by the device of paired epithets: φευκτέον καὶ ἀποτρεπτέον (3), ἱκετηρία καὶ πρεσβεῖα (10), οὐ πεπαύσεται . . . ἀδιαλειπτῶς (12), συμβαλλόμενον καὶ περισπουδαστόν (13). This practice is to be another of his most characteristic features of style, one derived from legal usage in which pairs of near-synonyms operate in tandem to define concepts by boxing them in so there can be no ambiguity. Not quite the same as a school figure of classical rhetoric, the legalistic doublet is at once decorative and effective. The paired terms can play off, one against the other, in passive versus active senses, in complementary buried metaphors in the words themselves, in juxtaposition of subtly different overtones. This procedure is, stylistically, the point where Dioscorus's working life as a jurist and his professional sense of literary language can be seen to fuse into one.

The matter at issue is one of six arouras of sown land that had been donated to the monastery by a widow, as an offering (προσφορὰ καὶ ἀγάπη) for her soul and that of her late husband. A certain Ezekiel, scornfully characterized in a triple crescendo as "a barber, a slanderer, a bad man" (κουρεὺς καὶ συκοφάντης καὶ πονηρός), is "unaccountably" trying to seize the land. The monks conclude their petition by invoking the aid of the Holy Trinity and by asking His Excellency to order the pagarch and the *topoteretes* to drive Ezekiel off. (One wonders, in view of the known behavior of the pagarch of Antaeopolis, just how much attention he will pay to the duke. But it is very much Dioscorus's job to request that the duke curb the pagarch.) In thus knitting his themes together, Dioscorus deploys his language—here in a chain of dependent infinitives of purpose—for maximum point.

Already by late 567, Dioscorus had made his reputation as a lawyer at Antinoë. Ensconced as a νομικός on the ducal *taxis*, he was retained as arbiter[46] in a complex case involving, as so often in Coptic society, a

----

46. On arbitration in Coptic law, I am indebted to the late A. Arthur Schiller for his unpublished papers that are kept in the Columbia University Law Library; and I am grateful to Roger and Whitney Bagnall for the opportunity to work on this material.

disputed inheritance. The proceedings of this case are recorded in a long text in Dioscorus's hand, *P.Lond.* V 1708.

Psates of Antinoë, who describes himself as working at the trade of making τζαγκάρια (Persian shoes, perhaps an upscale specialty that would have sold well in the fashionable society of the ducal seat), is being sued by his sisters and brothers-in-law. Dioscorus devotes most of the document, which numbers more than 260 lines, to recording the parties' statements; the world of family disputes within Coptic society is one he knows well. Yet even within the factual confines of a legal proceeding, he is flexing the sinews of his language with evident delight.

The present arbitration, in Greek, does not begin with a technical operative verb equivalent to ⲁⲓⲥⲱⲧⲙ, but rather with a (fragmentary) dating clause. Line 3 mentions a first indiction (567), calling it by the term ἐπινέμησις. If Bell's placement of the fragments at the beginning of the document is correct, this would appear to be an exception to Grenfell and Hunt's early observation (*P.Oxy.* I 126.10n., 1899)[47] that this word is never found in dating clauses at the heads of documents. (Dioscorus will use it thus again in 570, in *P.Cair.Masp.* II 67151.4.) It seems to be a self-consciously literary word, found in a Constantinopolitan milieu (John Lydus, *De mens.* 3.23; *Cod.Just.* X.16.13.5). Could Dioscorus have become familiar with it in his legal studies or on his trip to the capital, and be employing it as one of those classicizing devices by which a writer avoids the normal technical term for a common matter?[48] It gets borrowed into Coptic somewhat later (KRU 78.8). In any case, it is a touch of elegance in the tone of the opening formulas.

The greater part of this lengthy document consists of the statements of the parties to the dispute, told in a straightforward narrative fashion. Dioscorus, the arbiter, states their names and relationships, adding that, in the crossfire (ἀμφιβαλλομένων), God (τὸ θεῖον here) will make all plain to him (διασαφήσῃ μοι, a Cyrillian word). (He is to echo this sentiment in Coptic in *P.Lond.* V 1709.14–15 [discussed later]: ⲉⲧⲉⲣⲉ ⲡⲭⲟⲉⲓⲥ ⲛⲁⲧⲥⲁⲃⲟⲓ . . . ⲉⲃⲟⲗ ⲛ̄ϩⲏⲧⲥ̄.) The human intellect of the jurisprudent had powerful aid.

The dispute began after the death of Psates's father, the widower Apollos, and concerned the alleged squandering of his bequeathed property. The event of his death is rendered by an outstandingly appropriate metaphor (line 29): ἀπολειτουργήσαντα τὸν ἑαυτοῦ βίον ("he having laid

____

47. Repeated by Bagnall and Worp, *CSBE*, 5 n. 21.

48. Bagnall and Worp, *CSBE*, p. 5 n. 21 collected the uses of the word; they do not seem to fall into a perceptible pattern.

down the final liturgy, his life"). (Wilcken felt the force of the metaphor; Bell, surely not rightly, downplayed it.) Dioscorus hardly chose his metonymies at random: this one is deeply expressive of what was felt to be the very fabric of Egyptian city life at the time.

The parties carry on the story of their lives and wrongs, their thoughts moving in a world bounded by the expected horizons of economic class and personal concern. As craftsmen of Antinoë, they are concerned with keeping up appearances and with exact records of their finances; and, we can infer, they are aware of the bureaucracy that is set round and over them in the city. Such an awareness is probably what lies behind the repeated references in their testimony to the terms of office of certain officials. Psates ties events in his past to remembered markers: "in the second year that the *gloriosissimus* Apion was in office" (lines 82–83); "when recently Horion was taxiarch" (lines 86–87); "in Conon's time" (line 94). These signposts along the stream of memory, characteristic devices in a society that was so visibly a network of personal relations, led Bell to speculate on the possible "existence at Antinoopolis of a local system of dating by eponymous civic magistrates" (*P.Lond.* V p. 121). (Had that been the case, it would have had interesting consequences for the development of the eponymous Coptic *lashane* after the conquest.) It would seem that Antinoë had in fact no such official system. But we can unravel some of Bell's confusion about the presence and role of the taxiarch.

A military official called the $\tau\alpha\xi\iota\alpha\rho\chi\sigma$ had been known in Ptolemaic Egypt (*PSI* 513.12, *P.Mich. Zenon* 70.5); he was equated (later) with a centurion or *primipilus* (cf. *P.Ryl.* 627–634). But the title was evolving (as was the form—the later monastic prefect is a $\tau\alpha\xi\iota\alpha\rho\chi\eta s$).[49] Nevertheless, we can determine who the taxiarch was in the sixth-century Thebaid (after Justinian's Edict 13: *pace* Bell, hardly the duke).[50] In the world of the bureaucracy, taxiarch meant simply the head of the ducal *taxis* or *officium*, who was the *princeps* of the *schola* of the *agentes in rebus*.[51] It is logical that, in the "company town" atmosphere of Antinoë, the identity of this official remained in people's minds and formed a convenient marker by which to date their memories. Less directly, but just as visibly as the *protocometes* of

---

49. The root metaphor in the word gives it a literary life, in, e.g., Cyril and ps.-Dionysius.

50. Cf. John Lydus, *De Mag.* 1.46. For discussion of the Lydus passages, I am grateful to Michael Maas.

51. Maspero had already seen in 1912 (*Organisation militaire de l'Egypte byzantine* [Paris 1912] 85–88) that one can extrapolate from the Latin description of the office of the duke of the Thebaid in the *Notitia Dignitatum*. He was followed by G. Rouillard (*L'administration civile de l'Egypte byzantine*² [Paris 1928] 42–47).

a village, the chief *agens in rebus* marked off chapters in the histories of Antinoë's inhabitants.

The rest of the document is sprinkled with the occasional rare word or rhetorical figure from Dioscorus's pen. "And this," Psates is made to exclaim with a fine abstract noun, "this is the return I get for my φιλαδελφία: they are suing me!" (line 101). We find the *hapax* ἀπελλογαρίζειν 'to render an account' (line 104). The latter part of this form seems to anticipate the λογάριν/λογάριον of John Moschus and Leontius of Neapolis, and the later λογαριάζειν; these terms may well have originated in Byzantine Greek. (The double lambda is probably a spelling analogous to that in ἐλλογιμώτατος for εὐλογ-.) Dioscorus refers to the dividing up of the inheritance into equal shares—his contribution as arbiter—as an ἰσομοιρία (line 199)—not a legalism (at any rate, not a Justinianic one) but a Thucydideanism (7.75). In line 212, he tosses in the poetic μακαρίτης for the ordinary μακάριος. And he calls the Gospels (see later discussion) not εὐαγγέλια but μεγαλῖα (line 229), a word found not in Egyptian but in Palestinian authors (Moschus, Malalas, and Cyril of Scythopolis). Finally, he calls the "finalization" of the case a σβέσις 'quenching'—almost as though, with his sensitivity to metaphor, he saw the suits and countersuits as a fire raging in society.

The resolution of the parties' problems is bolstered at every turn by oaths: oaths on the Gospels (lines 228–229) and oaths taken in churches (lines 165–166, 243–244, 258). These sanctions are perfectly in line with, and acknowledged by, Justinian's Novel 74.5 of A.D. 538. They are equally natural to Coptic society (cf., later, CLT 5 [for Gospels] and BKU I 97 [for churches]).[52] But most of all, they tell us something about the values of all the parties to the case. The whole web of interlocking social relations is thus seen to be underpinned by a web of invisible constraints,[53] and made reliable thanks to these trusted points of reference. Matters are touched at their nodes of greatest tension by the felt power of that truth, which could simultaneously both prove and enforce the matter of the procedure.

Dioscorus was still busier in 568, being taken up with business affairs (as related in Chapter 1) and thus further exercising his style as a ducal lawyer who could be relied on to give of his best. But 569 was to be his *annus mirabilis*, the year of his most elaborate prose productions to date.

---

52. Cf. E. Seidl, *Der Eid im römisch-ägyptischen Provinzialrecht* (MB 24, Munich 1935) II 50–52; but we can discount his remarks about survival of Pharaonic "Aberglaube."

53. Compare again R. Colman, "Reason and unreason," esp. pp. 576–579, 586–587. One might almost discern the germ of something like an institution of "oath helpers" in Egypt.

His work visibly and expansively unites the Latin heritage of jurisprudence with the Greek-Coptic fabric of his culture.

P.Cair.Masp. III 67314 mentions a "coming fourth indiction" (III.16), which must be 570. Maspero termed the document a division of an inheritance, but in effect it really is a support agreement (ὁμολογία, III.7 and 41). Five brothers agree to maintain their mother Asteria for her lifetime on the income of some land in the Hermopolite[54] that she had received from her late husband. The yearly income and yield from that land are to be paid for Asteria's support, regardless of her health (an insurance policy), under the terms of what Dioscorus calls an *etesium peculium* (I.20, II.5) or a *legatum* (I.33, cf. II.5 restored).[55] These are not the only occurrences of Latin technical terms, albeit used in slightly unusual ways, in Dioscorus's text.[56]

The first part of this document is framed in the first person by Asteria, and the second part in the first person by her sons. She begins by describing the death (ἀποβίωσις, a very Dioscorian term) of her husband and the circumstances of the entrusted property. She directs her sons to see to the annual income with all care, "without εὑρεσιλογία or circumscribing (περιγραφή) the law in any way," even should she fall ill or become senile (hence, legally incompetent). In case of necessity, the sons are to see to the principal, the interest, and the "customary payments" (lines 31–32), indicating that sixth-century financial transactions took such gratuities for granted. The maintenance is called a *legatum;* this must be the *legatum annuum* of *Digest* 33.1, to which Dioscorus would naturally have referred in Latin.

Asteria goes on to make provision for the rent (στεγανόμιον, II.10) payable by her sister Maria, a provision that is not to be contested or overturned. Then her sons state their complementary agreement (ἀνθομολογοῦμεν, III.7), on which they take the awesome oath of *completio* (Maspero restored ἐκπληκτικόν, but it ought to be ἐκπληρωτικόν: ἐκπλήρωσις = *completio*). Now Dioscorus begins to employ more of his consciously elegant style: the agreement cannot be made light of by any σκοπῷ καὶ

54. Cf. M. Drew-Bear, *Le nome Hermopolite* (Missoula, Mont. 1979) 225.

55. The word λήγαδον first appears in the Gnomon of the Idios Logos. (And cf. *P.Grenf.* I 62.16.) Dioscorus will use it often; see later, in the testament of the physician Flavius Phoebammon of 570, *P.Cair.Masp.* II 67151.295, 299. He defines ἀννουάλια λήγατον as εϥμΗΝ and πεκούλιον λήγατον as Ν6ⲁⲅⲟ(Ν) in his glossary, lines 343, 346.

56. See N. van der Wal, "Die Schreibweise der dem lateinischen entlehnten Fachworte i.d. frühbyz. Juristensprache," *Scriptorium* 37 (1983) 29–53. The point is that Latinisms and technical terms were distinguished by their script in juristic *literary* texts; but in the everyday documents of the actual praxis, they were simply there, completely integrated into the usage, quite at home. From literary texts, see J. Horn, "Latino-Coptica," *Atti XVII congr.intl.papirol.* (Naples 1984) 1361–1376.

τρόπῳ, by any legal angle or loophole. And the sons agree to show "all good disposition and pure love of φιλομητορία" toward their mother, for whom they pray a long life (ζῆν καὶ ὑγιαίνειν, the Egyptian formula from ⲱⲛⲍ + ⲟⲩⲭⲁⲓ). *Philometoria*, a word from poetry and rhetoric, is a *hapax* in Dioscorus but represents the sort of abstract noun he often uses to carry the weight of the idea and adorn it with Christian semantic content (juxtaposing it here with ἀγάπη).[57]

In the splendid rhetorical conclusion of this document, Dioscorus uses his favorite procedural device of paired nouns, epithets, or phrases. Each son agrees to pay his yearly share at his own κινδύνῳ καὶ πόρῳ, γενικῶς καὶ ἰδικῶς, ἐνεχύρου λόγῳ καὶ ὑποθήκης δικαίῳ, εὐγνωμονῶς καὶ πληρωτικῶς (III.23–25); and to feed, comfort, and nurse their mother in her old age (here a triplet of literary words, γηροβοσκεῖσθαι, παρηγορεῖσθαι καὶ νοσοκομεῖσθαι) should any *malakia* or *arrostia* befall her. And Dioscorus's peroration is a balanced symphony of assonance (III.39–41): "We will make the payments," say the sons, "out of our own *periousia*, by/of our goods' *synkoinonia*, paying in *homonoia* [with the sixth century's itacizing pronunciation, the harmony would have been unbroken] in all the ways we have sworn to in this *homologia*." The very end is sewn together in true lawyer's fashion by a sextuple chain of verbs spelling out just how the contract will be kept. Dioscorus, careful professional guardian of the law, ends with the word δίκη. It is the theme of his prose as well as his poetry.

MAJOR WORKS PRESERVED IN COPTIC

The year 569 was also the year of a major and multidocumented law case, the affair of Anoup and Julius. Dioscorus acted twice as arbiter in their case, and recorded the depositions and his decisions in the matter in Coptic. It is really owing to the chances of preservation[58] that we know of this case in this language: in the bilingual society of Antinoë, where the same legal involvement could generate paperwork indifferently in Greek and Coptic,[59] things did not fall neatly along class or confessional lines. Hence, we cannot conclude automatically that the monks Anoup and Julius were

57. Did Dioscorus know enough Ptolemaic history to be making, as well, a bit of a pun?

58. See L. S. B. MacCoull, "The Coptic archive of Dioscorus of Aphrodito," *Cd'E* 56 (1981) 185–193.

59. For another example, see A. A. Schiller, "Interrelation of Coptic and Greek papyri," *Festschrift F. Oertel*, ed. H. Braunert (Bonn 1964) 107–119.

lower class or non-Chalcedonian: the old labels do not stick. This case, involving as it does a point of the law of monastic property, puts us right at the heart of Byzantine Egyptian society. Could those already in the monastic state own property at all?[60] Could monks inherit? Could they manage, and dispose of, their property?[61] In what sense were they the possessors of their monastic dwellings?[62] In a world where monasteries were, corporately, great landowners, the competence and activities of their members took on special importance.

Dioscorus begins recording the transactions of Anoup and Julius in a text dated 28 October 569, the divided *P.Cair.Masp.* II 67176r+P.Alex.inv. 689. The monastery involved is his family house, Pharoou (the Apostles, see previous discussion). In addition to the recently published text,[63] the following observations may illustrate Dioscorus's Coptic prose style of legal composition.

The beginning of the first half has been lost, and the text has suffered from abrasion in both parts, but enough can be read to yield connected sense. The text runs, in translation, as follows:

> "(having) established a cession (ⲡⲁⲣⲁⲭⲱⲣⲏⲥⲓⲥ) in the name (?) of Apa Papnoute . . . whether my sons also, having become monks, shall inherit the cell (room) or not.' She said, then, in the cession that if they become monks they will share in . . . (but) if not, no one shall inherit anything, neither my own nor a stranger. But if . . . there intervened another week of the fifteenth year (indiction [566]) of this assessment (?). When they heard these things, namely Anoup son of Apollo and Julius son of Sarapammon, they filed a countersuit against them, the mother not being the owner. But the sons agreed. . . . The cession was established with Apa Papnoute . . . showing that Apa Papnoute was made to agree . . . with the heirs.
>
> I, Papnoute, saw everything which you (pl.) . . . with improvement. . . . They did not sell (it) without consideration, but . . . with regard to what the Lord put into my mind . . . Apa Papnoute and Anoup son of Apollo and Julius son of Sarapammon are to inherit in common, half and half, accord-

60. See the paper of M. Krause, "Zur Möglichkeit apotaktischen Mönchtums," *II intl.congr.copt.stud.* (Rome 1985) 121–134. E. Wipszycka theorized, contrary to the earlier work of Krause, "Das Apa-Apollon-Kloster zu Bawit," that *apotaktikos* did not mean a special category of monks, let alone a legal status, but simply meant "coenobite" as opposed to *anachoretes;* see "Les terres de la congrégation pachomienne . . . ," in *Le monde grec. Hommages Cl. Préaux,* ed. J. Bingen, G. Cambier, and G. Nachtergael (Brussels 1975) 634.

61. See again, Steinwenter, "Byzantinische Mönchstestamente," *Aegyptus* 12 (1932) 55–64.

62. See the literature, esp. Steinwenter, "Rechtsstellung," and "Vermögensrechte."

63. L. S. B. MacCoull, "A Coptic cession of land by Dioscorus of Aphrodito," *II intl.congr.copt.stud.* (Rome 1985) 159–166.

> ing to the *dikaion* of my house(s). . . . If Apa Papnoute should transgress this document (lit. "sale"), he is not to . . . their deposit. . . . Only if no improvement has been made in . . . so that they show their zeal at all times, performing their service in proper order . . . with each other without quarreling. For it is agreed (ⲥⲩⲙⲫⲱⲛⲉ) according to our scrutiny (ⲇⲟⲕⲓⲙⲁⲥⲓⲁ) (and) our counsel . . . that the sons Anoup and Julius, having entered the monastic life (ⲧⲙⲛⲧ̄ⲙⲟⲛⲁⲭⲟⲥ) according to the advice of Mesiane their mother, . . . are to share with Apa Papnoute, rightly and justly, going halves together. Hereafter, then, according to this plan, we have made judgment without dissembling. ☧ Give it to the pious superior of the mount of Pharoou and its whole village, from Dioscorus, the humble son of Apa Apollos of Pharoou. The Holy Trinity. And may I be protected from above by your prayers. Hathyr, new moon, 3rd indiction, 4th year of the reign and consulship of Fl. Justin (II) semper Augustus.

It appears that three years previously Mesiane, the mother of two sons by different fathers, had wanted to make a written property disposition *(parachoresis)* on behalf of those sons before they entered, with her support, the monastic life. (She had reinforced their vocation with a stipulation that if they remained laymen they would forfeit their shares in a dwelling [*ri*] apparently handed down from a deceased relative.) This disposition entails two assumptions: first, that already professed monks could inherit immovable property; and second, that monks had some right of ownership over their cells. (Both these conditions are amply documented by the papyri.)[64] Later, the half-brothers Anoup and Julius have countersued (ⲁⲛⲧⲓⲇⲓⲕⲟⲗⲟⲅⲉⲓ [*sic*]) some unnamed parties, on the grounds that Mesiane, not having *dominium* (ⲣ̄ ϫⲟⲉⲓⲥ), had no right to make such a disposition. One Apa Papnoute, most likely the *oikonomos* of the monastery of Pharoou and hence representing its *dikaion* (II.9), had been party to the first arrangement. In the intervening three years, the brothers have apparently both made improvements *(philokalia)* to the property and tried to dispose of it (ⲧⲓ ⲉⲃⲟⲗ) for gain. Dioscorus, acting as arbiter (ⲁⲛⲕⲣⲓⲛⲉ), records his decision: the ownership is to be vested jointly in the brothers and in Apa Papnoute, simultaneously, by due process, and without further dispute.

The depositions of the parties are recorded in narrative fashion, giving the facts, whereas Dioscorus puts his judgment in slightly more rhetorical style. (Apa Papnoute, though, has a pious turn of phrase: ⲡϫⲟⲉⲓⲥ ⲛⲁϫϥ̄ ⲉⲡⲁϩⲏⲧ, II.5; Dioscorus will echo it later, in *P.Lond.* V 1709.14–15.) As temporal administrator of the monastery, Dioscorus is concerned above all with the smooth running of its affairs, both spiritual (ⲟⲩⲣⲟⲧ) and social

64. Steinwenter, "Rechtsstellung," "Vermögensrechte," and *Das Recht der koptischen Urkunden* (Munich 1955) 24–25, 50.

(ⲁⲗⲱⲧⲛ̄, ⲉⲡ ⲟⲣⲁⲓⲛⲟⲛ [a unique Latin-Greek hybrid], ⲁⲭⲛ ⲙⲓϣⲉ). His doublet ⲟⲣⲑⲱⲥ ⲕⲁⲓ ⲁⲓⲕⲁⲓⲱⲥ, naturalized as it is in a Coptic text, speaks to and answers his sense of role as arbiter ⲁⲭⲛ ⲩⲡⲟⲕⲣⲓⲥⲓⲥ (not at all a common loanword: ?cf. Ep 51.45). (He is very conscious of the pun in playing off ⲕⲣⲓⲛⲉ against ⲩⲡⲟ-ⲕⲣⲓⲥⲓⲥ.) He interjects the closing invocation-phrase, "The Holy Trinity," and we are reminded of the importance of Trinitarian formulas in his poetry.[65] He then adds a postscript, asking for the prayers of the house, mindful of its place in his life as a family foundation. Notable is the gentle tact with which he signs himself simply the "son of Apa Apollo of Pharoou," not "the former Flavius Apollos the *protocometes*," or "son of your founder," but an Apollos as he would have wished to be remembered, the holy old man of the house. The Coptic sense of *Eigenkloster* and *Eigenkirche*, whatever the actual juristic status of the entity, had very deep roots. And this case is, as we shall see, not yet over.

To reach its next phase, we have an intervening stage in Greek. The verso of *P.Cair.Masp.* III 67353 bears the earlier of Dioscorus's two versions of a disinheritance document, with a dating clause giving regnal Justin II 5, Hathyr 16, indiction 3 (12.xi.569). This, then, is Dioscorus's last major work of 569.

Since the first version of this genre of document appeared (in *P.Cair. Masp.* I 67097 v D, written later; see subsequent discussion), it has provoked lively discussion and comment from jurists (the literature is collected by Amelotti and Wurm).[66] The document in III 67353v is framed in the first person by an unnamed Antinoite; the named children, Dionysia, John, Paulina, and Andrew, are not identifiable from the papyri. Earlier opinion had held that this piece's companion never grew into an actual legal deed but was a rhetorical exercise on paper only. We cannot be certain, but I see no obstacle to there having occurred, in 569, an actual case;[67] the reuse of much of the material in the 570s, in longer and more ornamented form, would be due to Dioscorus's Handelian habit of self-borrowing, in poetry or prose, when inspired by a similar occasion. The style is Dioscorian: resounding abstract nouns, paired attributes, scriptural and old Roman allusions resonate throughout.

The text in III 67353v calls the piece a πρόγραμμα, a proclamation, of *apokeryxis* and *apagoreusis*, public disinheritance and renunciation; that in

<hr>

65. L. S. B. MacCoull, "A Trinitarian formula in Dioscorus of Aphrodito," *BSAC* 24 (1982) 103–110, and MacCoull, "μονοειδής," pp. 61–64.

66. M. Amelotti, *Le costituzioni giustinianee nei papiri* (Milan 1971) 74–75; M. Wurm, *Apokeryxis, abdicatio und exheredatio* (MB 60) (Munich 1972) 92–95.

67. So Wurm, *Apokeryxis,* p. 92.

I 67097 v D calls it a διήγημα, a detailed narrative, of *apokeryxis*. (This fits in with the earlier writing's having been indeed called forth by a real occasion. The secondary literature is mistaken about the date of I 67097 v D: the seventh and eighth indictions in v A must be 573–574,[68] and this dating agrees with the explicit siting at Aphrodito, where Dioscorus had returned, in line 79.) Note the pair of classical metaphors, of a herald proclaiming something aloud in the marketplace, buried in the technical terms. Operating as he is at a meeting place of *Reichsrecht* and *Volksrecht*, Dioscorus demonstrates his awareness of the classical past.

After a "being of sound mind" preamble, the framer of the document describes his grievances against his children. Dioscorus coins the word πατρολοός (?cf. the seventh-century πατρολύμας, PG 38.1032). None of them has been γηρόκομος: compare the γηροβοσκεῖσθαι in *P.Cair.Masp.* III 67314.28 (the noun γηροκομεῖον for an old people's home occurs in slightly later authors: see Cyril of Scythopolis, and Leontius's life of John the Almoner). The children have become ἀντίπαλοι (the agonistic image is alive to Dioscorus, as it was in his early poem on S. Senas) and μέγαιροι—that is, "too big for their britches." Ὁ ἀντίπαλος is also a patristic epithet for the devil: Dioscorus is indirectly alluding to the demonically unnatural way the children are said to have acted.

Then Dioscorus coins in succession three splendid abstract nouns: they have gone to the limits of πατροκτασία (which is ἄσπλαγχνον, as was the pagarch Menas in *P.Cair.Masp.* I 67002). And, in cutting the children off from all but what they must receive by law (the *lex Falcidia*), they are to become a state of ultimate rejection, κορακοβροσία and ὀμματωρυξία. This is a kind of scriptural phrase making (cf. Ps. 63:11, a psalm Dioscorus quoted in his verse letter to Philoponus,[69] and Herod's sticky end, eaten of worms). And he consciously puns in calling the children ἀπαίδευτοι—not only are they devoid of well-trained manners, they are not really the person's own children at all any more.

The document ends with an oath formula that invokes God and the imperial couple Justin and Sophia to see that the jurists of Antinoë continue to do their job of bringing settlement (ἀποδημίωσις, a *hapax*) to bad situations by arbitration and fearless pronouncement of decisions, banishing impious conduct. Then Dioscorus constructs a chiastically balanced summing up: "they should have honored their parents, according to the θεῖος νόμος (the Fifth Commandment), but they neglected even the πατρικὸς

---

68. Cf. L. S. B. MacCoull, "The imperial *chairetismos* of Dioscorus of Aphrodito," *JARCE* (1981) 46 n. 7.

69. L. S. B. MacCoull, "Dioscorus of Aphrodito and John Philoponus."

θεσμός (i.e., natural law)." Here in one graceful period is Dioscorus's meditation on divine law, natural law, and their interaction.[70]

On the other side of *P.Cair.Masp.* III 67353—the side with writing across the fibers, in *transversa charta* fashion—Dioscorus returned, in 569/70, to the case of Anoup and Julius and their property. (Maspero had noticed that this side bore a "long contract in Coptic," but could not read it.[71]) Much of the surface of the papyrus is faded and abraded (see Figure 5), but enough connected text can be read to yield further information about the outcome of the affair. I give first a transcription and translation of the fragments.

(Glass 5)

ΧΜΓ

† ΚΑΤΑ ΜΕСΙΤΙΑС ΤΡΟΠΟΝ ΑΙСШΤΜ ΕΘΥΠΟΘΕСΙС ΠΠΑΥΛΟС ΠϢΗΡΕ Ν[
ΘΕΟΦΙΛΟС ΠΕΠΡΕСΒΥΤΕΡΟС ΑΥШ ΜШΝΑΧΟС ΜΝΧΡΗСΤΗС ΠϢΗΡΕ
   ΠΠΑϨΑΜ[
ΜΝΛΕΟΝΤΙΟС ΠϢΗΡΕ ΝΑΠΟΛΛШ Ν . ΝΟΝΕ . . . . . . [
5   ΕΥΟ ΝΑΦΗΛΙϪΕ ΝСΟΒΕΚΕ ΑСΤ. [
   . . . . ϪΕ ΟΥϨΗΚΕ . . [
ΤΕϥϢΟ . ΕΠ . ΝΤΑ . . . . ΑΒ ΡΚΟСΜΙΚΟΝ ΑϥΚΑ ΠΛΑΝΙСΤΗС ΝСШС ΜΝΤΕϥ[
ΜΝΤΕϥΚΑΙСΕ ΜΝΤΜΝΤΑΤ. . . . . ΜΠΚΟΥΪ ΕΤΙ СΟΒΕΚΕ
   ΜΝϨΥΠΟСΤΑ[СΙС
ΝΤΑϥ . . . . ΝΑΠΑ ΠΑΠΝΟΥΤΕ ΤΟΟΥ ΝΤΡΙΜΗСΙΝ ΝΝΟΥ[Β

(Glass 6, fr. 2)
10   ΟΥΠΑΡΑΧШΗΡСΙС ΕϪΝ ΑΜΦΙ[ΒΟΛΙΑ
ΝΠΡΑСΙС ΝΑΠΑ ΠΑΠΝΟΥΤΕ ΝϢШΠΕ ΕΤΕ ΤΑΪ ΤΕ ΤΡΙ ΕΤΡΕ[
ΜΝΝΕϥΚΛΗΡΟΝΟΜΟС ϢΑ ΕΝΕϨ ΕСϨΟΜΟΛΟΓΕΙ ϪΕ Α ΠΑϨΑΪ ΔΙΑΤΙΘΕ
ΕΡΟΪ ΜϪΠΟС ΕΒΑΜΟΥ ϪΕ . . . . ΝΑϢΗΡΕ ΟΥШϢ ΕΡΜΟΝΑΧΟС[

(Glass 2)

   ΚΟΙΝШΝΕΙ ΝΕΜΑΚ

15   ΕΙΔΕ ΜΗ ΓΕ ΜΝΤΕΛΑΑΥ ΝΚΛΗΡΟΝΟΜΟС ϨШϥ ΝΕΜΑΚ ΕΠШΪΠΕ ΟΥΔΕ Ϣ. [
ΕϢШΠΕ ΔΕ ΕΡϢΑΝ ΝΑϢΗΡΕ ΕΙ ΕΤΜΝΤΜΟΝΑΧΟС ΝΕΚ6ΝΘΕ ΝϢΑΥ Ν . [
ΝΕΜΑΥ ϨΑΠΕϥΤΟΟΥ ΝΤΡΪΜΥСΙ ΝΤΕΙΤΕ ϨΑΦΙΛΟΚΑΛΕΪΑ ΕΚΑΑΒ
   ΕΤΡΕΪΕΥΤ[

<hr>

70. Much of the juristic discussion about this text and especially *P.Cair.Masp.* I 67097 v D has turned on the different meanings of θεῖος νόμος: in III 67353 v 33 it clearly means the commandment to honor father and mother, but in I 67097 v D it might or might not mean a particular piece of imperial legislation.

71. In October 1933, the late Charles Kuentz had tried to transcribe this side (a copy of his notes toward a transcription, sent to W. E. Crum, is in the Griffith Institute at Oxford), but, as he was an Ancient Egyptologist and neither a documentary papyrologist nor a social historian of the Late Antique period, without much success.

ⲉⲓϭⲉ ⲥⲟⲩ ⲣ̄ⲁⲗⲗⲟⲧⲣⲓⲟⲥ ⲉⲧⲣⲉⲓ ⲁⲓ̈ϣⲓⲛⲉ ⲇⲉ ⲥⲁ ⲧⲁⲡⲟⲇⲉⲓⲝⲓⲥ ⲛ̄ⲛⲓϣⲁϫⲉ
ϩⲱⲥ ⲁⲕⲣⲟⲁⲧⲏⲥ ⲕϛ (ⲁⲓ) ⲕⲣⲓ̈ⲧⲏⲥ ⲧⲏⲥ ⲩⲡⲟⲑⲉⲥⲉⲱⲥ ⲁⲩⲉⲙⲫⲁⲛⲉⲓⲥⲑⲁⲓ ⲛⲁⲓ̈ ⲛ̄ⲛ̄[
ⲧⲡⲁⲣⲁⲭⲱⲣⲏⲥⲓⲥ ⲉ̣ⲓ̣ⲧⲉ ⲣⲱⲙⲉ ⲉⲓⲧⲉ ⲥϩⲓⲙⲉ ⲛ̄ⲡⲉⲩⲣⲟⲧ ⲕⲁⲧⲁ ⲛⲓϣⲁϫⲉ ⲉⲥⲃⲉⲃⲁ[ⲓⲱ
. . . . . . ⲡⲣⲙ ⲧⲗⲕⲉ ⲛⲧⲁⲥϣⲱⲡⲉ ⲉⲡⲙⲉⲭⲉⲓⲣ ⲉⲃⲇⲟⲙⲏ ⲛ̄ⲧⲡⲉⲛⲧⲉ ⲕⲁⲓ
ⲇⲉⲕⲁⲧⲏ ⲧⲣⲟⲙⲡⲉ ⲛ̄ⲡⲁ . . . ⲉ ⲛⲁⲓ̈ ⲇⲉ ⲛ̄ⲧⲉⲣⲉⲩⲥⲱⲧⲙ̄ ⲉⲣⲟⲟⲩ ⲛ̄ϭⲓ ⲛⲁ ⲁⲛⲟⲩⲡ· ⲡϣⲏⲣⲉ
ⲛⲁⲡⲟⲗⲗⲱ ⲙⲛ̄ⲓ̈ⲟⲩⲗⲓⲟⲥ ⲡϣⲏⲣⲉ ⲛ̄ⲥⲁⲣⲁⲡⲁⲙⲱⲛ ⲁⲩⲁⲛⲧⲓⲇⲓⲕϛ (ⲁⲓ) ⲱ[ⲗⲟⲅⲉⲓ
ϣⲁⲣⲟⲟⲩ ϫⲉ ⲧⲙⲁⲁⲩ ⲱ ⲛ̄ⲡϫⲟⲉⲓⲥ ⲁⲛ ⲁⲗⲗⲁ ⲛ̄ϣⲏⲣⲉ ⲛⲉ ⲁⲩⲛ̄ⲑⲟⲙⲟⲗⲟⲅⲓⲁ
ⲁⲡⲁ ⲡⲁⲡⲛⲟⲩⲧⲉ ϣⲉ ⲛⲧⲙⲛⲧⲙⲁⲁⲩ ⲕⲁⲧⲁ ⲑⲉ ⲥⲩⲙⲫⲱⲛⲉⲓ ⲛⲉⲓ ϩⲛⲧⲡⲁⲣⲁⲭⲱⲣⲏⲥⲓⲥ

(Glass 5)

ⲁⲕⲣⲟⲁⲧⲏⲥ ⲉϫⲛ ⲛⲉⲩⲇⲓⲕⲁⲓⲟⲗⲟⲅⲓⲁ ⲛⲁⲛ . . . . . ⲗⲟⲥ
]ⲡⲉⲡⲣⲉⲥⲃⲩⲧⲉⲣⲟⲥ· ⲙⲛ̄ⲛ̄ ⲕⲁⲓ ⲥⲛⲏⲩ ⲉⲧⲛⲉⲙⲁⲩ ⲛ̄ⲧⲁⲛⲛϣⲁⲣⲉ ⲑⲟⲙⲟ[ⲗⲟⲅⲓⲁ
]ⲛ̄ⲙⲟⲟⲩ ⲉⲩϫⲱ ⲛ̄ⲙⲟⲥ ϫⲉ ⲉⲧⲓ ⲉⲣⲉ ⲡⲙⲁⲕ[ⲁⲣⲓⲟⲥ

(Glass 1, fr. 4)

ⲛ̄ⲧⲓⲙⲏ ⲛ̄ϩⲏⲧⲥ̄ ⲉⲁⲩϫⲓⲧⲟⲩ ϩⲁⲧⲣⲉ ϫⲓⲛⲧⲁ ⲧⲉⲩⲙⲁⲁⲩ ⲙⲟⲩ ⲉⲛⲧⲁⲩⲥⲙ̄ⲛ̄ⲧⲥ
ϩⲓⲡⲣⲱⲧⲏⲥⲓ̈ ⲛⲁⲩ ⲧⲉⲩⲧⲛⲥⲟⲟⲩⲧⲛ ⲧⲉⲛⲟⲩ ⲛ̄ⲧⲁⲥⲡⲁⲣⲉⲗⲑⲉ ⲧϩⲟⲙⲟⲗⲟⲅⲓⲁ ⲇⲉ
ⲛⲧⲁ ⲧⲉⲩⲙⲁⲁⲩ ϫⲓⲧⲥ ⲛ̄ⲧⲛ̄ⲡⲁⲡⲛⲟⲩⲧⲉ ⲕⲁⲧⲁ ⲧⲡⲁⲣⲁⲇⲟⲥⲓⲥ ⲛ̄ⲛⲉⲩⲉⲓⲱⲧ
ⲛ̄ⲑⲉ ⲛ̄ⲧⲁⲥϩⲟⲙⲟⲗⲟⲅⲉⲓ̈ ⲛ̄ⲧⲡⲁⲣⲁⲭⲱⲣⲏⲥⲓⲥ ⲛ̄ⲧⲁⲥϣⲱⲡⲉ ⲛ̄ⲧϩⲏⲙⲉⲣⲁ ⲡⲉϩⲱ .
ⲛ̄ⲧⲁ ⲧⲡⲁⲣⲁⲭⲱⲣⲏⲥⲓⲥ ϣⲱⲡⲉ ⲛ̄ϩⲏⲧⲥ̄ ⲛ̄ⲥⲟⲩⲥⲁϣϥ̄ ⲛ̄ⲙ̄ϣⲓⲣ ⲟⲛ ⲛⲧⲡⲉ . . . .
ⲧⲏⲥ ⲡⲣⲟⲡⲁⲣⲉⲗⲑⲟⲩⲥⲏⲥ ⲉⲥϫⲱ ⲙⲙⲟⲥ . . . .

(Glass 6, fr. 1)

ⲁϫⲛ ⲙⲓϣⲉ ⲉϫⲛ ⲛⲓⲥⲩⲙⲫⲱⲛⲟⲛ . . .
ⲁⲛⲕⲁⲁⲩ ⲉⲃⲟⲗ ⲛ̄ⲡⲙⲉⲣⲟⲥ ⲛⲉⲩⲇⲟⲕⲉⲓ ⲉⲡⲉⲛϣⲟϫⲛⲉ
ϫⲉ ⲁⲛⲟⲩⲡ ⲙⲛ̄ⲓⲟⲩⲗⲓⲟⲥ ⲛⲉⲛ̄ϣⲏⲣⲉ ⲛⲛⲉⲩⲣⲟⲧ′ ⲛ̄ⲧⲁⲩⲉⲓ ⲉⲧⲙⲏⲧⲙⲁⲛⲁⲭⲟⲥ
ⲕⲁⲧⲁ ⲡϣⲟϫⲛⲉ ⲛⲛⲉⲙⲉⲥⲓⲁⲛⲉ ⲧⲉⲩⲙⲁⲁⲩ ⲙⲛ̄ⲡⲉⲩⲣⲟⲧ ⲡⲉⲩⲉⲓⲱⲧ ⲉϣⲁⲛ̣
. . . . ⲟⲣⲑⲱⲥ ⲕⲁⲓ ⲇⲓⲕⲁⲓⲱⲥ . . . ⲡⲣⲓ ⲛ̄ⲡⲁϣⲉ
. . .
. . .
[M.2] ̣ⲇⲓⲟⲥⲕⲟⲣⲟⲥ ⲡ[ϣⲏⲣⲉ ⲛ̄ⲁⲡⲁ ⲁⲡⲟⲗⲗⲱⲥ ⲕⲧⲗ.

After the manner of an arbitration. I have heard the deposition of Paul son of N., (and) Theophilus the priest and monk, and Chrestes son of Paham, and Leontius son of Apollo. . . . They (Anoup and Julius) being minors . . . to live in the world. The creditor forgave it, with . . . the little ones still being minors, with property . . . (which?) Apa Papnoute gave trimesia of gold for . . . (Statement by Mesiane) . . . A cession without dispute . . . (the) sale which Apa Papnoute made . . . and his heirs for ever,

(I) agreeing that my husband bequeath to me and my children (?) . . . my sons wish to become monks. . . . if not, that no heir go to law with you over what is mine, nor . . . but if my sons enter upon the monastic life, you are to find the way to . . . them with respect to his five trimesia for this as concerns improving the property *(philokalia)*, putting it toward . . .

(Statements and summing up by Dioscorus) If, therefore, they alienate a part of it, I have sought for the documentary evidence *(apodeixis)* of these words, as arbiter (ⲁⲕⲣⲟⲁⲧⲏⲥ) and judge (ⲕⲣⲓⲧⲏⲥ) of the deposition. They produced it for me as regards the cession, whether man or woman, according to these guaranteed words . . . the man from Telke. It was on Mecheir 7 that it took place, in the fifteenth year [indiction, i.e., A.D. 566]. . . . But these, when they heard them, namely (the ones of) Anoup son of Apollo and Julius son of Sarapammon, they made a countersuit *(antidikaiologia)* against them to the effect that the mother was not the owner, but rather the sons were. They agreed (that) Apa Papnoute was to go and close the deal with the mother in the way they had agreed in the cession . . . (to be) arbiter over their case at law . . . the priest, and also those brothers . . . saying: "When the late (N.) was still alive . . . (?)" . . . Apa Papnoute . . . (the) price for it, which they received double since their mother died, they established it upon their proposal *(protasis)*. Now you are extending the agreement, though it has expired, which their mother accepted from Apa Papnoute according to the bequest *(paradosis)* of their fathers, as she agreed to the cession as it happened on the day that the cession took place, on the seventh of Mecheir. She having already come forward to speak (?) . . . and it had previously expired . . . without fighting about the agreements *(symphonon)*. We dissolved them, as to the portion which seemed right to our counsel, that Anoup and Julius the sons, being ready (eager) to go into monastic life according to the counsel of Mesiane their mother and the readiness of their fathers . . . rightly and justly . . . half . . . Dioscorus, son of Apa Apollos.

Dioscorus's Coptic style in this document is comparatively restrained, technical, and to the point. There is not much hypotaxis: his construction proceeds mainly by circumstantial clauses, straightforward conditions, and balancing of pairs. What relative clauses there are are deployed rationally, and he does not deliberately use "purple-patch" ornament. This thoroughly practical Coptic prose is studded with the Greek juristic loanwords that are by now totally at home in the language.

P.Cair.Masp. III 67353r begins with the exact same technically operative phrases as does *P.Lond.* V 1709 (see later discussion): ⲕⲁⲧⲁ ⲙⲉⲥⲓⲧⲉⲓⲁⲥ ⲧⲣⲟⲡⲟⲛ· ⲁⲓⲥⲱⲧⲙ. For ⲙⲉⲥⲓⲧ(ⲉ)ⲓⲁ as the technical term for arbitration, compare *P.Cair.Masp.* III 67313.24; and also the more informal usages in *P.Monac.* 6.4, 23, 7.34, 41, 14.48, and *P.Fouad* III 85.13–14 (Syene and Antinoë). (The noun in this period is also used as the theological word for mediation, viz., by Christ, as the noun μεσίτης is for the divine mediator, but this is by extension and by the way.) Compare also *SPP* X 115.1, 214.4, 250.18, XX 193.1 for the noun. Further in Coptic, it appears later spelled ⲙⲉⲥⲉⲧⲓⲁ in KRU 44.16, 19, 23, 35, 41. It was the primary role of the arbiter, before rendering judgment (doing the work of a ⲕⲣⲓⲧⲏⲥ), to *listen* to the depositions of the witnesses; hence, the other technical term (and Dioscorus's self description) for arbiter is ⲁⲕⲣⲟⲁⲧⲏⲥ (infrequently used, however, in texts of this period; it survives garbled in Ep 575.9, WS 100, 145n., perhaps in Krall 1). Hence, ⲁⲓⲥⲱⲧⲙ can be translated "I have heard, I have listened to." (He used ἀκροάτης in *P.Lond.* V 1708.151.[72])

None of the four witnesses named is known from other papyri from Antinoë or Aphrodito:[73] Paul son of N., Theophilus the priest and monk, Chrestes son of Paham, and Leontius son of Apollo are new to the prosopography of Dioscorus's life. New too are some of the verb coinages with ⲣ̄: ⲣ̄ⲕⲟⲥⲙⲓⲕⲟⲛ 'to be a layman, live in the world'; ⲣ̄ⲁⲗⲗⲟⲧⲣⲓⲟⲥ 'to alienate' in the legal sense (cf. ἀλλοτριάζω in *P.Oxy.* XX 2267.8). The latter lives on in Coptic; compare BM 439, BKU III 321.29, VC 6 v 11, ST 172.5. But ⲣ̄ + Greek verb is not a preferred formation in the Sahidic of Middle Egypt.[74] One has the feeling that Dioscorus is deliberately Hellenizing even more than the usual legal usages would have him do.

For matters of being of legal age, compare KRU 89.11, 100.25. And for that figure of fear in any village, the *danistes*, compare KRU 16.48, 67.41, CO 189, Ep 260.10, 272.6, 520.2. The references in the text to the past, to the *parachoresis* and the *philokalia* made to the property, firmly bind this text to its predecessor, *P.Cair.Masp.* II 67176r+P.Alex.inv. 689. The question remains whether Mesiane's statement is being repeated from a past occasion, if she is dead by the time Dioscorus is drawing up this final document: the ⲙⲟⲩ is very hard to read. But the judgment is clear: any previous arrangements are abrogated, and the *dominium* has passed from its former possessor, whether the mother or the two half-brothers by themselves, to be vested jointly in the two monks and the monastic superior Apa Papnoute, who has apparently already put money into the property.

Now Justinian's Novel 5.5 "defined the monk's profession as the

---

72. For an exact parallel cf. *SPP* III/VIII 402.3, ἀκροατὴς τῆς ὑποθέσεως; and in a literary text, Epiphanius *Haer.* 71.1 (PG 42.376A), κριτὰς καὶ ἀκροατάς, just as Dioscorus describes himself. Rouillard, *L'administration civile*, p. 136 with n. 5, calls attention to the administrative meaning of μεσίτης: the "middleman" in the annona shipment.

73. MacCoull, "Prosopography of Aphrodito," p. 92.

74. It is, however, characteristic of Akhmimic; and we can see from the strong Sa flavor of Dioscorus's Coptic as seen in his glossary that this feature was part of his speech and may well have been an Akhmimicism (or Lycopolitanism).

moment when *dominium* passed from the monk to the monastery."[75] This piece of legislation was designed for the West; and how far its writ ran in the neighborhood of Antinoë is not easy to see.[76] There is no simply corresponding definition of just what type of legal act was needed to have the ⲣ̄ϫⲟⲉⲓⲥ inhere in both the *dikaion* of the religious house and the professed former owners. As can be seen from the case of Anoup and Julius, arbitration by a skilled (and, we presume, trusted) jurist was resorted to. By the reign of Justin II, it is plain to see that Egyptian monks continued to manage their own immovable property under a variety of forms. Dioscorus's spare Coptic *Geschäftsprosa* is a useful and flexible instrument for spelling out the realities of the situation he was called on to understand.

The phrase ⲕⲁⲧⲁ ⲙⲉⲥⲓⲧⲓⲁⲥ ⲧⲣⲟⲡⲟⲛ also begins Dioscorus's latest preserved Coptic arbitration, *P.Lond.* V 1709 (probably from early 570). Dioscorus has been formally called in to act as arbiter (ⲁⲓⲥⲱⲧⲙ again, twice) in the case of Phoebammon and Victorine, a brother and sister originally from Lycopolis but at the present time residing in Antinoë, who are suing their stepmother and half-sister for misappropriation of their late father's inheritance. Unfortunately, Dioscorus's judgment rendered at the end has not been preserved, and the center portion of the papyrus—two pieces, joined with something missing—is fragmentary. But the remaining text contains enough of interest to form a fitting close to our consideration of his Coptic documentary works and their style and import.

Dioscorus's clients were from a not unrespectable stratum of society. The late John had been not only a deacon but also a former ⲡⲣⲟⲛⲟⲏⲧⲏⲥ on the staff (here called not ⲧⲁⲝⲓⲥ but ⲏⲓ 'house'—perhaps he was attached to the private chapel) of Athanasius, Duke of the Thebaid. (Athanasius, recipient of Dioscorus's poems and petitions, is here titled ⲡⲁⲛⲉⲩⲫⲏⲙⲟⲥ ⲡⲁⲧⲣⲓⲕⲓⲟⲥ.) After the death of his first wife, Phoebammon and Victorine's mother, he had married a woman called Amanias and fathered another daughter, Philadelphia. Dioscorus prefaces his arbitration of their case with a rhetorical preamble that describes the stages by which an arbitration was set in motion by plaintiffs who were connected in both the civil and the

75. R. Kay, "Benedict, Justinian, and donations 'mortis causa' in the 'Regula Magistri,'" *RB* 90 (1980) 169–193.

76. A. M. Demicheli, "La politica religiosa di Giustiniano in Egitto: riflessi sulla chiesa egiziana della legislazione ecclesiastica giustinianea," *Aegyptus* 63 (1983) 217–257 sees the question along the old, and wrong, lines of linguistic-equaling-confessional division, and does not consider the real praxis of the documentary papyri. Nor does E. R. Hardy, "The Egyptian policy of Justinian," *DOP* 22 (1968) 21–41, move from the political to the social sphere.

ecclesiastical sphere with "official" Antinoë. Phoebammon and Victorine put a request (ⲁⲓⲧⲉⲓ) to Dioscorus (with an oath, ⲁⲛⲁⲱ, presumably to abide by his decision) to provide the technical office of an arbiter, ⲉⲧⲣⲁⲥⲱⲧⲙ̅ ⲡⲉⲩ2ⲱⲃ—that is, listen to their case. This was followed by an invitation or summons (ⲡⲁⲣⲁⲕⲁⲗⲉⲓ), by their consent (ⲥⲩⲛⲁⲓⲛⲉⲥⲓⲥ); and it seems that this action amounted to or constituted (ⲥⲙⲓⲛⲉ) a *compromissum* (ⲕⲟⲙⲡⲣⲟⲙⲓⲥⲥⲟⲛ, a Dioscorian legal Latinism)—namely, that which enabled an arbiter to function. That function is called ⲉⲝⲉⲧⲁⲍⲉ 'scrutiny', and Dioscorus concludes his preamble with an invocation of divine aid (ⲉⲧⲉⲣⲉ ⲡⲭⲟⲉⲓⲥ ⲛⲁⲧⲥⲁⲃⲟⲓ̈ . . .) in that business of scrutiny and resolution. The whole series of technical terms, most of which are Greek, is in effect a set of juristic "dominoes" that act to get the arbitration process moving.

On his deathbed and in front of witnesses, the late John had made an oral disposition (ⲉⲝ ⲁⲅⲣⲁⲫⲟⲩ ⲃⲟⲩⲗⲏⲥⲉⲱⲥ) of his household goods (ⲥⲕⲉⲩⲏ). The legal ramifications of this act have been treated at some length by Leopold Wenger.[77] His conclusions are that John's deathbed declaration constituted a *testamentum ruri conditum*, and that the dying man's presumed use of spoken Coptic constituted, *qua* language, an ancient local custom that would have been tolerable under that head. John's intentions were clear: his children were to share his property. (To try and resolve the difficulties of previous textual critics, I should propose to read the word divisions in lines 29–30 of the papyrus as [ⲙⲁ]ⲣⲉ ⲛⲁⲱⲏⲣⲉ 6ⲉ ⲣ ⲉⲛⲉⲩⲉⲣⲏⲩ | ⲡⲉⲧⲉⲡⲱⲓ̈ ⲡⲉ ⲧⲏⲣ̅ϥ̅ ["Let my children, therefore, apportion with one another everything that is mine"]. ⲣ̅ ⲉⲛⲉⲩⲉⲣⲏⲩ construes plainly as "deal to or with one another, share out.") The portions are to be thirds (ⲛ̅ⲱⲟⲙⲛ̅ⲧ̅, line 31), as there are three ⲱⲏⲣⲉ.

Later the claim is made that Philadelphia, the new daughter, was not intended to receive any portion (lines 83–84, meaning that the last third would have been for Amanias). But this absurdity is, it seems, overturned by the seven witnesses to John's deathbed words, who have been fetched from Lycopolis/Siout to testify in the arbitration proceeding,[78] backed by the ⲡⲁⲛⲧⲉⲕⲁⲓⲕⲟⲥ of that city. Wenger sees it, I think quite rightly, as a tribute to Dioscorus's reputation in Upper Egypt as a fair and efficient jurist that these people would have made the trip to his office in Antinoë.

After a further narrative of details, including Victorine's plea of her inability to obtain a marriage portion, the papyrus breaks off. But a case like

77. L. Wenger, "Ein mündliches Testament in koptischer Sprache (P.Lond. V 1709)," *Aus Novellenindex u. Papyruswörterbuch* (Munich 1928) 45–58.

78. Cf. Wenger, "Mündliches Testament," pp. 49, 58.

this is not just another example of the Coptic national sport of suing one's relatives. It is a window into a society in which minor clerics and officials, literate and at home with a bilingual bureaucracy,[79] were accustomed to having access to a dependable and trustworthy machinery for the redress of grievances. The history of Coptic (i.e., Coptophone) law, and Dioscorus's part in it, do not amount to only the creation of rhetorical *flosculi*. The Coptic legal documents from before the conquest—when the lively provincial culture of Egypt coruscated with every fashionable development, every trendy novelty, in literary and religious life—illustrate on the most basic level what Late Antique society was like where town life went on, where classical and Christian elements were totally blended into a civilized vehicle for dealing with ordinary human stubbornness. At about age fifty, Dioscorus of Antinoë could well feel that he had arrived in that society.

FROM ANTINOË BACK TO APHRODITO, 570–573 AND AFTER

Later in 570 the inhabitants of Aphrodito had occasion once more to complain of the misconduct of the Antaeopolitan pagarch. They turned, naturally, to someone with ample experience in matters of this kind, who was competently representing their interests at the ducal capital. Dioscorus composed their petition *P.Lond.* V 1674 in Greek in his most highly colored rhetorical style, using old and new elements to paint a striking picture of society, its ills and its possibilities for good. Like his encomiastic poems, his practical prose pieces (like this one) were always fitted to the needs and patterns of the moment.

Somewhat in the manner of Handel called upon to produce an oratorio for the defeat of the Jacobites, or Bach having to put together the St. Mark Passion, Dioscorus was to reuse, or use in parallel, material from a companion piece, the draft petition *P.Cair.Masp.* I 67009, for his opening. And what an opening it is: like a fanfare, a joining of God and emperor, heaven and earth. "Divine Providence and our Christ-loving emperor," he begins, addressing the duke of the Thebaid, "have graciously deigned to proclaim

---

79. Relevant here are the fascinating, and sometimes debatable, conclusions of E. Wipszycka in "Le degré d'alphabétisation en Egypte byzantine," *Rev.Et.Aug.* 30 (1984) 279–296. She concludes that there is a feeling that the combination of literacy and Christianity opened up ways of upward social mobility not previously open to lower-middle-class Egyptians. But she underestimates the pervasiveness of bilingualism; the use of Greek did not automatically imply "snob value" by any means. Nor did the use of Coptic stamp the user as "not quite."

your most eminent philanthropy as a gift to the struggling Thebaid. And they have deemed you (lit. "it," i.e., "Your Philanthropy")[80] worthy of rule, as being able to alleviate the bitter injustices (ἀδικήματα) of the Thebans." For "to proclaim" Dioscorus uses the highly charged θεσπίσαι: when the voices of Providence (θεία πρόνοια) and the emperor have spoken as one, the proclamation is certainly oracular, divine, a "word of power."[81] And so the petitioners fall at the duke's feet, pleading that the matter at hand turns on a question of their ancestral rights: ὡς ἀπὸ γονέων καὶ προγόν[ων . . .[82] Not only have the Aphroditans met their yearly tax quotas with prudence and thoroughness, but they know how they want to live and go on living: εὐγενῶς καὶ ἐλευθερικῶς, like gentlemen and "the right sort."[83] Dioscorus puts into their mouths a formula for the Good Life that is at once thoroughly classical-Hellenic in feeling and value, and perfectly expresses the opulent tone of Late Antique civic men.

But under the yoke of the pagarchy, the text continues, their life has been (line 17) ἀποφθαλμιωσαμένων, blasted and withered by the evil eye of envy; we know this concept well from Dioscorus's poetry (see Chapter 3, comments on H12, H23). Again, what they have suffered has been worse than a barbarian raid (lines 21–22, echoing the sentiments of earlier petitions). They are in a state of ἀκαρπία, one of the abstract nouns Dioscorus favors (it is used by Cyril and Severus of Antioch): the irrigation works have been ruined, and the tax assessment has been disproportionately and disastrously raised. The new pagarch is called, it appears, Julian,[84] and, thanks to him, not even the whole officialdom of the province can expect to see its quotas met. (Dioscorus uses the rare word πληναρία, found in Justinian's Novel 128—a word he could have known only from legal sources originating in the capital.)

Once again, the ultimate outrage has taken place—violence against women religious. They are designated as τὰς κόρας καὶ τὰς ἀσκητρίας

---

80. For the use of this word as a title of address, see Zilliacus, *Abundanz*, p. 107.

81. One might also speculate that *theia pronoia* was in people's minds in Egypt, in the third quarter of the sixth century, not only in an imperial and public context. There were gaps in the ecclesiastical rule, too: Dioscorus had lived much of his life in a world of *sede vacante*, Chalcedonian and non-Chalcedonian. The patriarchate also came under the scope of *theia pronoia*. Ever present beneath the this-worldly troubles of Aphrodito was the whisper of a sense of awareness that the web of visible Christendom was sometimes tenuous.

82. Cf. again Keenan, "Village shepherds," pp. 245–259.

83. The work of Till and Drescher has elucidated the meaning of *eleutheros* in Late Antiquity. See W. C. Till, "ελεγθεροc = 'unbescholten'," *Muséon* 64 (1951) 251–259; J. Drescher, "ελεγθεροc once more," *BSAC* 20 (1969/70) 251–259.

84. Another text from his dossier is contained in Cairo Museum S.R. 3733 (unnumbered text); cf. *BIFAO Bulletin du Centenaire* (Cairo 1981) 427–435.

παρθένους. (Do these terms, in part so classical, denote two different categories or states, perhaps young novices and older professed?) But the violence this time may be more economic than physical. The harm to the nuns is simply listed as one item of several deprivations of livelihood, as the text goes on, "and bringing ruin upon the nuns and taking away our livestock and using up the fodder for them that we had so laboriously planted, and even parching the seed grain, to our complete *bouleversement* (ἀναστροφή) and severe damage (λύμη) to the *demosios logos*." Perhaps there was felt to be such a strong obligation to support houses of women religious, who were less able to do their own farm work, that damage to their livelihood was felt to be as destructive as outright physical maltreatment. (Note the way Dioscorus uses the tragic word λύμη 'maiming', to denote a shortfall in the tax roll.)

To reinforce their claims, the Aphroditans have taken a double oath. They have sworn ἔμπροσθεν τοῖς ἁγίοις, in the presence of (*coram*, ⲘⲠⲈⲘⲦⲞ [ⲈⲂⲞⲗ]) the saints, under the *praesidium* (viz. the superiorship, implied) of the devout father and *hegoumenos* of the holy monastery of Apa Macrobius (lines 73–74). I take "in the presence of the saints" to mean that the formal action of the oath was made before ikons, or perhaps relics, in the Macrobius monastery,[85] with the superior being present. They call to witness the Lord God and Christ the βασιλέα βασιλευόντων (lines 83–84, a reference surely of interest to numismatists as well as political historians). The essence of their hope for redress of their wrongs is that there is One Who both is above all earthly rule and works through it (as in the coupling of *theia pronoia* and *philochristos basileus* in the opening phrase).

After a final summation of the problem, Dioscorus composes a rhetorical close to the petition, proleptically thanking the duke for comforting the *leptoktetores* of Aphrodito and entering in his *deltion* the particulars of what they have suffered. He constructs his sentences by his favorite method of pairs of epithets, thanking the duke's ἐκδίκησις (what a *defensor* does) and κατόρθωσις (really his Christian moral sense) for the possibility of a stable situation at Aphrodito. The landowners can remain on their properties ἀδιαστροφῶς καὶ ἀταραχῶς 'without confusion or disturbance', Cyrillian words that ring, in this post-Chalcedon world, with all the sounds of a theological definition. And his peroration is gracefully scriptural: "Though we have been left, as it were, orphans" (cf. John 14:18, which is itself a beautiful echo of the *Phaedo*), Dioscorus continues, ". . . we have now, as you see, come of age" (cf. Eph. 4:13). The implication is that in our responsi-

---

85. For the monastery of Apa Macrobius in the Antaeopolite, cf. Barison, "Ricerche," p. 96; and for a possible parallel to the oath form, in the greeting of a letter, cf. *P.Haun.* 31.2, . . . καὶ τῶν ἁγίων τῆς πόλε[ως.

bilities we have the duke to rely on. Dioscorus had, in his position, the duke's ear; and that ear could hardly have been deaf to the echoes of the classics and the New Testament.

On 16 November 570, Dioscorus produced his longest and most elaborate prose composition. He had been retained by Flavius Phoebammon, physician of Antinoë, to write his will.[86] Phoebammon was the son of the late Euprepeios, *archiatros* of Antinoë; that the profession ran in the family was not unusual.[87] He frames his will in the first person, terming it not just a *diatheke* but a *diathekimaia boulesis* (line 7), a will-and-testament, in the shape (*taxis* 'format') of a final written *diatyposis*, to be left unsealed for convenience (and with a disclaiming plea that his property [*periousia*] is, after all, not much). The shaping of this document leads Dioscorus to create an intricate structure that, in all its rhetorical parts, serves a practical legal end.

After the dating clause and the statement of intent, the will really begins with a typical *sententia*: "The end of all things and of the human race is death, and it is totally impossible to escape; but for those rightly disposed (τοῖς καλῶς φρονοῦσι), to make advance provision for it and to act prudently/piously (εὐλαβεῖσθαι) is the best plan of all (εὐτυχέστερον)" (lines 17–20). This rational preamble, with its elegiac tone and its hendiadys, is elegantly constructed with interlocking pairs of μέν . . . δέ and καί . . . καί groups. It introduces the expected nexus of "being of sound mind" clauses that set the scene for the framing of a valid will (lines 22–35, a striking list of all the classical qualities, like a λογισμός variously qualified as ἀκριβής and σώφρων and ἀπαθείς, that inhabited a Late Antique psyche). Being, then, in good health thanks to "Almighty God, the all-powerful Lord of all things" (a trope we know from Dioscorus's poetry), and lest he depart (ὑπαναγχωρῆσαι; so also line 74 later on) unprepared (cf. Ps. 39:13), Phoebammon sets about disposing of his ancestral property, Antinoite and other.

As all mortals that exist are permitted by heaven to do (lines 42–43), the physician makes his will: it is to be πολιτικοπραιτωρίαν, conforming to the requirements of the city *praetorium*, and witnessed by the seven witnesses required by *Cod.Just.* VI.23.21. These witnesses are Roman citizens (of course) and ἔφηβοι (i.e., "those of the gymnasium," or their sixth-century analogues), as "the power of the laws" (line 49) enjoins. The will is made in

86. For the literature on *P.Cair.Masp.* II 67151, see Amelotti, *Le costituzioni*, pp. 62–63; especially the early work of H. Kreller, *Erbrechtliche Untersuchungen auf Grund der graeco-aegyptischen Papyrusurkunden* (Leipzig 1915).

87. On physicians, see the work of T. S. Miller, *The birth of the hospital in the Byzantine empire* (Baltimore 1985). Cf. *P.Cair.Masp.* I 67006 v 6, 18, 20–21, 37, 57; 67057 I 13; II 67121.4; 67141 I v 22; 67155.1–2, at Aphrodito.

Greek,[88] and destined for a lawful place for the deposit of documents. In the still introductory next section, Dioscorus, the composer of the will, really excels as a painstaking writer of legal prose. The whole section (lines 51–73) that spells out the validity to be possessed in all contexts by every single particular of the will relies totally on Latinisms: κωδίκιλλος, φιδεϊκομισσαρία (ἐπιστολή), and even *confirmateumenous* and *ousufructu* written out in Latin letters[89]—which are, of course, simply letters in Dioscorus's normal hand. (A little later, line 130, we have *inter vivos* in the same continuity of ductus.)

Phoebammon has enjoyed his life and property (cf. lines 209–210, discussed later, and Eccl. 5:18) thanks to the mighty Lord God and in a law-abiding manner (lines 67–71; Dioscorus stresses κατὰ νόμους). After his death ("Should I undergo ἀνθρώπινόν τι and depart"), the physician wants his sons to be his heirs. Dioscorus spells out the nature of his property in a web of phrases designed to let nothing slip through a loophole (lines 87–95, the standard Byzantine *repertorium*). Should there be debts, in either direction (nicely playing, ὡς εἰπεῖν ἔπος [line 96], on active/passive verb endings), the sons are to see to them. Next come the bequests. The physician leaves one aroura of vineland in the Hermopolite, which he had inherited from his father, to the monastery (εὐαγὲς καὶ πάνσεπτον) of Apa Jeremias.[90] The irrigation machinery and similar necessary appurtenances come with the land (lines 101–124). This bequest is made piously, "for an eternal memorial and a share of honor, for the salvation of my soul and a holy offering (προσφορά) on behalf of the departed" (lines 122–124; cf. 126–127 and 145–146: "for the repose of my soul and the forgiveness of my sins" [not ἁμαρτίαι but πλημμελήματα, an oratorical word]). The long string of conditions in alpha-privatives (lines 142–144), spelling out the inviolability of the monastery's title, recalls similar Coptic formations in ⲁϫⲛ̅- familiar from the technical clauses of Coptic legal documents, of the sixth century and much later. The bequest is to be administered by the superior of Apa Jeremias. The present κοινοβιάρχης is one Apa Besas, in whom is to be vested every legal right of ownership (προπριαιταρίας δίκαιον, another Latin legalism, line 150). The land is not to be alienated, but to be ἐπίμονον καὶ παραμόνιμον, for it is his *prosphora*.

Next come directions for Phoebammon's funeral. His sons are to do the

88. On the preeminent validity of Greek, see Wenger, "Mündliches Testament," pp. 50–53.

89. Van der Wal, "Die Schreibweise," does not take these documentary examples into account. In documents, the Latin words are not singled out by any special writing system or device.

90. Possibly the famous one at Saqqara.

52 DIOSCORUS OF APHRODITO

περιστολή of his body (elaborate wrapping, we may assume, not physical mummification at this date). He adjures the superior of the monastery "by the holy, consubstantial and invincible (ἀήττητος) Trinity" (lines 163–164), to provide him with burial *ad sanctos*.[91] The abbot is "to receive my remains into the holy monastery at a memorial, for a commemoration of my all-too-short life, and to reckon my name in the catalogue of all the saints who are at rest, when you make a recital of them by name (ἐνεραδνούμιον, from *ad nomen*)" (lines 164–168). His μνῆμα would have been with that of the other benefactors, adorned with just the sort of inscription we are familiar with from Egyptian monastic sites: "Phoebammon son of Euprepeios, physician, who fell asleep on the Xth of (month), indiction Y . . ." He will rank as a benefactor when the diptychs are read out in the liturgy of the house.

Charitable works are characteristic of this family of physicians. Phoebammon's next act in his will is to provide for the further endowing and running of the hospital (ξενεών) his father had founded (lines 182–184).[92] Its "management, care, and supervision" are to be carried on with an eye to "improvement *(philokalia)*, good care, and organization of treatments (διαιτοχορηγία)"—note this triple set of Dioscorian triplets—"carefully, painstakingly, and without negligence" (lines 185–187). This is theologically a good work (καλλιεργουμένην), and must be done with piety and fear of God (two, after all, of the seven gifts of the Holy Spirit). As administrator of the hospital, Phoebammon designates his brother John, and adjures him "by the eternal God . . . not to be lazy where the work of God, which is zealously to be promoted, is concerned; for if you are negligent, God will see" (lines 193–195). The testator adjures (again by the Holy Trinity) the ecclesiastical (θεοπίστους καὶ ἐλεήμονας), legal (λαμπροὺς καὶ σοφωτάτους συνηγόρους), and civil authorities to abide by these provisions, "without any opposition or recalcitrance, without the syllogisms of rhetors or the quibbling subtleties (λεπτολογία) of councilmen." In putting these words and sentiments into Phoebammon's mouth, Dioscorus, the writer, shows an almost painful awareness of the ins and outs, the string pullings and the byways, of Byzantine Egyptian society. Product as he was of an educational system that made one of necessity expert in the rhetorical figure and the persuasive device, of the Philoponian school of Aristotelian categorization that had discovered how powerful a tool the *Organon* really was, Dioscorus is telling his contemporaries (and, by implication, posterity) that

91. On burial *ad sanctos*, see P. R. L. Brown, *The cult of the saints* (Chicago 1980) 27, 31–35; also on inclusion of the deceased in the commemorations.

92. See H.-R. Hagemann, *Die Stellung der Piae Causae nach justinianischem Rechte* (Basel 1953) 53–54; and the work of Miller, *Birth of the hospital*. For another ξενεών in the area, that of Apa Dios in the Synoria, see *P. Freer* 08.45 (A+B) III.15, 18, IV.13, V.2, 4.

running beneath it all like an unmoving pedal point is the law—that Law, indeed, which it was his delight to meditate, and to articulate, day and night.

Phoebammon designates a tutor for his minor sons, the heirs (πατρω-νεύεσθαι καὶ κουρατορεύεσθαι, rich Latinisms; lines 229–230), namely, Apa Besas again, abbot of the same house.[93] The superior is to function in surrogate kinship as a *curator*, and legally as a guardian (κηδεμών), as Dioscorus puts it in balanced parallel phrases. Again we find an oath, adjuring Besas "by the *prosopon* of Almighty God and His honored and preeminent salvation" to fulfill the charge laid on him "as a good work heartily acceptable to God, availing for the soul in reverence and love of humanity" (lines 235–239; and cf. 250–251). Clearly, the choice of a cleric—an abbot, one used to authority and direction—as a guardian came naturally to a man who looked after a charity hospital and intended to be buried *ad sanctos*. The prestige of Apa Besas and his community shine out of the stately phrases. The abbot will, after all, have to answer before "the fearful tribunal *(bema)* of God"—an image that is to live throughout Coptic law—"to Almighty God Who is Himself the *orphanotrophos*." And if he has done well, God will be his rewarder (ἱκανοδότης) (a phrase taken directly from the language of New Testament parables), "with a bountiful hand making recompense μυριανταπλασίως and giving him long life" (lines 256–258). This language of reward is that of Dioscorus's poems of noble patronage, as he again couples *apolausis* and *soteria*.

Phoebammon, getting his breath, as it were, prepares to make another pious bequest to Apa Jeremias, "as I, ὁ δείλαιος (a word out of the vocabulary of classical tragedy), prepare to go the road of all men,[94] in need of comfort and intercession" (lines 259–260). He wishes to present to the monastery a new boat (σκαφίδιον),[95] fully equipped (lines 275–285), together with the bill of sale proving that he had duly bought it from Antinoite citizens ἀπὸ ἀγοραστικοῦ δικαίου. And this, too, is done out of pious motives, for the forgiveness of his sins and the repose of his soul (lines 284–285). The rest of the text of the will is taken up with specific

93. For this and the later period, compare A. Masi, "L'*actio protutelae* nella compilazione giustinianea e nella dottrina bizantina," in *Studi Senesi* (Siena 1962) 197–218. An ecclesiastic was a good choice for *epitropos*.

94. Compare the observations of W. C. Till on later documents in *Erbrechtliche Untersuchungen auf Grund der koptischen Rechtsurkunden* [he deliberately patterned his title after that of Kreller] (Vienna 1954) 65–66.

95. On monastic boat services, cf. R. Remondon, "Le monastère alexandrin de la Métanoia était-il bénéficiaire du fisc ou à son service?" in *Studi Volterra* 5 (Milan 1971) 769–781. For *skaphidia*, see M. Merzagora, "La navigazione in Egitto nell' età greco-romana," *Aegyptus* 10 (1929) 125.

financial provisions, including one for a mysterious dependent called Athanasius (could it have been a love child?). The closing—Dioscorus's closing—is, as preserved, comparatively brief, stating that the will has been written with ἀκριβολογία, and finishing with the usual κύριον clause and a second dating clause. The subscriptions are lost.

In composing this will and expressing his client's wishes, Dioscorus blends elements from Roman law, classical literature, school philosophy, and the Bible into a highly colored and effective whole. By this period, true, it had become the done thing to use the writing of a will as an occasion for sententious meditations on death, eternity, and the evanescence of life. Dioscorus correctly follows the legal prescriptions for drawing up a will, while constructing his own variations on the theme of mortality and mutability. Much of the 307-line length of this document is taken up with pious foundations, a deeply embedded feature of Byzantine Egyptian society. With each contribution the testator makes to the Christian institutions of his world, new expressions of splendid reverence are found, not like adventitious ornaments stuck on, but like transparent windows, *oeils-de-boeuf* set with mica, in the text, through which quite another light diffuses. (We see here a little of the mental habit that by reflex adds "Blessed be He" to the divine names whenever they are spoken.) Dioscorus unrolls his prose rather like the unfolding of an inhabited vine scroll in the sort of Coptic sculpture with which Antinoë's great public buildings were covered—at every new curve there lurks another heraldic life form. The happy fusion of classical allusion and scriptural familiarity is alive and well in this kind of writing. It is hard to detect, in A.D. 570, the seeds in this society of something that will begin, in only another two hundred years, to jettison its languages and its memory, and huddle away with Arabic, in itself the carrier of totally alien values. The range of human possibilities we see in the Coptic society that produced this document was to be withered utterly. As yet, though, there is no shadow across the sun.

In the course of his life and activities, Dioscorus produced, along the way, a number of nondocumentary works in prose: his Greek-Coptic glossary,[96] paradigms in Greek grammar,[97] and marginalia to a life of Isocrates

---

96. An indispensable tool, yes, for the interpretation of his poetry and the characterization of his dialect (and other things); but the article of B. Baldwin, "Notes on the Greek-Coptic glossary of Dioscorus of Aphrodito," *Glotta* 60 (1982) 79–81, is written by an author who has no Coptic. See my study, "Further notes on the Greek-Coptic glossary of Dioscorus of Aphrodito," *Glotta* 64 (1986) 253–257. The original publication is H. I. Bell and W. E. Crum, "A Greek-Coptic glossary," *Aegyptus* 6 (1925) 177–226.

97. I am grateful to Professor A. Wouters of Leuven, author of *The grammatical papyri from Graeco-Roman Egypt* (Brussels 1979) (see esp. p. 18, n. 17), for corresponding with me

(*P.Cair.Masp.* II 67175).[98] Even the last of these is of interest, as a kind of
coda, in the way it lets us see Dioscorus's mind at work. To the left of the
main narrative text are workpoints naming the classical categories that the
orator (and often the jurist too) sought to embody: $\pi\epsilon\iota\theta\acute{\omega}$, $\tau\grave{o}$ $\sigma\acute{v}\mu\phi\epsilon\rho o\nu$, $\tau\grave{o}$
$\kappa\alpha\lambda\acute{o}\nu$, $\tau\grave{o}$ $\delta\acute{\iota}\kappa\alpha\iota o\nu$. They are not a bad outline of Dioscorus's career goals. As
later topics, we find listed $\sigma\upsilon\mu\pi\acute{\epsilon}\rho\alpha\sigma\mu\alpha$, the conclusion of a syllogism, and
$\delta\iota\acute{\alpha}\kappa\rho\iota\sigma\iota s$, a legal *sententia* (Dioscorus used it in *P.Lond.* V 1708.126). The
term $\sigma\upsilon\mu\pi\acute{\epsilon}\rho\alpha\sigma\mu\alpha$ 'that which necessarily follows' was obviously a technical expression that Dioscorus had learned from the work of Philoponus;
the Alexandrian teacher uses it often in his commentaries on the Prior and
Posterior Analytics (55.26, 58.8, 64.4, 76.27–28, 93.12, 194.19), and else-
where in his writings.[99] Finally, the legal term $\delta\iota\acute{\alpha}\kappa\rho\iota\sigma\iota s$ (cf. *Cod.Just.* I.33.5,
34.3) lives on as a loanword in Coptic (e.g., VC 3.12, and possibly cf. Bal
136.2, 143.2). When Dioscorus kept a study text among his professional
papers, it is visible on the papyrus page that he assimilated what it was
about.

On the recto of the fourth leaf of *P.Cair.Masp.* III 67325, we find a
dating clause (in a land lease) giving the third regnal year of Maurice,
Pharmouthi 10, indiction 3 (5.iv.585). The locality is Aphrodito.[100] On the
first two leaves, in Dioscorus's hand, are a series of accounts of grain,
fodder, wine, vegetable crops, and seed grain for holdings in the Aphrodito
area for dates from a sixth to an eighth indiction—that is, 572/3–574/5—
when Dioscorus had returned to his home village. The places are often
familiar, the people less so, for example, the *topoi* Pherko (II r 11) and
Victoros (II v 1), the holding $'O\alpha\sigma\iota\tau\hat{\omega}\nu$ (I 4 26, v 5). There are women
religious (Ama Eirene, I r 13; Ama Helene, II v 4), and even an "Apa John,
my in-law" (II v 11—a connection by marriage of Dioscorus himself or one

---

about his proposed edition, with comments, of all of Dioscorus's *grammatica*. If only more
of his Coptic had survived.

98. There is also his syncretistic invocation, *P.Cair.Masp.* II 67188: see L. S. B.
MacCoull, "P.Cair.Masp. II 67188 Verso 1–5: the *Gnostica* of Dioscorus of Aphrodito," *Tyche*
2 (1987) 95–97. On his well-known ownership of the Homer and Menander codices, and
their place in his life, cf. W. Clarysse, "Literary papyri in documentary 'archives,'" in *Egypt
and the Hellenistic world*, ed. E. van 't Dack, P. Van Dessel, W. Van Gucht, [*StudHell* 27]
(Louvain 1983) 43–61, esp. 55–57; cf. 73.

99. On the impact of the syllogism as a tool for Late Antique thought, see F. E. Peters,
Aristotle and the Arabs (New York and London 1968) 19–20.

100. Formula (9) of Maurice in R. S. Bagnall and K. A. Worp, *Regnal formulas in
Byzantine Egypt* (BASP suppl. 2; Missoula, Mont. 1979) p. 63. Also in *P.Cair.Masp.* I 67111.
Why was Maurice styled a $\mu\acute{\epsilon}\gamma\iota\sigma\tau os$ $\epsilon\grave{v}\epsilon\rho\gamma\acute{\epsilon}\tau\eta s$? Surely not for his pro-Chalcedonian bias.
(One day someone will explain why it was Maurice who instituted the practice of requiring
all documents to begin with a Christian invocation.)

of his children?). Camel herds, chickpeas, wine; so passed the days of an Aphroditan *syntelestes*. In a manner not unbefitting a Coptic grandee of fifties Assiut, the last in history that we see of Dioscorus, he is keeping his books. As Josephine Tey wrote in *The Daughter of Time*, "Truth is not in accounts, but in account books."

· III ·

THE GREEK POEMS

In this chapter, Dioscorus's Greek verse works are presented in chronological order, with historical and literary parallels, in an effort to make his amalgam of rhetorical, classical, and Christian ways of looking at the world intelligible to the reader in their context and against their background of the culture of sixth-century Egypt. These works are a rich source, an open window into the life of that Late Antique society. Dioscorus, the bilingual poet of that bilingual society, expresses the interrelatedness of his world through a wealth of figures of speech drawn from the classics (and his poetic predecessors), the law, and the Scriptures. The poems may be read as a sensitive, living witness to the values and the preoccupations of a Mediterranean way of life that was undergirded with the ancient humane learning and shot through with the colors and scents of Christianity's insights into the spirit.

These poems have grown organically out of the same world we have already come to know in Dioscorus's documents. The writing of poetry itself was an act of high status in Byzantine Egyptian culture, and to display one's learning in both administrative prose and encomiastic verse was a most desirable ornament of public life. A lawyer like Dioscorus drew on his own experience in choosing the governing metaphors in which to express the realities it was his role to interpret and to praise.

As in the rhetorically composed documents, so in the poetry: master images, leading images that sum up a whole concern of Dioscorus's society, leap out and strike the reader. At the governor's arrival, the life-giving Nile rises for the inundation; the fallen walls of troubled cities rise up, prompted by justice; the "great captains" stretch out "the hand of plenty" to their clients; "blonde Demeter" and Dionysus join in a Christian wedding procession; rulers and ruled share in the "faith of the single-essenced Trinity." Each image translates into a theme: Dioscorus's principal themes of rulership, the role of the city, patronage, the great clan of *dynatoi*, and the continuing life of the church. All of these interact in the polyphonic texture of the physical and mental world of Dioscorus's era. These themes articulate the deepest preoccupations of the local elite culture of Late Antique Egypt. They are neither simply Egyptian notions wearing Greek dress, nor Greek commonplaces projected on the local color of the background: each element in the amalgam has acted on and altered the rest. The poems written on these themes are not remote *jeux d'esprit*; they speak the living language of political and social relations in an Egyptian provincial city. As has been recently, and brilliantly, written, "The hellenized Egyptian wrote the Greek language, to whose expressiveness he was sensitive, and thought in Greek categories, whose subtlety he exploited. But once he had been moulded by that culture, he became first its bearer, then its arbiter."[1] In his poetry, Dioscorus took up this role with intensity and distinction.

Dioscorus's poetic craft has many and deep roots. As recently as twenty years ago it was still the conventional wisdom to place him at the very end of a tradition and then judge him negatively as a degenerate epigone of that tradition.[2] But taking into account the emphases and the results of modern scholarship, we can take the time to view his background and his preoccupations on their own terms.

Dioscorus was, it is true, one of the last of the poets who were also men of affairs in Late Antique Egypt. He was also something of an anomaly in sixth-century literature,[3] at least as it is viewed in the Greek and Latin spheres. Far from separating the classical and the Christian in his writings, he combines them with rare felicity, especially in panegyrics and epithalamia. He does not use the purist, classicizing Greek favored by the elite, but, as a Copt and a practicing jurist, the "papyrological Greek" of his own speech, complete with technical terms, Latinisms, and words from rhetoric,

1. G. Fowden, *The Egyptian Hermes* (Cambridge 1986) 73.

2. Alan Cameron, "Wandering poets: A literary movement in Byzantine Egypt," *Historia* 14 (1965) 470–509. The remarks of B. Baldwin, "Dioscorus of Aphrodito: the worst poet of antiquity?" *Atti XVII congr.intl.papirol.* (Naples 1984) 327–331 add nothing.

3. See Averil Cameron, *Procopius and the sixth century* (Berkeley 1985) 19–25, for what she terms the "crisis of sixth-century literature," and for her very acute remarks about panegyric, p. 25 n. 44. This is exactly what I have been concerned with for nearly nineteen years, since my very first readings in Dioscorus and his period.

philosophy, the Scriptures, and the discourse of growing Monophysite self-awareness. As will be shown in the commentaries, his poems are intelligible only in the context of all his works, including prose and including writings in Coptic as well as Greek. As a man of his time and place, he was preoccupied with the land, with his locality and the changing nature of urban life, and with right belief and how it permeated and affected his society. He was also concerned with the past.

In Egypt there was not so much a conscious need to strive after evoking the past, or to conform to the norms of the past; the past was, to an overwhelming degree, all around, as anyone sees who goes looking for the living realities of "hellenistische Landwirtschaft."[4] Rather, there were in Late Antique Egypt three "pasts" to contend with: the Graeco-Roman past, the pharaonic past, and the biblical and Christian past. The first and the third blaze forth from Dioscorus's poetry; there are even traces of the second (as when he calls Duke John "Ammon of the Nile").

In a way, what Dioscorus was doing in composing poems was writing, in bits and pieces, a *Patria* of Aphrodito, "the Paphian land," and of Antinoë, Hadrian's city (he calls a monastic novice the "son of Hadrian," and a bridegroom "sprung from Antinous's eagle"). He wrote these poems in Greek, in a form of the learned tradition that served local identity and guaranteed local culture.[5] He celebrated the mythology of these towns and the reputations and deeds of their citizens, of those local *dynatoi* who made the culture of Byzantine Egypt work.

Dioscorus's line of poetic descent[6] began with Triphiodorus, whom we now know to have written ca. 300,[7] and who came from Atripe (later the site of Shenoute's monastery), just across the river from Panopolis. Immediately we are located right in the heartland of the Egyptian "poets' country." Next in the line comes Harpocration of Panopolis (fl. 330–348), whose poems are lost, but whose career has emerged from the papyri.[8] Writing of

4. The phrase is from the title of Martin Schnebel's classic monograph of 1925 (*Münchener Beiträge zur Papyrusforschung u. antiken Rechtsgeschichte*, Bd. 7 [Munich 1925]).

5. I am indebted to Professor Glen Bowersock's lecture, "Poets and patronage in Byzantine Egypt," Dumbarton Oaks, 8 May 1986.

6. I gratefully follow Alan Cameron, "The empress and the poet," *YCS* 27 (1982) 217–289, esp. 217–221 and 235–239, for chronology of the poets. I also thank Dr. Catherine Brown Tkacz of the *Oxford Dictionary of Byzantium* for the chance to check the latest information on these figures.

7. Thanks to *P.Oxy.* XLI 2946, published in 1972; see E. Livrea, "*P.Oxy.* 2946 e la constitutio textus di Trifiodoro," *ZPE* 33 (1979) 54–74.

8. G. M. Browne, "A panegyrist from Panopolis," *Proc. XIV intl.congr.papyrol.* (London 1975) 29–33, and idem, "Harpocration panegyrista," *Ill.Cl.Stud.* 2 (1977) 184–196; cf. W. H. Willis, "Two literary papyri in an archive from Panopolis," ibid. 3 (1978) 140–153, and idem,

events from the 420s to the 440s, and originating in Thebes to the south, was Olympiodorus, now shown to be the probable author of the poem known as the *Blemyomachia*,[9] of which papyrus fragments were found at the site of the Theban monastery of St. Phoebammon. Also most likely from the early fifth century is the poem called the *Vision of Dorotheos*,[10] recently thought to have come from the Pachomian library at nearby Pbow.[11] Holding the consulship in 441 was Cyrus of Panopolis, later a bishop and hagiographer who remembered the saint's legend of his Egyptian hometown.[12] And looming largest of all is the dominant figure of Nonnus of Panopolis, whose *Dionysiaka* and *Metabole* (or *Paraphrasis*) *of the Gospel of John* are thought to have been written in the period 450–470,[13] sparking an even greater period of creativity in Egyptian poetry.

Nonnus's slightly younger contemporary, Pamprepius (440–484),[14] also came from Panopolis; and to the period just before and just after 500 can be dated the works of Colluthus (namesake of the martyr and patron saint of Antinoë) from Lycopolis (Assiut), and Christodorus of Coptos (Qeft), who wrote the *ekphraseis* of Constantinopolitan statues contained in *AP* II and, most probably, a papyrus encomium on Anastasius (or Zeno).[15] Also writing at about the turn of the fifth to sixth century in Egypt were the author of the pseudo-Apollinarian Psalter paraphrase[16] and, I believe, the author of the Euripidean cento known as the *Christus Patiens*[17]; their cities of origin are not known, but their works bear the Egyptian stamp. Musaeus, an Egyptian from an unspecified region who used the Nonnus St. John

---

"The letter of Ammon of Panopolis to his mother," *Actes XVᵉ congr.intl.papyrol.* 2 (Brussels 1979) 98–115.

9. Edited by E. Livrea (Meisenheim 1978); cf. L. S. B. MacCoull, "Papyrus fragments from the monastery of Phoebammon," *Proc. XVI intl.congr.papyrol.* (Chico, Calif. 1981) 491–498.

10. Edited by A. Hurst et al., in *P.Bodmer XXIX* (Geneva 1984). I am grateful to Mirrit Boutros Ghali and the director and staff of the Bibliothèque Bodmer in Cologny for the opportunity to see the papyrus at first hand.

11. J. M. Robinson, "Reconstructing the first Christian monastic library," Smithsonian Institution Libraries lecture, 15 September 1986.

12. Above n. 6.

13. The late dating suggested by B. Baldwin, "Nonnus and Agathias: two problems in literary chronology," *Eranos* 84 (1986) 60–61, does not seem to hold up.

14. Edited by E. Livrea (Teubner, Leipzig 1979). He may also be the author of the panegyric fragment *P.Flor.* II 114 (Heitsch 36); the papyri are physically very similar.

15. Cf. R. C. McCail, "P.Gr.Vindob. 29788C: Hexameter encomium on an unnamed emperor," *JHS* 98 (1978) 38–63; E. Livrea, "Pamprepio ed il P.Vindob. 29788A–C," *ZPE* 25 (1977) 121–134.

16. J. Golega, *Der homerische Psalter* (Ettal 1960).

17. L. S. B. MacCoull, "Egyptian elements in the *Christus Patiens*," *BSAC* 27 (1985) 45–51.

and the Psalter paraphrase in his poetry,[18] came either just before or just after this group of writers.

Of Dioscorus's poetic predecessors, he seems to have taken most from Nonnus, specifically from the Gospel paraphrase.[19] Among his sixth-century contemporaries, only Julian the Egyptian[20] shared his nationality; there seem to be not many mutual borrowings between Dioscorus and the Syro-Constantinopolitan group of John of Gaza, Agathias, and Paul the Silentiary. (The most stri king comparison seems to be the "new Phaethon" of Dioscorus's H14.1 and H24.5, and the Φαέθων νέος of John of Gaza's *Anacreontea*.[21]) After his return to Upper Egypt from the capital by 553, Dioscorus worked mostly alone and in the interstices of a busy legal career. What texts of the νέοι he may have had before him we do not know from his surviving archive. But read them he had, and he had been born and reared right in the center of that Egyptian poetic heartland that extended from Thebes to Hermopolis.

Of Christian influences on Dioscorus's poetry, the Scriptures take pride of place; the Psalter and the Old and New Testaments were probably the most influential, as he would have been steeped in their texts through participation in the Copto-Alexandrian liturgy. Time and again we meet echoes: of the Exodus story (the Tables of the Law), of parables and sayings of Christ ('love thy neighbor'), of the psalmist's invocations. Dioscorus borrows from the Christian Aristotelianism of his teacher, John Philoponus, to describe the Trinity.[22] He most probably knew of the obscure Egyptian saint Senas from local Coptic legend.[23] His non-epic Greek vocabulary echoes Cyril[24] and Athanasius; it is even possible that some of

18. Th. Gelzer, in Th. Gelzer and C. H. Whitman, *Musaeus: Hero and Leander* (Loeb, Cambridge, Mass. 1975) 297–299; now edited by E. Livrea (Teubner, Leipzig 1982).

19. There is a shared thought between the σαόπτολις of *P.Flor.* II 114.3.16 and Dioscorus's ῥυσίπτολις (an Aeschylean word) in the encomium on Victor (and compare the thought at the end of his Anacreontic); this was a preoccupation of the Egyptian poets. We still need an adequate study of the Nonnus St. John paraphrase; the Oxford thesis of C. Marnau, "Nonnos's paraphrase of St. John's Gospel: introduction and commentary on books I and II" (1982), perpetuates outmoded value judgments on Late Antique Egyptian literature and society. The new critical edition of the text by Professor Enrico Livrea is eagerly awaited; see his paper "Towards a new edition of Nonnus' Paraphrase of St. John's Gospel," *XVII international Byzantine congress abstracts* (Washington, D.C. 1986) 198–199.

20. See K. Hartigan, "Julian the Egyptian," *Eranos* 63 (1975) 43–54.

21. Edited by K. Abel (Berlin 1882) III.6.

22. L. S. B. MacCoull, "μονοειδής in Dioscorus of Aphrodito: an addendum," *BSAC* 25 (1983) 61–64.

23. L. S. B. MacCoull, "The isopsephistic poem on St. Senas by Dioscorus of Aphrodito," *ZPE* 62 (1986) 51–53.

24. MacCoull, "μονοειδής," p. 61; cf. L. S. B. MacCoull, "A Trinitarian formula in Dioscorus of Aphrodito," *BSAC* 24 (1982) 106 with n. 22. It would help our understanding if

his employments of mood and tense reflect the usages of Coptic verbal conjugations and converters as we see them in Shenoute's *Lobreden*,[25] though this is a matter for further philological research on a minutely close level. Whether Dioscorus knew of the exegetical work of Rufus of Hypselis (Shotep, just north of Aphrodito), who flourished in the patriarchate of Damian, after 578,[26] or, from nearby Antaeopolis, of the ps.-Dioscorian (the patriarch; actually sixth-century) *Panegyric on Macarius of Tkow*,[27] remains conjectural. Further philological research will no doubt reveal additional sources reflected in Dioscorus's writings.

Something remains to be said on Dioscorus's use of meter. The most recent treatment of this subject,[28] taking into account the hexameters, iambics, and Anacreontic, still speaks of "orribili *monstra*."[29] But the understanding of Greek meter in Coptic-speaking sixth-century Egypt is not that simple; and when the pervasive Greek-Coptic bilingualism of the time and place is taken adequately into account, judgments of "howlers" will be seen to be somewhat beside the point. It is acknowledged that by the reign of Justin II we are dealing with an advanced stage of the transition from quantitative to accentual/stress rhythm. What cannot be insisted upon too strongly in any consideration of Egyptian Greek, in language and prosody, is the fact of interference from Coptic,[30] which changed the shape and sound of the spoken language of the province; and of all writers, Dioscorus in particular used the spoken language in his poetry. In the society of Egypt above all, we can see bilingualism in action. The interchanges of ε/н and o/ω, of τ/ⲁ and ⲗ/ⲣ, the fluid state of short and long vowels as they were heard by the Egyptian ear, the influence on notions of hiatus of the Sahidic and Lycopolitan[31] (Assiutic) pronunciation of double vowels (e.g., ⲁⲁ = ⲁ'ⲁ), the native habits of stress in word groups—all these factors changed

---

more of Cyril were extant in Coptic (cf. L. S. B. MacCoull, "Coptic sources: A problem in the sociology of knowledge," *BSAC* 26 [1984] 1–2).

25. A. Shisha-Halevy, *Coptic grammatical categories* (Rome 1986) 64–75.

26. See G. Garitte, "Rufus de Shotep," *Muséon* 69 (1956) 11–33. My own search for Rufus material in the Coptic Orthodox Patriarchate at Cairo was without results.

27. Edited by D. W. Johnson, *CSCO* 415–416 (Scr.copt. 41–42; Louvain 1980).

28. A. Saija, "La metrica di Dioscoro di Afroditopoli," in *Studi A. Ardizzone* 2 (Rome and Messina 1978) 823–849. (The wrong form of the name of Dioscorus's city, leading to confusion with the city near Memphis, Atfih, is unfortunate.)

29. Ibid. pp. 823, 843.

30. F. T. Gignac, *Grammar of the Greek papyri of the Roman and Byzantine periods* I (Milan 1976) 46–53.

31. Saija, "La metrica," p. 829, writes, "in Dioscoro non è ammissible parlare di dorismi." Indeed not. The outstanding feature of the Lycopolitan (Assiut) dialect is ⲁ-vocalization.

the way quantity and position were conceived of and handled by Egyptian writers of Greek. To quote Thomas Gelzer in his comments on Nonnian metrical rules: "For the calculation of word-lengths not only single words, but also "word-groups" with internal relationships, such as preposition and noun, or epithet and proper name, must be taken into account."[32] This is pure Coptic philology.[33] What is understood of Coptic meter (not much Coptic poetry survives) is indeed based on grasping the modifier group as a unity for prosodic purposes.[34] The Coptic background is essential for any attempt to scan Dioscorus.

In the following pages are commentaries on the individual poems, in chronological order. These commentaries contain material from many areas of sixth-century culture, Egyptian and empire-wide; they attempt to show the interrelatedness of the fabric of Dioscorus's world, and his works' reflection of the society and life of his times.

H6. Encomium. A.D. 551–553. *P.Cair.Masp.* II 67177
(See Figure 6)

Ὦ γέν[ος] ἀφράστοιο μελισταγέος Μελε[
κυδαλί[μ]ων πατέρων ἀπὸ ῥίζης ὀλβισ[τήρων,
ὧν ἀ[ρ]ε[τ]ῆς κα[μ]άτοισιν ἀ[γά]λματα κο[σμ
Βασίλιος π[ρ]οπά[τωρ ἐπαοίδ[ι]μος ἐκ θ[ε]ο[ῦ ἦλθεν
5 . . . .] . . . βίην πανολέ[θ]ριον . σ. . . . π[
εὐ[σεβί]ης ἀλύ[τ]οι[ο δικαιοσ[υν
τούνεκα καὶ σύ, φέριστε, παν[ίκε]λος ἔσκ[ες ἐ]κείνῳ,
πίσ[τιν] ἀ[ε]ρτάζων Τριάδ[ος μονο]ειδέος ὀρθήν.
οὐ πέλεν, οὐ πέλεν ἄλλ[ος ὁμοίιος ὔμμι] γεν[έθλη,
10 τῆς πολυκαλλίστης σοφίης ἐγκύμονι πάσης.
Αἰακίδη[ς] ἀδάμαντι βεβαμμένος οὐ πέλεν ἶσος,
οὐδ' Αἴας Τελαμώνιος, οὐ κρατερὸς Διομήδης.
τολμήεις γενόμην· πόθεν ἤλυθον ὑμνοπολεῦσαι
τοσσατίην ἀρετήν, ἄπερ ἀστέρες ἄκριτοι ἦσαν,
15 ἠδ' ἁλὸς ἀτρυγέτοιο τὰ κύματα τ' ἐξονομῆναι;
οὕτως ἀτρεκέως, προφερέστατε, μῆτις ἀνάκ[τ]ων,
παντοίων ἐπέων πανυπέρτατος ἔπλεο τιμῆς.
τούνεκα μεῦ φόρμιγγι πολύστονι τ' ἵλαος ἴσθι·
ἄρκια πήματ' ἔπασχον ἐνὶ ῥοθίοισι θαλάσσης,

32. Th. Gelzer, in Musaeus: Hero and Leander, p. 329 n. (b).

33. See Shisha-Halevy, *Coptic grammatical categories*, pp. 11–14, 15–60 on the modifier; 163–164 on not "word" but "syntagm."

34. T. Säve-Söderbergh, *Studies in the Coptic Manichaean psalm book* (Uppsala 1949), esp. 1–10, 88–90. H. Junker's metrical comments in *Koptische Poesie des 10. Jhdts.* (Berlin 1908–1911) deal with much later material; but even there the concepts of "modifier" and "syntagm" apply.

20　Πενταπολιήτου Θεοδώρου οὕνεκα βίης.
　　τέτταρας, ἐξεδάμασσεν ἐμέ, χρυσῶν λάβε λίτρας,
　　ἔκτοτε ἡμετέρου χρήστης ἐδίωξε μελάθρ[ο]υ.
　　ἐν χθονὶ παμβασιλῆος ἐλήλυθον ἔκτοθι τ[έ]κνων·
　　ἤλυθον οὐκ ὄλβον διζήμενος οἱάπερ ἅ[λ]λοι,
25　ἀλλὰ πόρον βιότοιο καὶ υἱήεσσιν ἐμοῖσι,
　　μὴ σφέας ὀλλυμένους ἀέκων βλεφάροισι νοήσω.
　　τούνεκα σῆς ἀρετῆς γουνάζομαι, ὥς κεν ἀνάγκῃ
　　τειρομένῳ σὺν παισὶν ἀρηγόνα χεῖρ᾽ ἀτανύσ[σ]ῃς.

1 cf. P. Cairo Cat. II 67184 B 16 ῳ γενος αφρα[σ]τοιο νοος κα. ν. ο[|
Μελεαγρου sup. Ma　2 cf. 4,4　3 κοσμια στησαν sup. Ma　4 cf. 14,4 | ad
hunc versum in margine dextro verticaliter hae litterae scriptae sunt: ο
με . . υμε . . δην . αρχ. μων. . . ν. . [ε]χθαι[ρ]ων [πε]νιχ[ρο]ισι[ν . απε. . ισι[ο]ν
ε[ς χ]ρον[ον] ελθοις　6 cf. 3,69　8 cf. 1 verso 6 et 3,41　9 cf. 2,3　10 cf.
1,18　13 cf. 12 B 18 et 5,11s　16 cf. 2,1　17 cf. 4β 9　18 πολυστων =
πολυστονος　19 ενιρροθιοισι Π　21 εμε aut εμοι Π　23 cf. 2,4 | πατρης
supra τεκνων Π　24–26 cf. 4,17–19　28 cf. 3,24

O descendant of Mele(), honey-sweet beyond words, sprung from
renowned ancestors from the stock of the blessed, from among whom
your famous forebear Basil came from God, (bringing) the ornaments of
excellence (out) of troubles, . . . destructive force . . . the justice of indissoluble piety. . . . And so you too, honored one, have come, so like him,
exalting the right faith of the Trinity, single in essence. Never, never was
there anyone like you in noble birth, quick with every kind of beautiful
wisdom. Even when Achilles was dipped in the fire he was not equal to
your unconquerable self, nor was Telamonian Ajax, nor brave Diomedes.
Let me be bold: whence should I begin to celebrate such great excellence,
great as the stars are numberless, as if I could name the waves of the
unharvested sea? In so accurate a sense are you, Your Excellency, craft of
rulers, exalted and fully worthy of eloquence of every kind. Wherefore be
gracious to my loud lyre; I have suffered enough troubles on the breakers
of the sea, because of the violence of Theodore of the Pentapolis. They
overwhelmed me (saying) "Take four pounds of gold," since when my
creditors have driven me from my house. In the land of the emperor I have
been (like) one without a fatherland; I have come, not, like others, seeking
riches, but seeking a means of living for my sons as well, so that I do not
with my eyes behold them perishing. And so I beseech Your Excellency,
stretch out a helping hand to one who, together with his sons, is oppressed
by need.

In this poem, Dioscorus's earliest, the autobiographical element is
strong. He is seen here to make first use of elements and themes that will
appear in his oeuvre for more than twenty years.

1. Besides Maspero's Μελε[άγρου, also possible are Μελε[σίππου (cf.
SPP III 253), or perhaps even Μελε[τίου (cf. PLRE II, p. 753, and BGU 1630).

It is not certain if the addressee was a duke of the Thebaid. Cf. J. Diethart, *Prosopographia Arsinoitica* (Vienna 1980), no. 3471.

4. The Basilius in question may be a member of one of the most powerful families in Late Antiquity; see A. Cameron and D. Schauer, "The last consul: Basilius and his diptych," *JHS* 102 (1982) 33–59; cf. D. Schauer, "The consular diptych of Basilius (V5) re-evaluated," *Seventh BSC Abstracts* (Boston 1981) 56–57, and now R. S. Bagnall, A. Cameron, S. R. Schwartz, and K. A. Worp, *Consuls of the Later Roman Empire* (Atlanta, 1987) 616–17. Cf. also Vettius Agorius Basilius Mavortius, cos. 527 (*PLRE* II, pp. 736–737).

6. For εὐσεβίης, a central concept in Dioscorus's thought, cf. *P.Cair. Masp.* II 67184 B 4, 67183 r 12 (see H1).

8. Cf. H3.41; see L. S. B. MacCoull, "A Trinitarian formula in Dioscorus of Aphrodito," *BSAC* 24 (1982) 103–110, and eadem, "μονοειδής in Dioscorus of Aphrodito: An addendum," ibid. 25 (1983) 61–64. The word comes from John Philoponus; it occurs also in the Greek of Severus of Antioch.[35] And ὀρθὴ πίστις is Athanasian and Cyrillian, and is quoted as such by Justinian in his *De recta fide* of 551.

10. σοφίης ἐγκύμονι: cf. *P.Cair.Masp.* II 67184 11, 15; 67183 r 18 (and commentary on H1); similar, Nonnus *Metabole* 7.29, 8.59.

11. Cf. Apollonius Rhodius 4.869–879 (ed. F. Vian [Paris 1981], 178).

13. ὑμνοπολεύειν: cf. J. Golega, *Der homerische Psalter* (Ettal 1960), p. 44.

19. . . . θαλάσσης, i.e., Dioscorus's journey to Constantinople in 551. Compare line 23.

20. For Theodore, bishop of the Pentapolis, see *P.Cair.Masp.* II 67168 (undated), and J. G. Keenan, "The Aphrodite papyri and village life in Byzantine Egypt," *BSAC* 26 (1984) 51–63. The "five cities" were Ptolemais Hermiou, the metropolis, south of Atripe (Sohag) on the west bank, famous for its heritage as an autonomous Greek city; Thinis, the old nome capital; and probably Diospolis Parva, Tentyra, and perhaps Abydos. For Ptolemais, see *P.Flor.* III 377.21; for the Pentapolis, see *P.Fuad* 86.2 and J. Gascou's comments in "*P.Fouad* 87: les monastères pachômiens et l'état byzantin," *BIFAO* 76 (1976) 159–160. We do not know why Bishop Theodore, a businessman who dealt in wine with a Pachomian house in the Hermopolite, had demanded the sum of 288 solidi from Dioscorus.

21. The large sum of 288 solidi apparently was a bone of contention in the matter of Dioscorus's journey to the capital. Compare *PSI* I 76, the case of Fl. Christodote in A.D. 574; and J. G. Keenan, "The Case of Flavia Christodote," *ZPE* 29 (1978) 191–209.

23. Read Dioscorus's own correction πάτρης for τέκνων.

---

35. See R. Reidinger, ed., *Concilium Lateranense 649* (*ACO* II 1, Berlin 1984) 425.

παμβασιλεύς (reused later in H2.4 and elsewhere); a word characteristic of the Coptic liturgy; see Golega, *Der homerische Psalter*, pp. 124, 172, citing A. Buckel, *Die Gottesbezeichnungen in den Liturgien der Ostkirchen* (Würzburg 1938), not available to me. Here the word is applied to the emperor, not the deity. Cf. Nonnus *Metabole* 1.85, 5.162; in an oath, *P.Cair.Masp.* I 67097 v D 79.

24. On this *topos*, cf. C. B. Welles, "The garden of Ptolemagrios at Panopolis," *TAPA* 77 (1946) 192–206, esp. 202–203.

In combining the craft of poetry (to ameliorate his condition) with a local public career and with travel, Dioscorus was following in the footsteps of his illustrious earlier countrymen Olympiodorus, Pamprepius, Cyrus, and, of course, Nonnus, as described at the beginning of this chapter.[36] Dioscorus can now be seen as not unworthy of that company. He is using hexameter form for a rhetorical production embodying Menander Rhetor's prescriptions for an epideictic praise speech: γένος, φύσις, ἐπιτηδεύματα, virtues, συγκρίσεις.[37] This sort of pattern will be seen to underlie most of his poetic work. Rhetorical training had formed both the lawyer and the creative writer.

<table><tr><td>H8. Encomium. A.D. 553?</td><td align="right">*P. Walters* 517</td></tr></table>

᾿Ω πτολίαρχε μέγιστε βοηθόε πᾶσιν ἀνάγκης,
κλῦθι πονιομένου Παφίης χθονὸς ἐνναετῆρος.
δέξεο ᾿μῆς γενιῆς τὰ δυσίμερα δάκρυα μόχθων.
πολλὰ μοὶ ἐν γραφίδεσσι χαράγματα οἴκοθεν ἤχθη,
5   ὅττι καὶ Γαβριῆλις χερείονα τῶν πρὶν ἔερξεν
Πενταπολίτης Θεόδωρος ἀτάσθαλα ἔργα καὶ αὐτός
ἡμετέρων σφετέρισσεν ἀλωῶν καρπὸν ἀπούρας.
χῶρον ἄ[π]αντα θέριζε μελισταγέων σταφυλάων.
θρέμματα ἠδὲ βόας πόρεν ἄρσα⟨ς⟩ κτήματα πάντα,
10 οὔν[ε]κεν ἐνδεκάτης Θεοδόσσιος ὧν λάβε χρυσῶν
ἡμετ]έρης [γ]ενιῆς βιοτήσιον. νῦν δὲ φαεινῶν
σοῦ πρ]ο̣κυλ[ιν]δόμε[ν]ος πόδας ἴχνων ὕψος ῎Αρειον . . .

2 cf. 3,54   **4** cf. 3,34   **6** cf. 6,20   **8** cf. 25,5   **9** add. Ke   **10** cf. 6,21 l ad causam v. P. Cairo Cat. 67024,1–17 et Mal l.c.   **12** cf. XXXVI *recto* a 18

O lord of cities, great helper of all in need, hear a troubled dweller in the land of Aphrodito. Receive the tormented tears of my family's troubles. I

36. This world has been elucidated by Alan Cameron from "Wandering poets," pp. 470–509, to "The empress and the poet," pp. 217–289.

37. See now L. Pernot, "Les τόποι de l'éloge chez Ménandros le rhéteur," *REG* 99 (1986) 33–53.

brought many stamped documents from home, which Gabriel dismissed as worse than the old ones.

Theodore of the Pentapolis himself in his presumptuous evil deeds stole for himself the harvest of my threshing floors. (Do you) reap the whole estate of honey-sweet grape clusters. Come and water all the property that raises cattle, on account of which Theodosius took the revenue of the eleventh indiction, my family's support. And now I prostrate myself at your feet, before the warlike grandeur of your shining footsteps. . . .

2. Παφίης χθονός, a learned and charming pun on the name of Aphrodito (cf. H24.7, H14.2). The many representations (even from Aphrodito itself; see J. Quibell, "Kom Ishgaw," *Annales du service des antiquités* 3 [1902], pl. II) of Aphrodite in Coptic art of the period show that this association would have been very much alive in the minds of Dioscorus's audience. See H. Torp, "Leda Christiana: The problem of the interpretation of Coptic sculpture with mythological motifs," *Acta Inst.Rom.Norv.* 4 (1969) 101–112, esp. 102–103.[38] We may even compare the Dumbarton Oaks Aphrodite pendant[39] as an illustration of this thought. There was a sense of the abiding presence of the name patron of Dioscorus's city (a subject that will be discussed later), from Hathor to Aphrodite to the Blessed Virgin.

3. δυσίμερα: a Nonnian word, redolent of unhappy love (Peek *Lexikon* s.v., used of Ariadne, Orion, and others), here applied to Dioscorus's frustrations.

4. χαράγματα: cf. Heitsch S10 r 16. See G. Vikan and J. Nesbitt, *Security in Byzantium: locking, sealing, and weighing* (Washington, D.C. 1980); and G. Vikan, "Security in Byzantium: keys," *Akten d. XVI. Intl. Byzantinistenkongress* II/3 (Vienna 1982) 503–511. Dioscorus will use this formulation again, in the 570s, in the encomium to Duke John. The concept of evidence, weight, and worthiness of evidence that is to be used in proof, and of precedent is uppermost in the mind of Dioscorus the lawyer. Cf. H3.34, and Romanos 39.11.1, θεῖα ἐγχαράγματα.

5. Gabriel, and **10.** Theodosius, cannot be identified from the papyri as yet.

6. Once more Theodore of the Pentapolis, Dioscorus's clerical villain.

38. Compare also Torp's shorter article, "Coptic mythological reliefs: Pagan or Christian?", Βυζαντινα 2 (1973) 15–17; and now T. Säve-Söderbergh, "The pagan elements in early Christianity and Gnosticism," in *Colloque international sur les textes de Nag Hammadi*, ed. B. Barc (Quebec and Louvain 1981) 71–85, esp. 80–81.

39. K. Weitzmann, ed., *Age of Spirituality: A symposium* (New York and Princeton 1979) no. 288, pl. IX, pp. 313–314; M. C. Ross, *Catalogue of the Dumbarton Oaks Collection* II (Washington, D.C. 1965) no. 12. Compare the Coptic Museum Aphrodite-on-shell: J. Beckwith, *Coptic sculpture* (London 1963) pl. 62. See also K. Wessel, *Coptic art* (New York 1965) pl. 38 and 39.

Does the mention of grapes in line 8 suggest that Theodore was again dealing in wine at Dioscorus's expense?

10. The eleventh indiction in question is doubtless A.D. 547 (Bagnall and Worp, *CSBE*, 88).

11–12. Salutations to the addressee's "footsteps" have many parallels in Coptic epistolography; e.g., Ep 247, 300. Cf. H. Zilliacus, *Zur Abundanz der spätgriechischen Gebrauchssprache* (Helsinki 1967) 79. On the beauty of woman's feet in Late Antiquity, cf. Colluthus 135.

12. ὕψος is also a term of address in epistolography. See H. Zilliacus, *Untersuchungen zu den abstrakten Anredeformen u. Höflichkeitstiteln im Griechischen* (Helsinki 1949) 91, with references.

H12. Iambic prologue and hexameter encomium on Romanos. A.D. 553/4?	*P.Rein.* II 82 + *P.Lit.Lond.* 98

A

   Ὄλβιε πανόλβιε τῷ γένει κ[α]ὶ τοῖς λόγοις
   κάλλιστά σοι πρέπει, δέχο[υ], ὦ δέσποτα·
   ὑμῶν τὰς ἀξίας λέγειν οὐ β[ά]σκανος,
   ῥήτωρ ἄριστος εἰ μὴ εὐφυὴς πανύ,
5 ι . . . .] λογισμὸν ἀκριβῆ
   ο]τα[.]σινωεπε . ετ . [. . . . . .]ε . [.] . . την
   σο]φὸς παλαιὸς ὦ Μένανδρος τοῖς λόγοις
   ρ .]μην Μενανδρείαν Ἰσοκράτης λέγει.
   ω . .]ε δὲ γ[ὰ]ρ ἡμῖν ἡ πόλις σωφροσύνης.
10 μ . .]εδων ἔπαινον τετελεσμένος φύσει
   ἄ]κριτος ἔφυς τὰ διπλᾶ τῶν ἀρετάων,
   ν]εώτερος παν[έ]ντιμος τύχης [καὶ] γένους,
   ὀ]λβιοδαίμων ὁ δημοκηδεμὼν μέγας,
   σ]οφὸς σοφωτάτων ὑπερέβησα[ς λ]όγον.
15 τ]οίνυν σύ γ᾽ αὐτὸς συνδραμὼν τῷ ᾽μῷ σκοπῷ
   κ]αὶ μὴ κατόκνει συγκροτεῖν ξ[έ]νους ποτέ.
   ἁ]γίως ὁ γράψας ποτὲ τοὺς δύο π[λ]άκας
   κ]αὶ σοῦ χαράξει τοὺς χρόνους διπλώματι.

acrostichum: ο κυριος Ρωμανος.— 3 cf. 1 verso 2s et XXX 28 7s codex Menandri Cairensis (v. A. Koerte, Menander I, ³ 1957, p. VIII) et vita Isocratis (P. Cairo Cat. 67175) Dioscori fuisse verisimile est. cf. etiam 9,16 l γνωμην sup. Co contra acrostichum; ρυμην, ρημην (= ρημα), ρωμην? 12 cf. 10,6 14 cf. 4β 9 15 cf. 10,19 17s cf. 5,38s

B

   Ῥήτρης εὐρυνόο[ι]ο διαμπερὲς ἔμπλεος ἦσθα,
   ὦ βαθέης σοφίης πολυήρατον εὖχος ἐρώτων,

Μουσάων θεράπων καὶ Ἄρεος ἠδὲ Χαρίτων·
ἄλλον Ὅμηρον ἴδον καὶ Ἄρεα ἠδὲ τ' Ἔρωτα
5   νυμφίον ἀγλαίης πανομοίιον Ἡελίωνι.
νοῦσον ἐμὴν [π]ρήυνον, ἐπεὶ φρένα οὐκέτ' ἀείρω,
ὄλβιον εἰσορόων πατέρων γόνον ὀλβιστήρων
σώφρονα δημοτελῆ πανυπείροχον ἐγγὺς ἀνάκτων.
θάλλε μοι, εἰσέτι θάλλοις, ἕως ὅτε κέδρον ἱκάνῃς·
10 ἀντ' εὐεργεσίης τετανυμμένης πάντοθεν οἰκτρῷ
ὕμμι θεὸς πανεπόπτης διπλόον ἐγγυαλίξῃ
μακροπόρευτον ἔχειν ἄλυπον βίον ἐκτὸς ἀνίης
ἄφθονον αὐτοτέλεστον ἐπ' αὐχένι δυσμενέεσσιν.
σωροτέρην ἀτάνυσσον ἐμοὶ παλάμηφιν ἐάων
15 τὸν φίλα τέκνα σαώσοντ' ἠδὲ τεκοῦσαν ἀρίστην,
ὅττι βίης ἐπίηρα παρ' ἐλπίδα πήματα πάσχω.
σὸν κλέος ἀμφιβόητον ἐπὶ χρόνον ἄσπετον ἔλθοι.
τολμήεις γενόμην· πόθεν ἤλυθον εὐκλέα μορφῆς
ὑμνεῦσαι Ἄδονιν πεφιλημένον ἠδ' Ὑάκινθον;
20 ἀγλαίην ἐνίκησας ἐρωτοτόκου μελεδῶνος.

acrostichum: Ρωμαννος θαυμαστος.—   2 β supra ζαθεης Π cf. Eurip.
Med. 844   3 e.g. cf. I 443, h. Ap. 131, Archil. fr. 1   4 cf. 25,6   5 cf.
Septuag. Ps. 18,6 (? v. 1 verso 8)   5s alter versus delendus?   8 cf. 3,36
9 cf. 2,29 | cf. 2,25; 3,36; 4,12 | κεδρον v. e.g. Septuag. 3. Reg. 5,13; Ps. 91,13
13 cf. 4,11   14 cf. 3,24 | σωροτερην a verbo σωρος derivatum esse videtur;
cf. ογκοτερος.   16 επιηρα cf. 3,88   18s cf. 6,13s

Blessed one, all-blessed, in lineage and in mind, receive, my lord, the
beauty that is your due. It is not for the envious to recite your worth. The
most skilled of speakers, let alone the most eloquent, . . . (would hardly
frame) an accurate speech (about you). Menander, the ancient thinker,
(might have) in his sayings, and Isocrates (would have) echoed Menander.
(You are) to us the City of Wisdom. By your nature reckoned among those
worthy of a panegyric, and subject to no judge, you furnish a double kind
of excellence, (being) a young man all-honored by fortune and by descent,
great patron of the people, blessed in spirit; in your wisdom you have
surpassed the thought of the wisest. And now you yourself, deigning to
behold me, do not shrink from helping strangers. May He who in His
holiness once wrote the two Tables of the Law write many years in your
Book of Life.

You were totally filled with an ordinance of far-ranging intent, O much-
loved answer to the prayers of those who love divine wisdom, serving the
Muses and the Graces as well as War; I have seen a second Homer, and
Ares, and Love, Festivity's bridegroom, namesake of the sun. Soothe my
illness, since I am not in my right senses, beholding the blessed descendant of most blessed ancestors, the wise ruler, who is close to the supreme
sovereign himself. Flourish, and may you again flourish, till you resemble
a cedar; for God Who sees all things has put into your hands a double

return for your beneficence, in mercy extended everywhere, and granted you a long and painless life, free from grief, unblighted by envy and rounded in accomplishment, free from troubles round your neck. Stretch out to me your hand that heaps up good fortune, saving my dear children and their excellent mother, because in my land tenure I am suffering the unexpected troubles of violence. May your renowned glory continue to an innumerable time. Let me be bold: Where should I begin to sing of Adonis, famous for his beauty, or beloved Hyacinth? You have surpassed the splendor of Aphrodite in her care.

Romanos unfortunately cannot be identified from the papyri; he is likely to have been a duke of the Thebaid (cf. A13, B8).

A1. A brilliant opening line, praising just those qualities most desired in an Egyptian noble: it creates a world of highly visible opulence that reaches back to the praise poems of Pindar. The delight in noble lineage and fine speaking (following the rhetorical precepts of γένος and ἀνατροφή) (cf. line 14, the praise of wise eloquence), so often present in Dioscorus's poetry, is here compressed into a succession of images of great splendor. πανόλβιος, a word used by Quintus Smyrnaeus, may also here be in part a local pun, with a possible reminiscence of the fifth-century poet Panolbios (*PLRE* II, p. 829) who wrote verses to an Egyptian called Erythrius (*PLRE* II, pp. 401–402). As proper names, these seem to be indigenous to the area; cf. the Fl. Panolbios, *politeuomenos*, in *P. Freer* 1 IV 4³,[40] and count Erythrios in *P. Freer* 1 V 5–6, 12, VI 17; 2 I 11, 17 (cf. E. Bernand, *Inscriptions métriques de l'Egypte gréco-romaine* [Paris 1969] no. 123, an Erythrios from Antinoë). A form of local patriotism may have been at work (cf. P. Wormald, review of *Western Aristocracies and Imperial Court* by J. Matthews, *JRS* 66 [1976] 222). Cf. also Ps.-Apoll. *Metaphr.Pss.* 1.1 and 22.3; and the epigram cited by Golega, *Der homerische Psalter*, p. 8, line 11: ὄλβιε καὶ ζωῆς, ὄλβιε καὶ θανατοῦ. Also compare the Hestia Polyolbos tapestry at Dumbarton Oaks (from Sohag) (K. Wessel, *Koptische Kunst* [Recklinghausen 1963] pl. 132); cf. line 13, ὀλβιοδαίμων, and B7, itself a brilliant allegorization of Late Antique Egyptian aristocratic life. The "hearth full of blessings" is the noble house— the house of the patron. (P. Friedländer, *Documents of dying paganism* [Berkeley 1945] was overly concerned to emphasize the pagan content of this image. A Christian noble house like that of the Apions would have hung this tapestry with complete comfort and naturalness.[41])

40. J. Gascou and L. S. B. MacCoull, "Le cadastre d'Aphroditô," *Trav. et Mém.* 10 (1988) 103–158, esp. here 136. See H. Geremek, "Les πολιτευόμενοι égyptiens sont-ils identiques aux βουλευταί?," *Anagennesis* 1 (1981) 231–247.

41. Compare the remarks of Cameron, "The empress and the poet," p. 272; and P. R. L. Brown, *The making of late antiquity* (Cambridge, Mass. 1978) 81–82, with n. 2 (quoting H.

3. On the evil eye, cf. H23.21, and see D. Bonneau, "L'apotropaïque 'abaskantos' en Egypte," *RHR* 199 (1982) 23–36.

7–8. As A. Körte noticed in *Archiv* 14 (1941) 111, Dioscorus owned both the codex of Menander now at Cairo, see L. Koenen et al., *The Cairo codex of Menander (P.Cair.J.* 43227 [London 1978]), and the papyrus containing a life of Isocrates (*P.Cair.Masp.* II 67175; see chapter II). The implication is of excellence in both (gnomic) wisdom and statecraft. For Dioscorus and the *Menandri Sententiae*, see my comments on H10.25.

9. ἡ πόλις σωφροσύνης: a transcendent image of both the Redeemed City and some glorified Alexandria, or Constantinople, of the mind, all at once. (H. North, *Sophrosyne* [Ithaca 1966] 312–379, does not go later than Augustine.) Cf. Isa 1:26 (and 21), [ⲧⲡⲟⲗⲓⲥ ⲛ̄ⲧⲇⲓⲕ]ⲁⲓⲟⲥⲩⲛⲏ in *P.Köln* IV 169. See now W.-P. Funk, "Πόλις, πολίτης und πολιτεία im Koptischen," in *Soziale Typenbegriffe im alten Griechenland u. ihre Fortleben i.d. Sprachen der Welt* 7, ed. E. Ch. Welskopf (Berlin, DDR 1982) 283–320.

13. The noble patron par excellence, opulent and magnanimous.

17–18. Previous critics appear to have missed the point of this original and striking image. Collart in *P.Rein.* II (1940) thought the reference paralleled that of ἐγκώμια (pl.) in the title, i.e., the iambics plus the hexameters (following A. Körte in *Archiv* 10 [1932] 29; cf. Alan Cameron, "*Pap.Ant.* III.115 and the iambic prologue in late Greek poetry," *CQ* 64 [1970] 119–129), but confessed himself unable to interpret the lines. C. B. Welles, in his review of *P.Reinach* by P. Collart, *AJP* 68 (1947) 96–97, was also thinking of the present poet and his work. ῾Ο γράψας is God himself. The reference is to the two Tables of the Law written by the finger of God. The poet is dovetailing Scripture imagery with Roman chancery terminology (δίπλω-μα). See my comments on H10.17–18. Dioscorus will use the figure on several occasions: besides H10, also see H11.13–14, cf. H5.38–39. Cf. *Ep.Barnabas* 14.2. The Law, either New or Old, can be represented in Late Antique iconography as either a roll or a codex or diptych (δύο πλάκας): compare the sixth-century ivory pyxis in the Hermitage (W. F. Volbach, *Elfenbeinarbeiten der Spätantike*³ [Mainz 1976] no. 190) and the Moses cross at Sinai (K. Weitzman and I. Ševčenko, "The Moses cross at Sinai," *DOP* 17 [1963] 385–398). Here the visualization is clear. Dioscorus the *nomikos* has made the *diploma* into an appropriate metaphor for complimenting an official.

Torp). The persistent drawing of false antitheses (of "Christian/pagan," "Hellenic/Coptic" and the like) by critics perpetuates the value judgments of earlier periods. The present work seeks to free the reader's mind from such built-in idiosyncrasies.

B1. ῥήτρα is perhaps a deliberate archaism. εὐρύνοος is a *hapax* for Dioscorus here.

2. Read the poet's original ζαθεής here: the poem is about the splendor of divine wisdom as manifested in one person.

3. The μουσικὸς ἀνήρ is a man of action as well.

4. On Dioscorus as owner of Homer MSS, cf. *P.Cair.Masp.* II 67172, 67173, 67174.

5. The "bridegroom of Festivity/Splendor": cf. Ps. 18:6 LXX, the unforgettable image of the sun as a bridegroom, "rejoicing as a giant to run his course."

8. πανυπείροχος: cf. Oppian *Hal.* 1.311.

9. The cedar is of course a biblical (Old Testament) image (so Keydell in *RE* Suppl. 6 [1935] 28); to Heitsch's note, add Num. 24:6, Cant. 5:15, Ezek. 17:23.

11. Note again the juxtaposition of Christian and Roman-law terminology.

12. μακροπόρευτον is a *hapax* for Dioscorus here.

15. We do not know the identity of Dioscorus's wife.

16. I take this to be a reference again to the oppressions of Theodore of the Pentapolis (see my comments on H6 and H8). Such an identification would date the poem, and Romanos, to the early period, about 553/4, considerably before Dioscorus's move to Antinoë.

19. Hyacinthus: cf. comments on H27. Perhaps there was also an implied assimilation of the figure of Antinous to that of Apollo's beloved.

H1. Panegyric on the emperor Justin II.   *P.Cair.Masp.* II 67183
A.D. 565/6

recto

Ἰούστι]νος ἄμμνι ἵκανε φερέσβιος ἐσθλοσυνάω[ν,
Ἰούστινος] ἄμμιν ἵκανεν, ἐλευθερίης καὶ ἀρωγ[ῆς
δεινῶν σφ]αλμάτων λαθικηδέος ἤγαγε τέρψιν
ἀνδράσι τε κρατ]εροῖς πολυτ[ερπ]έσιν ἠδὲ γυναῖξί[ν.
5 [λώϊόν ἐστιν ἐὸν παναοίδιμον οὔνομα μέλψαι],
[ὅττι χάρις καὶ] χάρμα καὶ ε[ὐ]πίης [φίλον] ἄνθο[ς,
ὑμνε]ῦσαι νέον υἷα πολυσκήπτρου παλλατίου,
τὸν πολυ]κυδήεντα φιλόχριστον βασιλῆα,
οἷον δῶρο]ν ἐπήρατον ὃν θεὸς ὤπασε κόσμῳ.
10 ἤλυθεν] οὐ κατὰ [κ]όσμον ἀληθέα πάντα ν[ο]μεύει[ν].
κλεινότ]ατον δ' ἀτίταλλε θ[εοφρ]αδέεσσιν βουλαῖς
σώφρον]ος εὐσεβίης Θεοδοσίου πάνσοφον ἄσθμα,
ἐκ γέν]νης μεθέποντα θεοῦ δέος ἠδὲ καὶ θεσμούς,

θείω]ν χριστοφόρων ὃς ἀλουργίδα οἶδε φορῆναι.
15 σπεύδεο] νῦν, στρατίαρχε, σέθεν καλέειν ναετῆρας.
. . . . .]ος ἔπλ[ε]ο μοῦνος, ἀ[γ]ακλυτὰ δῶρα κομ[ί]ζῃς.
πάντ]ῃ κοιρανίης σκοπιάζετε πυθμένα [ῥ]ίζης
σώφ]ρονα, κυδαλίμης σοφίης ἐγκύμονα θεσμῶν,
τοῖς προτέρο]ι[ς] βασιλεῦσιν ἀοίδιμον ἐς θρόνον υἷα.

Iustinus II (aa. 565–578) Aegyptum numquam adiit; quare carmen ad adventum effigiei imperatoriae pertinet.—omnia sup. Ma.— 5s e 20,5s sup. Ma, cf. 3,13 7 cf. E. Kornemann, Weltgesch. d. Mittelmeerraumes II 445 10 cf. 2,23; 3,50; (14,2); 21,26; B 214 11 θεορρητοι[ς σεο in margine dextro sup. Cr 12 Theodosius I. (379–395) 16 αφθιτος sup. Ma l cf. Nonn. D. 37, 103 18 cf. 6,10

verso

χαίρε]τε μο[ι], βασιλῆες, ἐπὶ χρόνον ἄσπετον εὕδης.
κοιρα]νίης [ἀ]πάνευθε τεῆς φθόνος αἰὲν ἀλάσθω.
ἐκ σέο] κο[ιρα]νίης φθόνος ἔρπελος α[ἰ]ὲν ἀλάσθω
. . . .]λιν ὑμετέρῃσιν ὑ[πέ]σσε[τ]αι δέσμια χερσίν
5 . . . . . . π]εφρικότα τραγικώτερα δάκρυα λείβειν.
πίστ]ιν ἀερτάζεις θεοδέγμονα κυδιανείρην.
μὴ τ]ρομέοις, σκηπτοῦχε, τὸ σὸν κλέος οὔποτ᾽ ὀλεῖται·
ὡς] στέφος [ὑ]ψι[κ]άρηνον πάμφυλον ἔσσι κίβωτιν,
ἀκτ]ῖνες ἀστράπτουσ[ι τε]ῆς περικαλλέος μορφῆς
10 ὡς στ]έφος ὑψικά[ρηνο]ν . λαυ . . τα . . . κατ . . αφ . . . [
. . . .] . . ς ἱμ[εί]ρων φιλο[π]άρθενος ε . . . . τιν
οὐδαμὸς] δὲ ἄναξ πανομο[ίι]ος ἔπλετο σεῖο.
οὐραν]όθεν θε[ὸ]ς ὕμμι πόρεν διαδήματα φωτός
. . . . . .] . . . . . λεν . . . . . αφθιται . . ατα . ε[
15 . . . .] . . . [. . . .]λη[. . χθον]ὸς ἠδὲ θαλάσσης
. . . .]τατου τ[. . . . . . ὑπει]ρόχη [

1 de confusione plural. et sing. cf. e.g. 5,33; 6,9s; 17,14s; 23,14; 24,18.21 l ενδεις Π 2s alter versus delendus, cf. 8. 10; 2,2.7s–11s; 4,3; 10,33; 12B 5s; 13,9s: 17,15s. 23s; 19,8.11; 24,12s l cf. 23,21 et 12,3 5 cf. Nonn. D. 47,228 6 cf. 6,8 7 τρομεεις Π, cf. Nonn. D. 29,56 l cf. 4,7; 7,10; 20,1 8 κιβωτιν = arca Noae (Ke); cf. 12B 5.9 9 ομφης Π, cor. Ke cl. 20,3

Further notes: r1 read ἄμμιν 11 in apparatus add [σιν Ma. 13 εκ γεν] ῾γε῾ Pap. v2 ερπελος εια. in right margin 9 read ὁμῆς

Justin is come to us, the life-giver, bringer of good, Justin is come to us: he has brought to brave men and their happy wives the joy of freedom to banish care and of help for our painful failures. It is a fine thing to celebrate his name, worthy of poetic praise, as Grace does and Joy and the lovely flower of Eloquence, to sing the young son of the many-sceptred palace, the much-praised Emperor who loves Christ, which delightful gift God has granted to the world. He has come to shepherd all truth, not according to worldly standards. He has cherished with his divinely spoken counsels the most renowned wise breath of prudent and pious Theodosius, following from his birth the fear and the ordinances of God, and he knows how to wear the purple robe of the holy bearers of Christ. Come now, Duke of the Thebaid, call your subjects. You alone are . . . , and you bring gifts of renown. Behold everywhere the wise root of the stock of sovereignty, big with the statutes of glorious wisdom, a splendid successor to the throne of former Emperors. Rejoice with me, O sovereigns; may you reach a boundless length of life. May the evil eye ever be banished far from your reign (may creeping Envy ever be banished from your reign). It is in your hands to loose our bonds . . . (as) in our fear we shed tears of sorrow. You exalt the divine faith which glorifies mankind. You who bear the sceptre, do not fear, your glory shall never fade: like a crowning garland, you are the universal Ark of the Covenant, and the rays of your beautiful voice flash out, like a crowning garland . . . lover of Our Lady. . . . Never has there been a ruler like you. God has sent you from heaven a crown of light. . . .

Dioscorus began his "Antinoë period" in 566, with this poetic work celebrating the *adventus* of the emperor's image (most likely a panel-painted icon) at the capital of the duke of the Thebaid, in honor of the new reign. Fittingly, in a poem on an imperial subject by a writer who had personally seen the imperial capital, it is filled with striking imagery rooted in the Egyptian poetic tradition, the Scriptures, and Dioscorus's own experience. Most abundant are epithets shared with the Nonnus *Paraphrasis of St. John* (e.g., φερέσβιος, also used by the author of P.Vindob.Gr. 29788C; θεοφραδής; σκηπτοῦχος; φιλοπάρθενος). The new emperor, both royal in background and pious in convictions, is hailed as a wise Christian legislator in the great Theodosian tradition (r 10–12)—a motif dear to the heart of Dioscorus the jurist. As an expression of hope for a possible ecclesiastical rapprochement, and an affirmation of the first priority of the imperial role, Dioscorus praises the new emperor as "exalting the divine faith which glorifies mankind" (v 6). With great originality he compares the emperor to the Ark of the Covenant (v 8), and recreates the brilliance of the *adventus* procession with its public acclamations and outdoor pageantry in phrases shot through with ringing sound and light (ἀκτ]ῖνες . . . [τε]ῆς περικαλλέος ὀμφῆς, v 9). The whole poem acclaims the imperial *praesentia* as it is seen at work, in local color, among the Coptic people, and illustrates the prominence of Antinoë as the ceremonial center of Upper Egypt. See L. S. B. MacCoull, "The panegyric on Justin II by Dioscorus of Aphrodito," *Byzantion* 54 (1984) 575–585.

r1. φερέσβιος: cf. *P.Cair.Masp.* II 67178 A 13.

7. *palatium:* one of several examples of how Dioscorus was making

Latinisms respectable in poetry (e.g., *P.Cair.Masp.* II 67185 A1, ἐξκουβίτωρ; 67185 B13, καγκελλάριος, cf. 67316.9; 67185 B, ὀφφίκιον, cf. 67126.58). Such a list as that of J. D. C. Frendo, "The significance of technical terms in the poems of George of Pisidia," *Orpheus* 21 (1974) 53 is rather beside the point.

8. On φιλόχριστον βασιλῆα, see also Golega, *Der homerische Psalter*, pp. 33–34; and Weitzmann and Ševčenko, "The Moses cross at Sinai," esp. 395–398; if the authors had been aware of papyrological sources, they would have expressed less astonishment at the phraseology of this inscription. Cf. Dioscorus himself in *P.Lond.* V 1674.1 (A.D. 570)[42] and cf. *P.Cair.Masp.* I 67009.1.

πολυκυδήεις: cf. Golega, *Der homerische Psalter*, p. 107, citing Ps.-Apoll. *Metaphr.Pss.* 10.7, 63.20, 88.4, 97.4.

12. On the legislation, especially the novels, of Justin II, see Zepos and Zachariae v. Lingenthal, *Jus graecoromanum* I (Athens 1931, reprint Aalen 1962) 1–13: the emperor reintroduced divorce by consent. Novel 2 attests the presence of the σκαιὸς δαίμων so often invoked in the divorce contracts written by Dioscorus (*P.Cair.Masp.* I 67004.8, 67121.9, II 67153.12, 67154r9, 67155, III 67311.16, 67321.9; *P.Lond.* V 1712, 1713; cf. H. Zilliacus, *Zur Abundanz der spätgriechischen Gebrauchssprache* [Helsinki 1967] 15). Cf. P. R. L. Brown, *The making of late antiquity* (Cambridge, Mass. 1978) 10, with n. 33.

v2–3. "Alternate" lines in Dioscorus are not always to be discarded, in the manner of earlier critics: cf. Nonnus *Paraphr.* 18.33–34. The repetition is effective.

8. The most famous sixth-century Ark of the Covenant was of course that of the theories of Cosmas Indicopleustes, a figure of the universe: W. Wolska-Conus, *Cosmas Indicopleustès: Topographie chrétienne* III (SC 197, Paris 1973) 124–125 and pl. 6a.

15. Cf. Heitsch II S 10 (*P.Berol.* 9799) r14, with T. Viljamaa, *Studies in Greek encomiastic poetry of the early Byzantine period* (Helsinki 1968) 52. For a possible echo of the Coptic legal phrase ϩⲙ̄ⲡⲧⲟⲟⲩ ϩⲙ̄ⲡⲙⲟⲟⲩ, cf. Satzinger BKU III 350.11 with n. 6, and P. Yale inv. 1862 (L. S. B. MacCoull, "Coptic papyri in the Beinecke collection at Yale University," *Proc. XIV intl.congr.papyrol.* [London 1975] 218).

With this poem and the next (H10, to Victor the *praeses*) begins Dios-

---

42. The phrase was normal and well established at the Antinoë chancery; cf. *P.Cair.Masp.* I 67009 I 1, 67005.5 (restored), 67019.6, 22, III 67289B. It is found in chancery Greek as late as *P.Apoll.* 69.3. In Coptic, and from a nearby area, it is found at Bala'izah: Bal 191, 197, 227, 273. Other Coptic evidence is late and rather peripheral: BM 449.2 and 450.1 from Syene, 464.1 from Jeme (cf. 514, ninth-century liturgical).

corus's Antinoë period, upon his change of residence from Aphrodito to the seat of the duke of the Thebaid (cf. L. S. B. MacCoull, "Dioscorus and the dukes: an aspect of Coptic hellenism in the sixth century," *BS/EB* 14 [1988]).

H10. Encomium on Victor the prefect. A.D. 566/7.   *P.Cair.Masp.* II 67131

A

Θήβ]η πᾶσα χόρ[ευ]σ[ο]ν, ε[ἰ]ρήν[ην] δέ[χου,
οὐ γ]ὰρ θε[ωρήσεις] κακουργικὴν ἔτ[ι·
πάν]τη δέος πέ[φυκεν ἀσπίλου δίκ]ης
τοῦ] πανταρίστου καὶ διεσμιλευγμένου,
5   τ]οῦ ἡγεμῶνος Βίκτορος τοῦ πανσόφου,
ἀ]εὶ βραβευτοῦ ἔκ τε τύχης καὶ γέν[ου]s,
ἀνίσου [ἐ]κ πρέ[μνου, δ]ικαιο[τ]άτου πάνυ.
ὡς ... τυχοίης αγ[
ἔχεις, ἄριστο[s γόνος τῶν] ὀλ[β]ιστ[ήρων,
10   τοῦ ἡγεμῶνος καὶ [δ]ομ[ε]στίκου [τ]ύχην,
δίδυμα τῆς ἀρχῆς παναξιώματα.
οὐκ ἂν δυνήσεται †μεγειρα καρτερεῖν
θ]εοῦ διδόντος εὐδοκιμῆσαι ὑμῖν.
φιλ]εῖς τὸ θεῖον κ[αὶ] φιλ[εῖς] τοὺς πλησίους,
15   μ]ᾶλλον σεαυτοῦ τοὺς ξένους ποούμενος,
καὶ] εὖ σκοπεῖς ἐλεήμων εἰς τοὺς ἀθλίους.
ὁ γ]ράψας ἡδέως δακτύλῳ δύο πλακάς
κ]αὶ σοῦ χαράξει τοὺς χρόνους δι[π]λώματι.
νῦν μὴ κατόκνει συγκροτεῖν με δυστυχῆ
20   τὸν [πρ]ολαχόντα τὸν βίο[ν ἀπ]ορώτερον.
[
ε[ὐ]δαιμ[ον]ίης πατρ[ικῆς] πεσούμε[νος
                              ] τα π[α]νταχῆ
...... φ]υλαχθὲν τῇ σῇ αρ.. μ .. σπαθω
25   ἀργὸς π[ο]λίτης τῇ πόλε[ι] κακὸν μ[έ]γα.
ὅπως τύχοιμι τῆς [ὑμῶν] εὐερ[γεί]ης,
ἄπαντα τὸν .... [π]ολ[ί]ταις
π]ρὸς τὸν θεὸν τὰς ἱκεσίας ἐκ[φ]έρων·
ἀ]νθ' ὧν τὰ συμφέροντα .... ι ὑμῖν ... α . ειν.
30   ψῆφον δό[τ]ε [γ]ε τὴν [π]αροῦσαν, δέσποτα·
στ]ῆσον τὸν οἰ]κέτην νομικὸν τῇ πόλει,
ὑμῶν δ[ὲ] ταῖς χρείαις ἀεὶ ὑπηρέτην,
ἔχοντα τὸ πρόθυμον ηδ........

1–3 cf. 3,9–11   **4** cf. 3,5   **6** cf. 12,12   **10** domesticus: titulus   **12** με τειρ(ε)α coni. Ma   **14s** cf. 17,13; 18,4s Ι φιλ[τα]τους et αλλον σεαυτον olim Ma   **17s** cf. 5,38s Ι χαραξη Π   **19** cf. 12,16   **25** = P. Flor. III 295,6; cf. Eurip. fr. 512 αργος πολιτης κεινος, ως κακος γ' ανηρ (v. etiam Eurip. El. 80, fr. 187). post 25 paragraphus.   **33** αυταις δουλευειν in marg. dextro

B

versificator in margine dextro mutationem scripsit hanc:

] οὐκ ἀνεκπίπτει ποτέ.

ἔοικε σὸν τοὔνομ᾽ ἀεὶ πλημυρίῃ·

ὁ γὰρ σὸς ἀστὴρ νειλαγωγὸς πέφανται.

δοκεῖς σοι βρ . . . . εὐτυχέστερον βίον,

5   ὦ παντάριστε τῷ λόγῳ βουληφόρων.

ῥυσίπτολίν σε καὶ [

ὃν νῦν καλοῦσιν εὐσεβῆ σοφώτατοι,

στολιστὴν ἀσθενῶν, χολῶν, τυφλοῖν δοτήν,

ξήσεις θεοῦ δῶρον βιοσπόρον μέγαν

10   πανευτυχέστερος βασιλικῆς [

2s cf. 3,42s   5 cf. 17,1

Let the whole Thebaid dance and welcome peace, for you shall not behold evildoing any more; for fear of the spotless justice of the most excellent and polished prefect Victor the Wise has sprung up everywhere, who is ever a judge by fortune and descent, from unequaled stock, entirely most just. . . . You enjoy, O excellent descendant of blessed ancestors, the positions of both prefect (*hegemon*) and *domesticus*, twin high offices of state. I would not be able to bear . . . if God did (not) grant me to glory in you. You love God and you love your neighbor, and in your state of life you love strangers better than yourself, and in your generosity you look with kindness upon the poor. May He Who in His divine courtesy wrote with His finger the two Tables of the Law write many years in your Book of Life. Now do not shrink from helping me in my trouble, I who have hitherto had allotted to me quite a difficult life. I fall before your high-born prosperity. . . . (As the saying goes,) a lazy citizen is a great evil to his city. So let me obtain the benefit of your benefaction . . . bearing prayers to God. Instead of which events have. . . . Give me then your present resolve, my lord: establish your client as notary in the city, ever an attendant upon your wishes, willing to . . . (serve them . . .)

Your name is ever like the inundation of the Nile; and indeed your star has appeared to lead the Nile. You seem . . . a most happy life, O most excellent in mind of counselors. (I call you) savior of cities, and now the wise call you pious, who clothe the poor and the melancholy, benefactor to the blind; you shall obtain from God the great gift of propagating life, O most fortunate of royal . . .

In this poem Dioscorus is anticipating the beginning of his career as *nomikos* (A31) at Antinoë, a work he probably began in early 566 (or perhaps 567; cf. *P.Lond.* V 1674 pref.). It is a new poetic departure in several ways.

A1–2: This is the first time (of four) that Dioscorus will use his favorite opening line for iambics (cf. H9, H11, and culminating in H3, the ode to Duke John). For the Late Antique iambic, see Alan Cameron, "*Pap.Ant.* III.115 and the iambic prologue in late Greek poetry," *CQ* 64 (1970) 119–129. Because so much metaphrastic and cento poetic work has been shown to be Egyptian (Golega, *Der homerische Psalter*, pp. 31–34), the non-Euripidean portions of the *Christus Patiens* are also worth investigating from this perspective.[43]

On the iambics, see also A. Saija, "La metrica di Dioscoro di Afroditopoli," in *Studi in onore di A. Ardizzoni* 2, ed. E. Livrea and G. A. Privitera (Messina and Rome 1978) 840–844.

Compare Nonnus *Dion.* 5.119 (Thebes as the dancing-ground of the Olympian gods).[44]

3. ἄσπιλος is a New Testament word, e.g., 1 Pet. 1:19; cf. 2 Clem. 8:6.

4–9. The qualities of the *praeses* are described in proper rhetorical order. Cf. H11.4.

10. For *domestici* at Antinoë, cf. *P.Cair.Masp.* I 67005v3, II 67179.1, III 67330 IV 6; *P.Lond.* V 1672.4.

12. Probably μέγαιρα as in *P.Cair.Masp.* III 67353.11, hence "I could not endure the envy (of others), did not God grant me to praise you."

14–15. Cf. *P.Lit.Lond.* 100G, echoing Christ's teaching. On the problem of "who is my neighbor?" in Late Antiquity, especially in Egyptian village society, see Brown, *Making of late antiquity*, 77. On φιλοξενία, cf. H17.12–13, with star imagery (see later discussion); H18.4.

17–18. The reference, as in H12.17–18, is not to consular diptychs (so Maspero in *P.Cair.Masp.* II 67131, p. 15n.), but to the two Tables of the Law.

43. Treated by L. S. B. MacCoull, "Egyptian elements in the *Christus Patiens*," paper presented at the Tenth Byzantine Studies Conference, Cincinnati, November 1984; published in *BSAC* 27 (1985) 45–51. A. Tuilier's edition of the *Christus Patiens* (Paris 1969), in which he favored the traditional attribution to Gregory Nazianzen, was not well received; see the critique by J. Grosdidier de Matons in *Trav.etMém.* 5 (1973) 363–372. F. Trisoglio's edition (Rome 1979) was preceded by numerous articles but of a purely literary-critical nature. I hypothesize that the *Christus Patiens* was composed by an Egyptian poet ca. 500.

44. On the seven-gated Thebes of Hellas and the hundred-gated Egyptian Thebes in Late Antiquity, see K. Weitzmann, *Greek mythology in Byzantine art* (Princeton 1951) 35; cf. S. P. Brock, *The Syriac version of the pseudo-Nonnus mythological scholia* (Cambridge 1971) 81. On the Egyptian self-image as related to classical antiquity, cf. G. Bardy, "Le patriotisme égyptien dans la tradition patristique," *Rev.d'Hist.Eccl.* 45 (1950) 5–24, which stops before Chalcedon. Present-day scholarship would tend to disagree with his conclusions. It is also unfortunate that the paper by W. H. C. Frend, "Nationalism as a factor in anti-Chalcedonian feeling in Egypt," *SCH* 18 (1982) 21–38 is based only on the same old narrative sources, not on documentary papyri.

Compare also the iconography illustrated in Wolska-Conus, *Cosmas Indicopleustès: Topographie chrétienne* I (SC 141, Paris 1968) 99, 193, fig. 8.

19. συγκροτεῖν: cf. *P.Oxy.* XVIII 722.

25. This proverb in this form is not contained in the collections of Menander's *Monosticha* that we have (ed. S. Jaekel, Teubner, Leipzig, 1964); see D. Hagedorn and M. Weber, "Die griechisch-koptische Rezension der Menandersentenzen," *ZPE* 3 (1968) 15–50. Dioscorus uses it elsewhere, in prose, in *P.Flor.* III 295.6.[45] (Cf. W. Crönert in *Gnomon* 2 [1926] 660 adducing Vitelli's note to the line in *P.Flor.*, as well as the Euripides parallel noted by Heitsch.[46]) Dioscorus loved the proverbial (cf. the opening of *P.Cair.Masp.* II 67151, the will of Fl. Phoebammon); Zilliacus, *Abundanz*, pp. 13–14. A possible echo is preserved in the Arabic: M. Ullmann, *Die arabische Überlieferung der sogenannten Menandersentenzen* (AKM 34.1, Wiesbaden 1961) 33, no. 133 (but the Arabic word corresponding to ἀργός really means "profligate" rather than "lazy").[47] Even more distant echoes may be heard in the Syriac: see J.-P. Audet, "La sagesse de Menandre l'Egyptien," *Rev.Bibl.* 59 (1952) no. 12, p. 63; cf. no. 77 p. 74, on the notion "laziness is bad." On ἀργός, see T. Reekmans, "Ἀργός and its derivatives in the papyri," *Cd'E* 60 (1985) 275–281.

31. Dioscorus is asking for an official position at Antinoë. On the office, cf. H18 and *P.Lit.Lond.* 100F, on John the *nomikos*.

B3. ἀστὴρ νειλαγωγός: much can be said about Late Antique star imagery. Most apposite is still V. Stegemann, *Astrologie u. Universalgeschichte: Studien u. Interpretationen an den Dionysiaka des Nonnos* (Leipzig and Berlin 1930), esp. p. 60. Here, cf. H15.5 and H17.12–13. Dioscorus is referring to the connection between the rising of Sirius and the inundation. See D. Bonneau, *La crue du Nil* (Paris 1964) 314, with n. 3 (restoring βρ[έχειν) for this text. For the Christian Nile, see Bonneau, *Crue*, pp. 421–439; *P.Lit.Lond.* 239; *SPP* XV 250ab; and, most recently, *P.Turner* 10 (found at Antinoë; cf. the Antinoë Nilometer, in Bonneau, *Crue*, pl. X).[48] Dioscorus may possibly also

45. I am grateful to Dr. Rosario Pintaudi of Florence for providing a photograph. The Florence papyrus cannot be dated precisely from the prosopography (Apa Besas the *numerarius*, Thomas the pagarch of Antaeopolis), but probably belongs to before 551, hence containing Dioscorus's earlier use of this proverb; cf. the *oikos* Psintse, to be identified with the *topos* and monastery of Psintase in *P.Freer* 2 I 24, II 1; 1 VII 1 (?).

46. Compare also Ἀργὸς πολίτης κεῖνος ὡς κακός γ᾽ ἀνήρ, Eur.fr. *Mel.Vinct.* 21, from G. H. Opsimathes, ΓΝΩΜΑΙ (Leipzig 1884, reprint Amsterdam 1972) 148. I owe this reference to the kindness of Professor K. Snipes.

47. Cf. also G. Kraemer, "Arabische Homerverse," *ZDMG* N.F. 31 (1956) 259–316; H. Satzinger, "Zu den koptischen Menander-Sentenzen," *Cd'E* 47 (1972) 351–354.

48. Mention might also be made of the Coptic liturgy for the yearly blessing of the

be referring to the comet seen in Egypt from Mesore to Thoth of year 281 of Diocletian (September–October A.D. 565), recorded by Olympiodorus *In Meteor.* I.6 (ed. W. Stuve [*CAG* 12.2, Berlin 1900] 52.30–53.2), surely taken as a portent of the approaching death of Justinian. Star imagery was a graceful sort of compliment: cf. in W. M. Calder, *Monumenta Asiae Minoris Antiquae* 1:238 (Manchester 1928), the epitaph of a priest, ἀστὴρ ὃς ἐν[έλ]αμπεν ἐν ἐκλησίησιν Θεοῖο. . . .[49] See also Cameron, "*Pap.Ant.* III.115," pp. 125–126, with examples.

6. ῥυσίπτολιν: a central concept in Dioscorus's thought and in his world. Cf. H4.2, H28.16, H13.8–10, H2.24–26, and H3.38 (with my comments). The whole atmosphere of this subject is brought out with sensitivity and evocative power by P. R. L. Brown, "Art and society in Late Antiquity," in *Age of spirituality: A symposium*, ed. K. Weitzmann (New York and Princeton 1980) 17–27, esp. 19: "Throughout the Late Antique period, to 'renew' a city was the most praiseworthy achievement of the powerful." (Also Cameron, "*Pap.Ant.* III.115," pp. 126–127 treats this theme.) Representation of the Tyche of a city was alive and well in Coptic art: see examples in the British Museum, the Louvre, and at Milan (J. Beckwith, *Coptic sculpture* [London 1963] pl. 52, 94, 95); the Berlin head (Staatl. Mus. 4133; A. Effenberger, *Koptische Kunst* [Vienna 1976] Taf. 23); the Textile Museum tapestry (J. Trilling, *The Roman heritage: textiles from Egypt and the eastern Mediterranean, 300 to 600 A.D.* [Washington, D.C. 1982] no. 5, p. 32); the Tyche of Panopolis in the Victoria and Albert Museum (A. F. Kendrick, *Catalogue of textiles from burying-grounds in Egypt* I [London 1920] pl. XII, no. 51).[50] At the moment of uprooting himself from his native Aphrodito to the imposing ducal seat of Antinoë, Dioscorus is articulating the Egyptian citizen's sentiment of "what my city means to me."[51] One

---

Nile waters, transmitted, oddly enough, in Greek in the Melkite tradition. See H. Engberding, "Der Nil in der liturgischen Frömmigkeit des Christlichen Ostens," *Oriens Christianus* 37 (1953) 67–79; A. Dmitrievskii, *Opisanie* II (Kiev 1901, reprint Hildesheim 1965) 684–691, 981–989. For Monophysite liturgica for this feast, the most important text is *SPP* XV 250ab, a "farced" Trishagion with prayers to St. Shenoute (adding ὁ σταυρωθεὶς δι' ἡμᾶς), being published by the present writer in *JTS*. Another Greek papyrus (actually parchment) is *P.Lit.Lond.* 239. See also A. Hermann, "Der Nil und die Christen," *JbAC* 2 (1959) 30–69.

49. Cf. O. P. Nicholson, "Lactantius: Prophecy and politics in the age of Constantine the Great" (D.Phil. thesis, Oxford 1981) 130–133 with notes; L. S. B. MacCoull, "The imperial *chairetismos* of Dioscorus of Aphrodito," *JARCE* 18 (1981–85) 44–45 with nn. 20–21.

50. The Brooklyn Museum relief (acc. no. 62.45) may well be a city goddess or an allegorical representation of a personified Byzantine Egyptian city.

51. K. Hartigan, *The Poets and the cities* (Meisenheim 1979) does not treat Egypt; see

might recall also the concept of rejuvenation reflected in Pamprepius 3.11; cf. E. R. Curtius, *European literature and the Latin middle ages* (Princeton 1953) 103–105.

8. Cf. Mt 25:35–40.

H24. Epithalamium for Paul and Patricia. *P.Lit.Lond.* 100C
Ca. A.D. 566.

   Ἑρμείας προφέριστος ἐπ' ἀγλαίῃσιν ἐρίζων
   ἵστατο, Τριτογένεια, σέ[θε]ν μνημήϊα μέλψαι.
   σὸν μέλος ἀμφεβόησε καὶ ὤμοσε καρτερὸν ὅρκον
   παντοίης μεθέπεις ὁτ' ἀμετρήτων ἀρετάων
5 ἀτρεκέως Φαέθοντος ἐράσσατο, τίκτε σε μήτηρ.
   τοὔνομά σευ καλέω παναοίδιμον Ἀφρογενείην·
   ῥηιδίως Παφίης πολυή[ρατ]ος ἔπλεο κάλλει
   ἱσταμένης σὺν Ἔρωτι· [τεὴν] Πόθος ἤλασε μορφήν.
   Κάλλινον εὐπατέρεια τεὸν γενετῆρα μελάθροις
10 ἱμερόεντα πόσιν πολυφ[ίλ]τατον ἔλπεο Παῦλον,
   ἀντίθεον χαρίεντα πανίκελα Βελλεροφόντῃ,
   νυμφίον ἱμερόεντα κεχ. . . . . καις,
   νυμφίον ἱμερόεντα ποδῶν ἄπο μέχρι κομάων.
   νυμφίε, σεῖο γάμον γεραρώτερον ὑμνοπολεύω·
15 ὑμνοπόλων Χαρίτων νοαρωτέραν ἔχραο νύμφη[ν.
   μὴ τρομέεις λεχέων τέρεν' ἄντυγα σεμνοπολεύειν.
   φρουρὲ βίου, σῶτερ μ[εγά]ρων, σκηπτοῦ[χε. . . . ·
   ἠ]δέα Πατρικίης γάμον εὔνοον ἔκδοτε Παύλῳ
   νοῦσον ἄτερ βιότοιο διαμπερὲ[ς .]δε. θ. [. .]ων
20 Πατρικίης ἐρατῆς ὁμοῦ Παύλου [
   ἁρμονίης ἀλύτοιο δίδου σφίσιν ευ. αν. . . . ην,
   υἱέας υἱονοὺς γούνασιν σφοῖν ἀειρομένοισι,
   λαμπετόοντα βίον παναο[ίδι]μον εἰρήναισιν
   ὃν χρόνον . . . [
25 υπ. [

   acrostichum: εις Πατρικιαν{ν} νυμφην Παυλου.— 1 εριζων supra αρι[στος **3–5** 'Complete collapse of grammar. The idea appears to be that since Patricia is such a paragon, her existence can only be explained by supposing that her real father is Phaethon.' Mi **8** post ισταμενης interpungendum? **9s** ευπατερεια, ατε εκ Καλλινου ουσα, cf. 22,5 **11** cf. 2,20 **12s** alter versus delendus **13** in marg. dextro I cf. Π 640; AP V 194,3 **15** νοερωτεραν? **17** Iuppiter invocatur **19** νουσων? **22** cf. 23,17

pp. 3–4, 102–107. Compare the theoretical discussion in D. Claude, *Die byzantinische stadt im 6.Jhdt.* (Munich 1969) 195–229. Antinoë's special epithet was ἡ καλλίπολις: *P.Flor.* 93–7; *P.Lond.* V 1713.11, 1714.19; *P.Cair.Masp.* II 67151.7, 67155.5, 67156.5, 67159.8, 67163.9.

Come, Athena, who excelled when Hermes set up the contest of splendor; come to sing memories of you. So she cried your song aloud and swore a mighty oath to follow you everywhere, because clearly the mother who bore you was loved by Phaethon, so measureless is your excellence. I call upon your name as most worthy of song of all the daughters of Aphrodito; surely you are full of the beauty of beloved Aphrodite who stands by Love's side; longing has marked your loveliness. Your noble descent from the house of Callinus your father has given hope to beloved Paul, your dear husband, godlike in his grace, like Bellerophon, a desired bridegroom . . . with hair flowing down to his feet. Bridegroom, I praise your noble wedding; you have taken a bride wiser than the hymn-singing Graces. Do not be afraid of your soft marriage-bed's solemnity. Watch over their life together, O savior of homes, sceptered one. . . . Give Paul a pleasant and happy marriage with Patricia, a life quite without illness. . . . Paul and beloved Patricia. . . . Give them the . . . of indissoluble harmony, as they hold children and grandchildren on their laps, and a bright and peaceful life, worthy of poetic praise. . . .

This is Dioscorus's first epithalamium, a genre he will come to practice often. Milne's identification of the bride with Patricia the pagarch (cf. *P.Lond.* V 1660, ad *P.Lit.Lond.* 100C) makes sense and probably should be accepted.

1. One thinks of Hermes's role in the Judgment of Paris, conducting the goddesses to Mount Ida.[52] The same content is seen in Colluthus 77–79. Compare the Princeton relief of the Judgment, if this interpretation be correct; F. F. Jones, "Six pieces of sculpture," *Record Art Mus. Princeton Univ.* 21 (1962) 53–55; J. H. Turnure, "Princeton's 'enigmatic' relief," ibid. 22 (1963) 45–57, with a different, Christian interpretation; H. Zaloscer, *Die Kunst im christlichen Ägypten* (Vienna 1974) pl. 48: Athena stands in the central position, with a cross on her shield. Cf. also the Coptic textile of the Judgment of Paris in the Kevorkian Foundation (Brooklyn Museum, *Pagan and Christian Egypt* [New York 1941] no. 235), complete with star imagery. Read, as last word, ἐρίζειν.

3. Compare oath formulas in Byzantine Greek and Coptic papyri, e.g., the φρικτὸν καὶ σεβάσμιον ὅρκον sworn to a legal document; E. Seidl, *Der Eid*

<hr>

52. Disregarding Milne's "erotic associations." For Hermes's role in the Judgment of Paris in ancient art, see J. Henle, *Greek Myths: A vase painter's notebook* (Bloomington 1973) 127–130; 193 nn. 8–9, 13; cf. C. Clairmont, *Das Parisurteil in der antiken Kunst* (Frankfurt 1972) 22–23; F. Brommer, *Vasenlisten z.griech. Heldensage* (Marburg 1973) 459–460. Also cf. J. Trilling, *The Roman heritage: Textiles from Egypt and the eastern Mediterranean, 300–600 A.D.* (Washington, D.C. 1982) no. 25, p. 46; and the ivory pyxis (sixth century) in the Walters Art Gallery, W. F. Volbach, *Elfenbeinarbeiten der Spätantike*[3] (Mainz 1976) no. 104, p. 75 and Taf. 55.

im römisch-ägyptischen Provinzialrecht 2 (*MB* 24, Munich 1935), esp. 137–160.

4. ἀμετρήτων ἀρετάων: the first of several times Dioscorus will use this formulaic element to end a hexameter line; cf. H21.21, 25; 5.5; 2.15. See Golega, *Der homerische Psalter*, p. 97, n. 1.

5. Dioscorus is fond of the myth of Phaethon; cf. H20.3, which may provide an identification for the bridegroom in this poem, as it is addressed to one Paul, son of Domninus, *cancellarius* on the prefectural staff (see later comments). This Paul is probably the same person. Dioscorus had most likely read the Phaethon story in Nonnus *Dion.* 38.90–95. The young man fallen from the Sun's chariot does not seem to have been popular in Late Antique visual art (see Leclercq in *DACL* 14.1 [1939] 660–664, who does quote an undated inscription from Palestine containing the phrase νέος Φαέθων); I know of no Coptic representations.[53] (Cf. Pamprepius 3.16, 177.) Compare the "new Phaethon" of John of Gaza, *Anacreontea* III.6.

6–7. Note the sequence Ἀφρογενείην . . . Παφίης.

8. Πόθος . . . μορφήν: the poet is bringing out, not so much the metaphor of "forging" (Milne), as the idea of a special Late Antique type of beauty (with reminiscences of Alexander's *pothos*; see my comments on H26.1, the Achilles and Polyxena poem);[54] cf. H. P. L'Orange, "The antique origin of medieval portraiture," in *Likeness and icon: Selected studies* (Odense 1973) 96–102; H.-I. Marrou, "La civilisation de l'antiquité tardive," in *Christiana Tempora* (Rome 1978) 67–77, esp. 69, and 74–76.

9. Callinus: his identity cannot be fixed from the papyri of the Aphrodito/Antinoë region.

11. Bellerophon, first introduced here and later mentioned in other epithalamia and in an encomium (H21, H32, H2), is a favorite figure of Dioscorus. On the symbolism of "Bellerophon Christianus," taken as a type of the victory of good over evil, see G. M. A. Hanfmann, "The continuity of classical art: culture, myth, and faith," in Weitzmann, *Age of spirituality*, pp. 85–87, with figs. 19–21 and the literature cited in nn. 58–67, esp. M. Simon, "Bellerophon chrétien," in *Mélanges Carcopino* (Vendome 1966) 889–903;[55]

53. Dioscorus uses νέος Φαέθων in H14.1, to Dorotheos; H3.37 to Duke John. The Tortona Phaethon sarcophagus listed in *DACL* also depicts Leda and the Swan, a favorite figure in Dioscorus's poetry (see comment on H22.13, 15).

54. On *pothos*, see A. B. Bosworth, *A historical commentary on Arrian's history of Alexander* I (Oxford 1980) 35 n. 10, and esp. 62.

55. See H. Brandenburg, "Bellerophon christianus," *RomQ* 63 (1968) 49–86, esp. the literature cited p. 51 n. 6; idem, review of *Bellerophon* by S. Hiller, *JbAC* 14 (1971) 163–168; J. M. C. Toynbee, "The Christian mosaic pavement, Hinton St. Mary, Dorset," *JRS* 64 (1964) 7–14; cf. W. H. C. Frend, review of *Priscillian of Avila* by H. Chadwick, *JTS* 28 (1977) 564–

cf. I. Ševčenko, "A shadow outline of virtue: The classical heritage of Greek Christian literature (second to seventh century)," in Weitzmann, *Age of spirituality* 57, with nn. 34–35, citing Methodius of Olympus. This imagery was very much alive in Dioscorus's poetic mind. The beauty of the heroic young Bellerophon in the London ivory (Hanfmann, fig. 21) is what he is praising in the person of the young bridegroom Paul (and will later apply to others, including the duke of the Thebaid).

13. Cf. Cant. 5:11, in context.

15. Note that the bride is praised for her intelligence; the Christianization of σωφροσύνη is at work (see my comment on H12.9) (and cf. H22.8).

16. Either the σεμνονομένειν of Milne or the σεμνοπολέύειν of Heitsch would be compatible with the traces that remain on the papyrus. In either case, the word is a coinage by Dioscorus.

17. In spite of Milne's reservations, σκηπτοῦ[χε can be read; cf. H1 v 7.

H18. Encomium on John the notary.   *P.Lit.Lond.* 100F
Ca. A.D. 567.

Εἰς Ἰωάννην τὸν νομικὸν ἐγκώμιον
Ἐγὼ μὲν ἐν λόγοις τιμᾶν ἐβου[λ]όμην
τὸν αὐτάδελφον εὐμενῆ φιλόξενον,
τὸν ἀμίμητον ἐκ θεοῦ ὀνομαστικ[όν.
φιλεῖς τὸ θεῖον καὶ φιλεῖς τ[ὸν πλ]ησίον,
5   μᾶλλον σεαυτοῦ τοὺς ξ[ένους ποο]ύμενος,
ἀνθ' ὧν ἀγαθῶν εὖ πρ[. . . . .]ισου
τοῦ προσφιλεστάτου σ[. . . . . π]οθων.
ὅ δ' ἐκ . . [. . .]θεου δοτῆ[ρος] . . [
ἀντεισαγωγήν σοι ἀπείρα[τον φέρ]ει.
10   ἐγὼ γὰρ ἀντίποινα σ[ῆ]ς προθυμί[α]ς
οὐκ ἂν δυναίμην ἐνδεὴς ὢν ἐκτίσειν,
τρέφων δὲ μᾶλλον καὶ νέους ἀνηβίους
οὐ παύσομαι σ[έθεν ἀ]εὶ μεμνημένος
τοῦ δεσπ[ότου . .]οσελ[. .]πλη[. . .]ου φίλου
15   εὐχαῖς α[. . . . .] . ετων
ἐμ[. .] . . [. .]ομαιπω[.] . . . . [
μ[. .]ονασε πάντων γραμμ[ά]των καὶ χρη[μ]άτ[ων
τὸν εὐφυέστατον προσκυνητὸν δεσπότην.

    3 cf. Mi l.c. n. 100 G (encomium Johannis) ω πανταξιε της σης προσηγοριας τω οντι φιλαρετε φιλοξενε φιλοπτωχε. cf. etiam 15,2; 17,11   4s cf. 10,14s

---

 with n. 1. Bellerophon is depicted on the 'Shawl of Sabina' in the Louvre, from Antinoë: Weitzmann, *Age of spirituality*, no. 112. The plaque illustrated in Volbach, *Elfenbeinarbeiten*, no. 67, is not from Egypt.

I wanted to honor in words one who is as close as a brother to me, kind and a lover of strangers, matchless, named from God. You love God and you love your neighbor, and rather you love strangers better than yourself, and for these good deeds . . . of the most kindly . . . from God the giver . . . (for) bringing in someone inexperienced. For I, being needy, would not be able to pay full requital for your kindness; but since rather I am also bringing up my underage children, I shall not cease from ever remembering you, dear master, in my prayers . . . (you) with your skill in words, bowed down to, master of letters and of wealth.

This poem and its companion piece *P.Lit.Lond.* 100G (following), as well as its immediate predecessor H24, the epithalamium for Paul and Patricia, are all to be found on the horizontal-fibers side of *P.Lond.* V 1709, Dioscorus's first (of two) Coptic arbitration contract. This document is dated from its correlate *P.Cair.Masp.* I 67006.101, which mentions a coming fifteenth indiction (which must be A.D. 566). The poem H18 is a thanksgiving to John, a member of the notarial staff through whom it seems Dioscorus found a job. Hence this group of literary works, together with the other Coptic arbitration hearing in *P.Cair.Masp.* III 67353r, all fall into the period A.D. 566–570 (see Chapter 2).

2. φιλόξενον: cf. 4–5, *P.Lit.Lond.* 100G 1–2, H10 A 14–15. The desirable attributes of a scholarly host, a patron who can find an "inexperienced" (line 9) newcomer to the city a post fitted to his talents.

3. Like *P.Lit.Lond.* 100G 1 and 9 (θεόθεν), a play on the meaning of the name John. (Cf. Lk. 1:63.)

13. As so often in Coptic letters, ⲁⲣⲓⲡⲁⲙⲉⲉⲩⲉ . . .

17. The ideal patron, possessed of both learning and material influence.

18. εὐφυέστατον is a pleasing variation on epistolary form, praising John as being a notary good at his profession, one with a pretty turn of phrase.

To John. Ca. A.D. 567. *P.Lit.Lond.* 100G

+ τῷ τὰς τιμὰς λαχόντι καὶ ὑπερβαίνοντ[ι . . .]δε[. . .]λομω[
  Ἰωάννῃ ὁ ἐλεεινὸς καὶ ξένος ὑμέτερ(ος) προ[

Ɏ ὦ παντάξιε τῆς σῆς προσηγορίας τῷ ὄντι φιλάρετε
 φιλόξενε φιλόπτωχε φιλο[λ]αότεχνε· τί σοι εἴπω ἀξιέπαινε
 σκρῖβα τῶν κουβικούλια ἐγκω[μίων] μεμεστωμένων εἰς σέ
 . . . .[   ]ειν τοῖς πάσχουσι
5 πλέον εα[
 εὐεργέτημά σου· πάντων ὑποχερ. . . . τοῖς μὲν εὐπ. . .
 δεόντως αὐτεψυχαγώγεις ἐπιστέλλεις δὲ δῶρα
 προσήκοντα τρόφιμα τῆς τούτων συμπαθείας· εἴη 'ς' οὖν
 τοίνυν θεόθεν ἄλυπος ἄφθονος πολυ[χρονικὸς] . . . .

Heading. MS. ὑμετερ/.　**1** MS. ὦ παντ᾽αξιε, τῶ.　**2** MS. αξιεπαι. **3** 1.
κου βικουλίων.　**6** MS. σου·. ευπ: ευη or ευις possible.　**7** MS.
αυτ᾽εψυχαγωγεις.　**9** MS. ἄλυπος. πολυχρονικός from Cairo Masp. 67120
(F), 37, or πολυχρόνιος from Cairo Masp. 67315, 57. It is possible, however,
to read παντ . . .

To John, whose portion is honor, the surpassing . . . (from) your poor
stranger . . . O completely worthy of your name, in your being a lover of
excellence, of strangers, of the poor, you who love to instruct the people in
your craft: how, O praiseworthy one, shall I address you, as *scriba* of the
cubiculum, since you have had your fill of encomia upon you? . . . to those
who suffer . . . your benefaction . . . rightly you win over men's souls to
yourself, and you send as gifts fitting nourishment of sympathy with
these; so now may you be, from God, spared pain, generous, long-lived.
. . .

This piece is not a poem in classical meter, but a work of rhythmic
Kunstprosa similar to Dioscorus's *P.Cair.Masp.* I 67097 verso F, lines 17–27.

1–2. In the first two of these compounds, Dioscorus is praising John's
professional ability and his hospitality to the poet (as in the previous poem,
H18). On the connection of φιλόξενος and φιλόπτωχος, the specific term
ξενοδοχεῖον does not seem to be attested in the Aphrodito/Antinoë area
(see E. Wipszycka, *Les ressources et les activités économiques des églises en
Egypte du IVe au VIIIe siècle [Pap.Brux.* 10, Brussels 1972] 118–119). But such
institutions did exist: see T. S. Miller, *The birth of the hospital in the Byzantine empire* (Baltimore 1985) 107, 119. Φιλολαότεχνος is a telling coinage of
Dioscorus. Τεχνόω 'to instruct in one's τέχνη,' is derived from Nonnus
Dion. 25.413 and used by Philoponus's sixth-century Alexandrian Christian
disciple, Elias, in his commentary on Aristotle *Categories* (139.16).[56] The
λαός being instructed are of course not just anyone: they are John's, and
Dioscorus's, future *Fachmänner.*

3. *Scriba* is attested at Aphrodito in *P.Cair.Masp.* III 67353 v A 25;
cubiculum does not appear outside of this text. See S. Daris, *Il lessico latino
nel greco d'Egitto (Pap.Castr.* 3, Barcelona 1971) *s.vv.*

H25. Epithalamium for Athanasius, 566–570　　　　　　　　*P.Lit.Lond.* 100D

> . . . .]ηλον[
> . . . . .]ο. [. . . . . .]ων σθεναρω[.] . . [. . . ᾽Α]θανάσιον
> σε]ῖ[ο] γενεθλιάδος ῥοδοειδεῖς ἔσ[τε]ψαν ὧραι.
> ἀμφὶς ἐκυκλώσαντο χοριττίδες ἐννέα Μοῦσαι
> 5　καὶ Χαρίτων χόρος αὖτε μελισταγέων σταφυλάων.
> ὡς νέον ἄλλον ἴδον Διονύσιον· ἀτρεκέως γάρ
> ἀπρὶξ ἐν δεπάεσσιν ἐπ᾽ ἀλλήλοισιν ἰδόντες

56. Edited by A. Busse (*CAG* 18.1, Berlin 1900).

οἶνον, ἔρωτος ἄγαλμα, πολυτρεφέι Ποσιδῶνι
χερσὶν ἀειρόμενόν σεο, νυμφίε, [. . . . . . .] . . υρε.
10   ναὶ τάχα νῦν καλέω σε φυρο[. . . . .]καρων
Νεῖλον λ. . . . . . . ον θ[. .] . [. . . . .] . . .

3 cf. P. Cairo Cat. 67178 A σειο γενεθλιαδος ροδοειδεες εστεψαν ωραι και χρονιοις νιφαδεσσι νεφη ποτιζειν χθονα πασαν· τερπωλην ασκουσιν αει κατα γαιαν (Νειλον supra) εγειρειν.   6 cf. 12 B 4 I Διονυσος sc., cf. 23,11s   8 cf. 21,9 I Poseidon, fluminum dominus   11 cf. v. 6

. . . strong Athanasius . . . the rosy Hours crowned the day you were born. The nine Muses circled round you in their dance, and the chorus of the Graces, with clusters of grapes sweet as honey. I have beheld (you) as another new Dionysus; for truly those who looked upon the wine, Love's adornment, passing it closely in goblets one to another, have prayed to Poseidon the Nurturer for you, O bridegroom. . . . At once I call upon you . . . the Nile . . .

This Athanasius may be identified with the man of that name whom Dioscorus will later hail as duke of the Thebaid, ca. 571, in H25 (*P.Cair. Masp.* I 67097 v B–C). This poem as well is on the other side of *P.Lond.* V 1709.

3. On ῥοδοειδεῖς, see K. Kost, *Musaios: Hero und Leander* (Bonn 1971) 308, on Musaeus 119.

4. For the nine Muses in Late Antique art, cf. Volbach, *Elfenbeinarbeiten*, nos. 69–70.

6. Dionysiac imagery is beloved by Dioscorus (as noticed already by W. Crönert in *Gnomon* 2 [1926] 662–663, 666). The topic of Dionysiac imagery in Late Antiquity is vast; see V. F. Lenzen, *The triumph of Dionysos on textiles of Late Antique Egypt* (Berkeley and Los Angeles 1960). The subject, with comments, will recur in Dioscorus's later, and longer, encomiastic verses.

7–8. Cf. Proverbs 23:31 (Sahidic), . . . ⲙ̄ⲡⲉⲣ ϯϩⲉ ϩⲉⲛ ⲏⲣⲡ . . . (G. P. Sobhy, *The Proverbs of Solomon in the dialect of Upper Egypt* [Cairo 1927]),[57] for "look upon the wine."

<hr>

57. Also in W. H. Worrell, *The Proverbs of Solomon in Sahidic Coptic* (Chicago 1931). The text in verses 30 and 31 varies among ϩⲉⲛ ⲏⲣⲡ̄ / ϩⲛ ⲛⲏⲣⲡ / ϩ̄ⲛ ⲛ̄ⲏⲣⲡ̄ / ϩ̄ⲙ ⲡⲏⲣⲡ. A conspectus of texts is given in W. Kosack, *Proverbia Salomonis* (*VT Coptice* 1, Bonn 1973). The MS used by Sobhy in 1927 (G. P. Sobhy, *The book of the Proverbs of Solomon in the dialect of Upper Egypt* [Cairo 1927]) supposedly was a parchment codex found on the site of Fustat and dating to ca. 500; its present whereabouts is unknown, as is so often the case with anything in Egypt. Dialect texts are known: the Akhmimic was published by A. Böhlig, *Koptische Proverbien-Kodex* (Leipzig 1963), from a fifth-century Berlin MS, and the Lycopolitan is R. Kasser's *P. Bodmer VI: Livre des Proverbes* (Louvain 1960) from ca. 450.

8. Here Poseidon is assimilated to the Nile, father of rivers (line 11). The Nilotic river god is often depicted in Coptic art (Beckwith, *Coptic sculpture*, pl. 72–74; Zaloscer, *Kunst im christlichen Ägypten*, Taf. 30; Volbach, *Elfenbeinarbeiten*, no. 105).[58]

H21. Epithalamium for Count Callinicus and Theophile. Before A.D. 570   *P.Cair.Masp.* II 67179

᾿Επιθαλάμιον εἰς τὸν περίβλεπτον κόμετα Καλλίνικον

Νυμφίε, σεῖο γάμοι χαρίτων πλήθουσι χορείης,
σωφροσύνης μετὰ κάλλους ἀεὶ μεθέπουσιν ἀρωγήν.
νύμφης λέκτρα φέρεις παναριζήλης ᾿Αιάδνης,
τῆ[ς] χρυσ[οστ]εφάνου Θεοφίλης ἀργυροπέζης.
5   κ . λ . ιν [ἔρ]ωτος ἔχουσιν ὁμοῦ καὶ σώφρονος ὀσμήν.
χ[ρυσὸς χρυσὸν] ἔμαρπτε καὶ ἄργυρος ἄργυρον ηὗρεν.
κ[υ]πρισ[μ]ῶν νεαρῶν μελιηδέα βότρυν ἀείρεις·
ἐκ σέθεν ἀμφεκόμισσε γάμων Διόνυσος ὀπώρην,
οἶνον, ἔρωτος ἄγαλμα, μετ᾿ εὐθηνίας πόρ[ε] πᾶσιν,
10   καὶ ξανθὴ Δημήτηρ ἤγαγεν ἄ[ν]θος ἀ[ρούρης.
ἵστατο γὰρ στ[ε]φέεσσιν αλ . σ. ο[
σὸν θάλαμον ῥοδόεντα διέπλεκεν εἰρεσιώναις.
τὶς Μεμέλαος ἄριστος, ὅτι πλέον ἔπλεο κιρρός,
Τυνδαρέην μεθέπεις, ἀλλ᾿ οὐ φεύγουσαν, ἄκοιτιν.
15   ὄψεαι καὶ μετὰ ταῦτα φιλαίτατα τέκνα γονεῦ[σ]ι,
ἴκελα σαῖς ἀρεταῖς ἄμα εἰκόνι καὶ σέο νύμφης.
ζωγράφο[ν] ἀ[μ]φιβόητον ἐπίπνοον εἰκόνα πῆξαι
ἀτρεκέως ποθέω πολυήρατον [ε]ἶδος [ὑφαίν]ει[ν,

58. The "classic" representation is the ΝΕΙΛΟΣ tapestry in the Hermitage (K. Wessel, *Koptische Kunst* [Recklinghausen 1963] pl. 104), always viewed as an early Alexandrian masterpiece of Hellenistic realism as opposed to the later, less Greek and more stylized "Coptic" depictions of the bearded river deity. Elsewhere I hope to go more deeply into the pejorative connotations of "Coptic" and its connections with (1) the current debate over the definition of the word "Coptic" (see P. du Bourguet, "Une assimilation abusive: Copte-Chrétien (d'Egypte)," in *Actes XXIXe cong.intl.Orientalistes* [Paris 1975] 11–17, and "Le mot 'copte'," *BSAC* 25 [1983] 101–106; cf. S. L. Karren, "Near Eastern culture and Hellenic paideia in Damascius' Life of Isidore" [Diss., University of Wisconsin 1978] 22); and with (2) some present-day "anti-Fallmerayeresque" definitions (as in S. Vryonis, "Recent scholarship on continuity and discontinuity of culture," in *The "Past" in medieval and modern Greek culture*, ed. S. Vryonis [Malibu, Calif. 1978] 237–256). Here the methodology of illustrating Dioscorus's text with Late Antique Egyptian works of art of varying date and provenance may be called into question, especially in the light of the recent work of G. Vikan (e.g. "The so-called 'Sheikh Ibada group' of early Coptic sculptures," *Third Byzantine Studies Conference Abstracts* [New York 1977] 15–16) and L. Török (unpublished paper at the Third International Congress of Coptic Studies, Warsaw, August 1984), querying the authenticity of many well-known pieces. I am trying to bring out the interconnectedness of Late Antique Egyptian culture, with an eye on the roots of Coptic historical mythology.

χάρματι λαμπετόοντ' ἀμα[ρύγματα οἷα σελήνη.
20 ἡβήτην ἐ[νίκ]ησας ἀέθλιον Βελλεροφόντη[ν
εἰς δέμας, εἰ[ς] σέο κάλλος ἀμετρήτων ἀρετάων.
ἀκλιν[έω]ς ἐ[ν]ίκησας Ἀχιλλέα καὶ Διομήδην,
ῥηι]δίως τὸν Ἄρηα, πανάλκιμον Ἡρακλῆα.
ἵλα]θί μ[οι] τρομέοντι, τεὸν μέλος ὄφρα βοήσ[ω·
25 ἔμπλε[ος] εἰς πλό[ο]ν ἦλθον ἀμε[τρήτων ἀρετ]άων.
ἄσπετον οὐ κατὰ κό[σμ]ον ἐπὶ π[
σὴν σταφυλὴν επατη[ς
τί πλέον . . . [
[

1 cf. 22,1–3; Nonn. D. 47,474   3 cf. 22,4   6 cf. 22,9; 23,24; Callim. fr.
75,30s   7 cf. Nonn. D. 7,339   8 . . . οιδι . . . supra εκ σεθεν | cf. 3,42 | cf.
Nonn. D. 47,501   9 cf. 25,8; Musae. 8   10 sup. Ma e P. Cairo Cat.
67178A9   11s cf. 25,3   12 εις supra σον | -ξες ιμε[supra -πλεκεν | cf.
Nonn. D. 37,77   14 cf. 22,19 | ακοιτην Π   15 λεκτρα supra ταυτα, cf.
Nonn. D. 2,328   17–19 cf. 2,16–18   20 cf. 2,20   21 ομοιιος ουκ εφυ αλλος
in marg. dextro   22s cf. 2,19–21   24s cf. 2,14s   26 cf. 1,10

Bridegroom, may your wedding be filled with the dancing of the
Graces; may it ever seek the help of Wisdom after Beauty. You are marrying a bride who is an enviable Ariadne, silver-sandaled Theophile
wreathed in gold. (May your marriage) have the scent at once of love and
of wisdom. Gold has embraced gold, and silver has found silver. You raise
up the honey-sweet grape cluster, in its bloom of youth; Dionysus attends
the summer of your wedding, bearing wine, love's adornment, with
plenty for all, and blonde Demeter brings the flower of the field. . . . They
have woven holy wreaths round your rose-filled bedroom. Like splendid
Menelaus, but more tawny colored, follow your Helen, a wife who will
not leave you. And afterwards you shall see dear children on your lap, like
both your excellence and your wife's to look upon. I wish a famous painter
would accurately depict your lifelike image, with his craft to work your
beloved likeness, whose bright beams flash with joy like the moon. Your
young body has surpassed prize-winning Bellerophon, and your beauty is
that of measureless excellence. To judge impartially, you have outdone
Achilles and Diomedes, and easily outstripped Ares and brave Herakles.
Be gracious to me in my awe of you, so I may sing your song: I came sailing
on my voyage, inspired by your measureless excellence. Not in a worldly
sense . . .

For Count Callinicus, cf. *P.Antin.* III 189.1–2.

In line 13 Heitsch's text is misprinted: read Μενέλαος. Also in line 3
read Ἀριάδνης.

1. Dioscorus is fond of this opening; cf. H22.

3. παναρίζηλος: a *hapax* for Dioscorus. On the imagery of Ariadne and
Dionysus in Byzantine-Coptic Egypt, cf. the ivory Ariadne in the Cluny

Museum, Paris (Volbach, *Elfenbeinarbeiten*, no. 78, Taf. 44);[59] and Heitsch 39, a poem on the rising of the Nile, originally *PSI* VII (1925) 845.7 (dated by M. Norsa as fifth to sixth century [a papyrus codex leaf]).

4. We cannot identify Theophile or her family from the Aphrodito/Antinoë papyri. On ἀργυρόπεζα, cf. Nonnus *Dion.* 34.47. Did Dioscorus borrow from Homer directly? Triphiodorus uses χιονόπεζα.

5. Echoing line 2, ὀσμήν strongly points up the importance of scents in Late Antique aesthetics.[60] Compare Nonnus *Paraphr.* 18.7.

6. A favorite line of Dioscorus for epithalamia. Both Heitsch (citing Callimachus) and B. Baldwin, "Dioscorus of Aphrodito: the worst poet of antiquity?" *Atti XVII cong.intl.papirol.* (Naples 1984) 327–331, have missed the point. The allusion is to the sixth-century Alexandrian philosophical exegesis of the doctrine of the affinity of like with like. See John Philoponus, in *De Gen. et Corr.* II.2 (ed. G. Vitelli, *CAG* 16, Berlin 1887) 420, lines 7, 12–13. Callimachus's point was the union of superior as opposed to inferior elements. Dioscorus's Philoponian point is the union of two of the same kind.

For μάρπτω, the clear parallel is Ps. 84:11 LXX.

8. Here is Dioscorus's Dionysiac procession, like that of the thiasos tapestry in the Metropolitan Museum (cf. H. E. Winlock, "A Roman tapestry and a Roman rug," *Bull.Met.Mus.Art* 27 [1932] 157–158) in which face after face rejoices with the spectator, in the manner of the sculptured heads in the ceiling at Mshatta (cf. Plotinus, *Enn.* VI 7 [38] 15, 24–26; A. H. Armstrong in *The Cambridge history of later Greek and early Medieval philosophy* [Cambridge 1967] 221:[61] "a living sphere of varied color and pattern, or something all faces, shining with living faces").

10. Cant. 2:1; cf. *P.Cair.Masp.* 67178.9. On the presence of Demeter, cf. Pamprepius 3.115.

13. κῖρρος, cf. *P.Cair.Masp.* 67178.11, and Dioscorus's glossary, *P.Lond.* V 1821.313 ⲘⲢⲰ.

<hr>

59. Of course the most memorable Ariadne figures from Egypt are the Vienna textile (Wessel, *Coptic art*, pl. 113) and the Boston textile (Weitzmann, *Age of spirituality*, no. 125). The Cluny Museum ivory does not represent Ariadne, in the eyes of modern scholarship. Cf. also the ivory comb in Mainz: Volbach, *Elfenbeinarbeiten*, no. 88a.

60. Compare L. J. James, "The spread of effect of the aesthetics of Dionysius the Areopagite" (Diss., Ohio State University 1976) 12–13 with notes; R. F. Newbold, "Perception and sensory awareness among Latin writers in late antiquity," *Class.etMed.* 33 (1981–82) 169–190 (though not treating Greek material for comparison); P. R. L. Brown, *The cult of the saints* (Chicago 1980) pp. 76, 82. For the "göttliche Wohlgeruch" in Nonnus's *Metabole*, cf. K. Smolak, "Beiträge zur Erklärung der Metabole des Nonnos," *JÖB* 34 (1984) 4; cf. *Met.* 12.16.

61. Also compare the Antinoë Dionysiac tapestry—the *thiasos* in an Egyptian setting (Wessel, *Koptische Kunst*, pl. 107).

16. On children as *eikones* (images), in the *Life of S. Thecla* (ed. G. Dagron, *SH* 62, Brussels 1978) 5.37–38 we find, as a counter to the strange new Christian notion of the resurrection of the body, the widely held notion that the real resurrection is the natural human one through offspring: τῆς τῶν σπειράντων καὶ φυσάντων εἰκόνος ἐν τοῖς παισὶν αὖθις ἀνανεουμένης ἀεί . . .

17ff. On ἐπίπνοον, see C. A. Mango, "Antique statuary and the Byzantine beholder," *DOP* 17 (1963) 64–67.

20. On Bellerophon, cf. my comment on H24.11.

25. This too is a line Dioscorus will reuse often; cf. also Golega, *Der homerische Psalter*, p. 97, n. 1, with the literature there cited. ἔμπλεος recalls the Nonnian ἔμπνευστος; compare the notion of inspiration treated by Viljamaa, *Greek encomiastic poetry*, pp. 14, 77–79.

H5. Encomium on Duke Callinicus. Ca. A.D. 570+.   *P.Cair.Masp.* III 67315
(See Figure 7)

<pre>
    Ὕμνον ἀναστήσαιμι χοροστ[ασί]ης σέο δ[ό]ξης,
    τοῦ] πολυκυδήεντος Καλλινίκ[ου στρα]τιάρχου.
    θάλλε μοι, εἰσέτι θάλλεις, ἀμοίρ[α]τον ἐς χρόνον ἔλθοις,
    ὁ κλυτὸς ἐν μερόπεσσι καὶ ἐν χθονὶ παμβασιλῆος.
 5 ἔμπλεος εἰς πλόον ἦλθον ἀ[μετρ]ήτων ἀρετάων·
    οὐ πέλεν, οὐ πέλεν ἄλλος ὁμοίιος ὔμμι γενέθλῃ·
    τούνεκά σε προίαλλεν ἄναξ στρατίαρχον ἀμύμων
    πήματ᾽ ἀποπτοιεῖν ὅσα τέτληκε πότνια Θήβη.
    τούνεκα μὴν καλέω σε πανάλκιμον Ἡρακλῆα,
10 ὃς ῥα καμὼν πόρε πᾶσιν ἐλευθερ[ί]ης παναρώγην.
    τολμήεις γενόμην πανεπάξιον ὑμνοπολεύειν·
    τοσσατίην ἀρετὴν ἀνικάνετός εἰμι [λ]ιγαίνειν.
    μέτριος οὐκ ἐνόησα τόσον κλέος, μ[ῆ]τις [ἀ]νάκ[των·
    ἵλαθί μοι τρομέοντι, τεὸ[ν μέλος ὄφρα βοήσω.
15 τέττιξ τύτθ[ος ἔ]ην, καὶ ὄρ[γαν]όν ἐστι μ[ελί]σσης·
    καὶ θεὸν αὐτ[ὸν] ἄειδε πα[νάφ]θιτον α . . . . την.
    ὡς πέλε[ν] ἀγρ[ον]όμ[οισ]ι . . . .
    οὕτως ἄμμιν ἵκανες, καλλ[ίνι]κος στρατιάρχης,
    οὐ χρυσὸν ποθέων, ἀδίκω[ν] κρίσιν, ἀλλὰ θέμιστας.
20 ζωγράφον ἀμφιβόητον ἐπίγνοον εἰκόνα πῆξαι
    ἀτρεκέως ποθέω πολυήρατον εἶδος ὑφαίνειν,
    χάρματι λαμπετόοντ᾽ ἀμαρύγματα οἷα Σελήνη.
    ἀκλινέως ἐνί[κ]ησας Ἀχιλλέα καὶ Διομήδην,
    ῥηιδίως καὶ Ἀρῆα, κάλλει Βελλεροφόντην.
25 ἐκ σέθεν ἡγητείρας ἐπέδραμε πείρατα γαίης
    Νεῖλος ἀρουροβάτης· φιλοπάρθενος εἴς σε χορεύει
    ἀμφ[ὶς] καὶ Διόνυσος ἐυστεφάνοις ὑμεναίοις
    ἀφ[ν]ειὸν †καλεοντε [τὸ] σὸν κλέος ὀλβι[ό]δαιμον.
    οὕτως ἀεὶ ζώοις σὺ[ν ἀ]δέλφοις ε . το . . . .
</pre>

30 Ἀρκαδί[ην κα]ὶ Θήβην διαμπερ[ὲ]ς ἡν[ι]οχε[ύων,
πάντα φιλῶν καὶ πᾶσι φιλαί[τατο]ς, ὅττι ῥέ[ζε]σκ[ες.
εἰρήνη ταμίη θ[εοί]κε[λος] ἤνθε[ε] πάντη.
κλεπταδίην ἐδαμάσσα[τ]ε πε[ιρασμοῖ]ς σέο θ[ε]σμῶν.
γηοπόνοι γελόωσιν ἐπ᾽ ἐλπίσιν ἔργα τελέσσαι·
35 οὐκέτι γὰρ φρονέουσιν ἀτάσθαλα λῃστήρων
ἐν πεδίῳ διαλεύσειν, ἐπεὶ δέος ἔλλαβε πάντας
σῆς ἀρετῆς, προφέριστε, καὶ [ε]ὐνομίης διὰ κάλλος.
.. λ . . . . . [γρ]αφίδεσσι λιχάς ποτε θεσμοχαράξας
διπλόον ἀμφ[ι]βόητον ὅσον χρόνον ὔμμι χ[αρ]άσσει.
40 ὦ θεῖον ὄντως κ[αὶ ἀ]κριβῶς χ[ρ]υσοῦν γένος,
γουνάζο[μα]ί σε, [προσ]τάτη[ν τ]ῶν προστατῶν,
γουν[ά]ζομ[αί] σ[ε] . . . παν . . . . βασιλέω[ν.
εἴ τι[ς δυνή]σ[εται] ἀ[ριθμεῖν ἀστέρας
ἢ [τοῖς] κ[υ]άθ[οις τῆ]ς θ[αλάττης ῥεύματα,
45 ναί] πο[υ κἀγὼ π]άντω[ς δυνήσο]μαι μ[ετρεῖν
τὰς ἀ[ει]μ[νή]στ[ου]ς ἀρε[τὰς σ]οῦ, [δέσ]ποτ[α,
τοῦ πα]ν[τα]ρίσ[τ]ου κ[αὶ κλυτοῦ στρ]ατηλάτου.
[
πάρεστιν ἡμῖ[ν . . .
50 τὸ σὸν κλέος πανευτυχέστερον . ι[. . .]
εὐαγγ[ε]λίης ἐκ θεοῦ τὸ σημῖον
φανέν, δίκαιος συμφέρουσιν πραξε[.]ν.
Θήβη πᾶσα χόρευσον, εἰρήνην δέχου·
οὐ γὰρ θεωρήσεις κακουργικ[ὴν] ἔτι,
55 πά[ν]τῃ δέος πέφυκεν ἀσπίλου δίκης
τοῦ [ὀβριμω]τάτου στρατηγοῦ εὐμενοῦς.
εἴης π[ολ]υχρόνιος, ἄφθον[ο]ς πράττων,
νικ[ηφό]ρος, θρασύς, καταπατῶν ἐχθρούς,
νέος [Σόλ]ων, θεμίστια πιστὰ φυλάττων
60 τῷ εὐ[σε]βεῖ [ἄνα]κτι, πάντων δεσπότῃ.
. . . . ος γενναῖος στρατηγός
τ]ῷ [σῷ ὄρεξον οἰκέτῃ ὄλβου] χεῖρα.

3 cf. 2,29 et 2,12   4 cf. 2,4   5 cf. 2,15   6 cf. 2,3   7s cf. 2,6s   9s cf. 2,21s   11 cf. 6,13   12 cf. 6,14; 13,16; 23,16   13 cf. 2,1   14 cf. 2,14   17 cf. 3,45   18 cf. 2,8   19 cf. 13,11s; 14,5–7   20–24 cf. 2,16–20   24 cf. Z 156   25s cf. 3,42s | ηγητειρας = ηγεμονιας   28 καλεων? καλεοντες?   29 cf. 2,12   30 cf. 2,2   32 cf. 4 B 3   38s cf. 10,17s; 11,13s; 12,17s   40–42 cf. 3,1–3   43–46 cf. 9,10–13   51 ευ. αγγ Π   52 δικαιος vel δικαιας leg. Ma | πραξε . . ν vel πραξε . ν | πραυς σοφος τιμητικος φρονιμος ει in marg. dextro   53–55 cf. 3,9–11   59 cf. 3,12 (et 3,37!)   62 cf. 9,20

Let me raise a hymn of the dance to your glory, all-renowned Duke Callinicus. Flourish and again flourish, and may you attain to a boundless length of life, O famous among men in the land of the Emperor. I came sailing on my voyage, inspired by your measureless excellence. Never, never was there anyone like you in high descent: wherefore the noble lord has appointed you Duke, to drive away the troubles that Lady Thebes has endured. Therefore I call you all-brave Herakles, who has taken the trouble to bring the universal help of freedom to all. Let me be bold to celebrate (you), the all-worthy; I am not able to sing such excellence. Humbly I have not grasped such glory, craft of rulers; be gracious to me in my awe of you, so I may utter your song aloud. I wish I were a little cicada, or had the ability of the bee: even it sings of the imperishable God Himself. . . . So you have come to us, Duke Callinicus, fair in victory, not seeking money, the standard of the unjust, but seeking just judgments. I wish that a famous painter would accurately depict your recognizable image, with his craft to work your beloved likeness, whose bright beams flash with joy like the moon. To judge impartially, you have surpassed Achilles and Diomedes, and you have even outstripped Ares, and Beller-ophon in beauty. Under your leadership the Nile that covers Egypt's fields has flowed forth to the limits of our land; the lover of maidens dances before you, (namely) Dionysus with his wreathed revelers . . . (invoking?) your rich and blessed glory. So you may live forever, with your brothers, . . . ever charioteer of Arcadia and the Thebaid, loving all and beloved by all, which is your accomplishment. Peace who keeps God's house has flowered forth everywhere. You have subdued robbery by the trials of your judgments. The farmers are happy, looking forward to the fruition of their tasks; for they do not think they will see the presumptuous evils of thieves in their land, since fear of your excellence has seized everyone, Your Excellency, through the beauty of good government. As you have engraved laws in writing . . . so may you mark them out for a double length of renowned time. O descendant of a truly divine and really golden line, I beseech you, patron of patrons, I beseech you, . . . of kings. If someone could number the stars or measure out the sea's floods with a spoon, then I could measure your ever-memorable excellence, my lord, O best and most renowned Duke. Your most fortunate glory . . . The sign of God's Gospel is come, a just man with seemly actions. Let the whole Thebaid dance and welcome peace; for you shall not behold evildoing any more, since fear of the spotless justice of the most mighty and beneficent Duke has sprung up everywhere. May you be full of years, bounteous in actions, victorious, brave, treading down your enemies, O new Solon, keeping faithful judgments before the pious Emperor, the ruler of all. The noble Duke . . . stretch out the hand of blessing to one of your household.

This poem is Dioscorus's first real full-dress encomium on a local official; we can see how the poet is paying attention both to the prescriptions for an epideictic oration as set forth by Menander Rhetor and to the requirements for praising a holy man in a Coptic sermon (cf. C. D. G. Müller, "Einige Bemerkungen zur 'ars praedicandi' der alten koptischen Kirche," *Muséon* 67 [1954] 231–270). Dioscorus both was trained as a good classical rhetor and was influenced by the preaching he had heard and the hagiography he had read.

In this encomium Dioscorus originates much of the phraseology that he is later to rework in his praise of Duke John (see H2 and H3, A.D. 574–576). It is a poem about justice and good government, and their effect on the economic troubles of Aphrodito that had helped drive Dioscorus to move to Antinoë (cf. Cameron, "*Pap.Ant.* III.115," pp. 125–127: "administration of justice was felt to be the prime function of a provincial governor").

3a. Cf. H12 B 9; here not with an Old Testament image but with a conventional wish for long life (cf. lines 29, 57).

6. A line Dioscorus likes to use, in following the prescript of Menander Rhetor by first treating of his subject's γόνος (cf. line 40).

8. Lady Thebes is again personified in H4, the encomium on Duke Athanasius (cf. H4, with n. 6a above on the Egyptian Thebes). Such a classical figure (cf. H10 B 6 for cities personified) is a compliment to the duke, who is being regarded as a man of cosmopolitan culture (cf. line 4).

9. M. Simon in *Hercule et le christianisme* (Paris 1955) has described the nuances and the *Nachleben* of Herakles as a Christ-figure.

11. Compare the εὐτολμία of Pamprepius 3.4.

15. Here Dioscorus originates one of his most winning poetic figures, the hymn-singing cicada, a striking reworking of a Hellenistic conceit in a Christian context (see L. S. B. MacCoull, "John Philoponus and Dioscorus of Aphrodito," *Studia Patristica* 18 [Kalamazoo 1987] 1: 163–168, commenting on P.Berol. 13894). Since Plato (*Phdr.* 259) and Callimachus (*Aet.* 1.29–34, on the favorable atmosphere for poetry in Ptolemaic Alexandria), the cicada has been a metaphor for the poet (cf. Theocritus 1.148 and especially *Anacreontea* 34.18). Here the little insect sings καὶ Θεὸν αὐτόν (cf. P.Berol. 13894.18); also in H7.5–6. There are a few Late Antique parallels (Theophylact Simocatta, Letter 1; cf. A. Moffat, "The letters of Theophylaktos Simokatta, a 'Scriptor non iniucundus,'" *Seventh BSC Abstracts* [Boston 1981] 13) and patristic images (e.g., Chrysostom Hom. in Mt. 38 [*PG* 57.428]), though I have not found any specifically Coptic cicadas.[62] Think too of the Christian service of the asexual bee (*in hac cerei oblatione solemni, per ministrorum tuorum manus, de operibus apum sacrosancta reddit ecclesia*); see H. Douteil and F. Vongrey, *Exultet-Rolle: Kommentarband* (Graz 1975) 90–91 with the literature there cited.[63] The beehive is a type of the church.

---

62. Dioscorus very likely derived the figure most immediately from Menander Rhetor—a device of modesty; see the text edited by D. A. Russell and N. G. Wilson (Oxford 1981), sec. 391, pp. 118–119, 299. The commentators cite *AP* 9.380. See now L. S. B. MacCoull, "Dioscorus of Aphrodito and John Philoponus," *Studia Patristica* (Kalamazoo 1987), n. 19b, citing Jerome's cicada metaphor. P. Antin in *Recueil S. Jérôme* (Brussels 1968) 290n. gives numerous Late Antique literary references.

63. Cf. P. Lacau, *Fragments d'apocryphes coptes* (*Mémoires de l'Institut Français*

18. Note the pun on the duke's name.

19. Justice is once again the central theme of the poem.

20–21. Here again Dioscorus indicates what is regarded as desirable in portraiture (cf. L'Orange, "The antique origin of medieval portraiture"); to be compared with H21.17–18 immediately preceding. In the Callinicus epithalamium, H21, the likeness is to be ἐπίπνοον 'breathing'; here, ἐπί-γνοον 'lifelike'. These are the clichés of praise for a good portrait. (Cf. Mango, "Antique statuary," pp. 64–67.)

26. ἀρουροβάτης, evocative of the Egyptian landscape and the inundation (cf. H3.43).

Φιλοπάρθενος is here not the totally Christian usage of H1 v 11 (the Justin II encomium), but a more Nonnian, more ambivalent epithet, the new wine of a Christian overtone poured into the old bottle of the *Dionysiaka* (e.g., 2.122, 14.66). On the interrelation of the *Dionysiaka* and the *Paraphrasis*, see J. Golega, *Studien über die Evangeliendichtung des Nonnos von Panopolis* (Breslau 1930) 63–88, and Alan Cameron, "The empress and the poet," *YCS* 27 (1982) 237–238, 282, 284. Egypt of course was the γῆ φιλοπαρθένη par excellence since Cyril's triumph at Ephesus, to sensitize the ear to the Christian sense (see my comment on H1 v 11). In the midst of the Dionysiac imagery, Dioscorus's daily life was also surrounded by powerful images such as the magnificent tapestry of the Virgin at Cleveland, possibly from Panopolis (D. Shepherd, "An icon of the Virgin: A sixth-century tapestry panel from Egypt," *Bull.Cleveland Mus.Art* 56 [1969] 3 and 90–120).[64] In the present poem, the subtle ambiguity of this epithet is a credit to Dioscorus's sense of style. Cf. H. Jeanmaire, *Dionysos* (Paris 1951) 198–219.

29. σὺν ἀδέλφοις: see H13 and H17.

32. θ[εοί]κε[λος]: a striking and apposite conceit; cf. line 51. Here with an allusion to the idea of the imperial fisc: Peace enables the financial administration to proceed in a fashion that benefits everyone (cf. lines 34–35). Cf. also *Sinuthii opera* (ed. J. Leipoldt, Louvain and Paris 1913) IV, S. xii, 2–7 with the epithet "Hausvorsteherin" (ⲧⲣⲙⲛⲏⲓ).

33. πειρασμός carries, of course, its associations with the Lord's Prayer.

---

d'*Archéologie Orientale* 9, Cairo 1904) 86.20–24, the crowd clustering round Lazarus "like bees in a honeycomb": ⲛ̄ⲑⲏ ⲛⲟⲩⲁⲃ ⲛⲉϥⲓⲱ ϩⲉⲛⲟⲩⲙⲟⲩⲗϩ. Neither Dioscorus nor the Coptic fathers seem to be concerned with the purity symbolism of bees: their imagery is practical. Famous honey still comes from Egypt. Only after the conquest do we meet the bee's asexual reproduction as a type of the generation of the Son: van Lantschoot in *Coptic studies in honor of W. E. Crum* (Boston 1950) 343–344.

64. The inscription on this textile is *not* spelled incorrectly. Shepherd mistakes the gamma-iota digraph (ⲅ + ⲓ) for another eta (ⲏ).

37. προφέριστε: coined by Dioscorus.

38. λιχάs: cf. H11.13.

40. On this quasi-Vergilian "golden line," see L. Koenen, "Zwei Inschriften aus El-Bagawat," *ZPE* 2 (1968) 75–80, esp. 76; E. Bernand, *Inscriptions métriques de l'Egypte gréco-romaine* (Paris 1969) no. 173 (pp. 725–630); cf. *Christus Patiens* (ed. A. Tuilier, *SC* 149, Paris 1969) 116 (Euripidean): Γονᾶs γὰρ ἀπὸ χρυσέαs ἔβλαστέ μοι.[65] The contrasted adverbs in line 40 point up the close correspondence of the poetic description with the reality of the duke's noble lineage.

51. The justice of the duke, defender of the faith, is like the Good News (cf. *P.Cair.Masp.* I 67002 I 1–2, a passage treated by H. I. Bell, "An Egyptian village in the age of Justinian," *JHS* 64 [1944] 33).

53. νέος Σόλων: the duke upholds the right in both human and divine legislation, as in H11.5, and, elaborately, H3.12, 30.

60. On Justin II as both moderate (at least before 572) and pious, see Averil Cameron, "The early religious policies of Justin II," *SCH* 13 (1976) 51–67, reprinted in *Continuity and change in sixth-century Byzantium* (London 1981) no. 10.

H13. Birthday poem on Colluthus.   *P.Cair.Masp.* I 67120 v B
                                                            (See Figure 8)

```
    Κόλλουθε γλυκύμορφε, ὅλης ἀτὸς ᾽Αφρογενε⟨ί⟩ης,
    Κόλλουθε, χθόνα πᾶσαν ἐπέδραμεν οὔνομα σεῖο.
    οὔνομα σῆς γενεῆς πανεπέδραμε πείρατα Νείλου,
    κυδαλίμων πατέρων ἀπὸ ρίζης ὀλβιστήρων.
  5 οὐ πέλεν, οὐ [πέλεν] ἄλλος ὁμοίιος ὕμμι τὸ κῆ[δος
    . πα[ . . . . . . ]τωρ Αβαδιος ἐπὶ χθονὶ παμβασιλῆος
    ἔπλετο δωρ. . . . . . . . . . . . σιεω μῆτις ἀνάκτων.
    ἀμφότεροι γεγάασι κυβερνητῆρε πολήων,
    καὶ πτολίεθρον ἔσωσαν ἐύδμητον ᾽Αντινοῆος,
 10 καὶ πτόλιν ἐξεσάωσαν ἐύκτιτον ᾽Αντινοῆος.
    οὕτως ἄμμιν ἵκανες ὅλην Παφίην ἐλεαίρειν
    ἐκ μογερῶν καμάτων προηγητήρων ἀθεμίστων.
    ἀκτεάνους ἀτίταλλε το . . [ . . ]νος, οἱάπερ αὐτός
    πᾶσι πον⟨ε⟩ιομένοις [ἐλε]ήμο[να] χεῖρ᾽ ἀτανύσσεις.
 15 τούνεκ᾽ αν[ . ]ξ[
    τοσσατίην ἀρετὴν πανυπείροχον ἔμμεναι ἄλλων,
    ὁπλοτέροις περ ἐοῦσι πανάστεα Θήβης ἀρῆξαι.
    οὕτω[s ἀεὶ ζ]ώοις καὶ ἀμοίρατον ἐς χρόνον ἔλθοις,
```

65. On gold, see S. Averincev, "L'or dans le système des symboles de la culture protobyzantine," *Studi medievali* 20 (1979) 47–67—idiosyncratic but interesting. I owe this reference to Peter Brown.

σὺν τεκέεσσι φίλοισιν, ἀριζήλῃ σέο νύμφῃ,
20 ἠδὲ κασιγνήτοισιν Καλλινίκῳ, Δωροθείῳ,
καὶ Μάρκῳ τιμή⟨ε⟩ντι, περισσονόῳ δικασπώλῳ.

1 ατος = αετος, cognomen imperatorum 2s cf. 5,25 3 de composito cf. 2,22 4 cf. 4,4 5 cf. 2,3 6 cf. 2,4 | Αβαδιος cf. 17,5 9s mutationes 11 cf. 2,8 | cf. 14,5–7 12 εκ στυγερων supra μογερων Π 13 το σον μενος? Keyd 14 cf. 3,54 | cf. 3,24 16 cf. 5,12 17 cf. ad 3 18 cf. 2,12 19 cf. 2,30 20s cf. 17,20–24

Colluthus, fair to look upon, eagle of the whole land of Aphrodito, Colluthus, your name has overspread the whole earth. The fame of your lineage has reached as far as the sources of the Nile, O descendant of renowned ancestors, from the stock of the blessed. Never, never was there anyone like you in noble birth. . . . Abadios in the land of the Emperor . . . craft of rulers. Both were captains of cities, and saved well-built Antinoë (they saved Antinoë, good to dwell in). So you have come to us to take pity on the whole land of Aphrodito, suffering from lamentable troubles at the hands of unjust administrators. Be a foster father to the poor . . . , as you yourself stretch out a generous hand to those in trouble . . . that you are supreme over all others in such excellence, you who have helped all the cities of the Thebaid, poor though they be. So may you live forever and reach a boundless length of life, with your dear children and admirable wife, and your kinsmen Callinicus, Dorotheus, and honored Mark, the judge eminent for his understanding.

This birthday poem introduces a small group of encomia on the relatives of Duke Callinicus (cf. H5.29).

Colluthus (cf. W. E. Crum, "Colluthus, the martyr and his name," *BZ* 30 [1929–1930] 323–327), kinsman of Callinicus, Dorotheus, and Mark the judge, appears to have been an administrator at Antinoë (lines 9–10); he is also the recipient of H17, where he figures as pagarch of Antaeopolis. See L. S. B. MacCoull, "Additions to the prosopography of Aphrodito from the Coptic documents," *BSAC* 25 (1983) 91–94; and the forthcoming edition by L. Papini and L. S. B. MacCoull of P. Vaticani Copti Doresse, the Aphrodito Coptic papyri that were given by Jean Doresse to the Vatican Library. Colluthus and Mark together are mentioned in P.Vat.Copti Doresse 5 I 2–3, II 35; the signer, Taham daughter of Promauo, refers to her "late husband" Mark in I 8–9, II 32–33, which may date the Coptic document later if the identifications hold.

S. Colluthus was the patron saint of Antinoë (see L. Papini, "Due biglietti oracolari cristiani," in *Trenta papiri greci*, ed. M. Manfredi [Florence 1983] 68–70).

1. ἀτός 'eagle', perhaps a pun on ⲡⲁϩⲱⲙ (Pachomius) 'eagle'. The "land of Aphrodito" was overspread with monasteries (P. Barison,

"Ricerche sui monasteri dell' Egitto bizantino ed arabo," *Aegyptus* 18 [1938] 98–122 for Aphrodito, plus 95–98 for Antaeopolis and 86–90 for Antinoë); it is uncertain if they became divided along Monophysite/Chalcedonian lines in the disputes during the reign of Justinian (cf. J. Goehring, "Pachomius' vision of heresy," *Muséon* 95 [1982] 243–244). The local point of view in this dispute is exemplified in the *Panegyric on Apollo* (ed. K. H. Kuhn, *CSCO* 394 [Louvain 1978] 16–19, for the text, and 395 [Louvain 1978] 12–15, for the translation.

Ἀφρογενείης: cf. Παφίην in line 11, just as these two terms are juxtaposed in H24.6–7.

3. The sources of the Nile, a conundrum in the ancient world, were discussed in the schools of sixth-century Alexandria; Olympiodorus *in Meteor.* (ed. W. Stuve, [*CAG* XII.2, Berlin 1900] 105.25–28, 109.3–8, 132.14–15.

4–5. Again the praise of lineage (perhaps Dioscorus is thinking of Coptic kinship terminology),[66] given in accordance with the guidelines on how to do a *logos genethliakos* proposed by Menander Rhetor (ed. D. A. Russell and N. G. Wilson [Oxford 1981] 158–161, and 323–324).

6. Abadios must be the Apa Dios of H17. Coptic proper names incorporating this prefix are often found: G. Heuser, *Die Personennamen der Kopten* (Leipzig 1929) 125.

9–10. Antinoë too needed "saving" in the poet's view. See my comments on H10 B 6, and also references to the personifications of cities in Coptic art.

12. Again it is through justice that the city is to be saved.

20–21. An exact stemma showing the relationships of the four men cannot yet be drawn.

21. περισσόνοος, cf. Nonnus *Dion.* 5.222, 20.266, 22.129, 26.139, 37.176; *Paraphr.* 7.105, 16.64.

H14. Birthday poem for Count Dorotheos.   *P.Cair.Masp.* I 67120 v C

> Ἄρτι νέος Φαέθων ἐξάνθορες ἄμμι ἀρῆξαι,
> τιθήνην κατὰ κόσμον ἀεὶ Παφίης χθόνα τήνδε
> ἡμε[τέ]ρην κονίῃσιν ἀν[ο]ρθ[ῶσα]ι ἐρίπουσαν,
> Δωρόθεε προφέριστε. σὺ γὰρ δῶρον ἐκ θεοῦ ἦλθες.
> 5 ἤλυθες οὐκ ὄλβον διζήμενος οἱάπερ ἄλλοι,
> ἀλλὰ πόρον βιότοιο πενήτων ἐκτὸς ἀνίης
> εὐσεβίης πραπίδεσσι τεοῖς σφίσι σωοφυλάττειν.

1 cf. 3,37   3 cf. 2,24s   4 cf. 6,4   5s cf. 5,18s

66. Cf. M. Malinine, "Les noms de parenté en copte," *GLECS* 6 (1951–1954) 73–75.

Just now you have flowered forth like a new Phaethon to help us, to set upright and adorn this Aphrodito land of ours that nurtured us, though she had been thrown down in the dust, O excellent Dorotheos. For truly you come as a "gift from God." You have not come like others, seeking to get rich, but seeking a means of living for the poor, freed from grief, to keep your own people safe by your own understanding of piety.

1. On νεός Φαέθων, cf. my comments on H24.5.

4. The poem is really an extended pun (as is H19, Hypatius the *hypatos*).

7. The second of the twin pillars of good administration of the city is εὐσεβία.

H15. Birthday poem for Constantine.   *P.Cair.Masp.* I 67120 v D

   Εἴη τύχη πολλὴ κεχαριτωμένη
   τῇ σῇ γενεθλίῃ, βασιλικώνυμε.
   ὧραι πυκάζουσιν πάναγρον καὶ ἄνθη,
   ἐν αἷς ἐτέχθης, ὦ χαριέστατε πάνυ.
5 οὐκ ἀμβλυνεῖ ἄστρο[ν] τὸ σ[ὸν] πο[τ'] ἐκ θεο[ῦ·
   ῥέπει γὰρ εἰς χρηστάχους ἀργυρήμερες.
   θάλλοις ἑορταῖς εἰλαπίναις εὐπρεπές,
   εὐδαιμονῶν, ἀεὶ φιλαίτατος πᾶσι.

   3 de composito cf. 2,22   **3s** cf. 25,3   **5** cf. 17,12   **6** χρησταχους = χρηστους | αργυρημερες = 'saeculum aureum'   **7** θαλλεις Π

May there be great good fortune, full of grace, on your birthday, O imperially named. The Hours and flowers overshadowed the whole place where you were born, O most graced one. Your God-given star will not become dim, for the silver portion has inclined to good. May you rejoice, as befits you, in feasts and solemn banquets, happy and beloved by all.

1–3. The overtones of κεχαριτωμένη and the meaning of πυκάζω surely are deliberate echoes of the Angelic Salutation. Cf. the (unpublished) P. Robinson 29 (in the Duke University collection), a Trinitarian hymn to the Virgin.

2. The name Constantine retains its associations as the name of the first great Christian emperor.

5. Here is the Christian Late Antique notion of a star attached to a particular person, under God's dispensation;[67] cf. P. R. L. Brown, *The cult of the saints* (Chicago 1981) 73. In the *Life of Theodore of Sykeon* (ed. A.-J.

67. Dioscorus very likely knew the work of Paul of Alexandria and the related astrological writers from Egypt, traditional home of star lore; see W. Gundel and H. G. Gundel, *Astrologumena: Die astrologische Literatur in der Antike und ihre Geschichte* (Wiesbaden 1966) 236–254.

Festugière, *SH* 48, Brussels 1970) 4.6–7, we meet the idea of the star as a royal portent, and associated with the individual at birth.

6. Not as in Heitsch's note, but rather another allusion to the Neoplatonic doctrine of affinity, according to which like gravitates toward like; as in H21.6; Philoponus in *De Gen. et. Corr.* 218.17–20. On scales and weighing, see the study of E. Livrea in *Studia Cercidei* (Bonn 1986) 13, 44–48.

Constantine is not mentioned as one of the relations of Callinicus, Colluthus, Dorotheos, and Mark; but his poem is included in the same papyrus and must date from the same time in Dioscorus's production of occasional verse at Antinoë. The group continues with the next two poems.

H16. Birthday poem for an unnamed recipient.   *P.Cair.Masp.* I 67120 v E

> Χθὲς ἐς φίλους τὴν τέρψιν ἀνυψώσατε,
> τήμερον χαρίτων στέμματα τῆς σῆς νίκης.
> θεία πρόνοια δ' εὐτρεπῆ ποουμένη·
> οὐκ ἀστοχήσητε κρατοῦντες ἐκ θεοῦ
> 5 τὰς ἐντολὰς πρὸς ἐνδεεῖς ἠδὲ ξένους.
> ζώο[ις] ἀλύπως εὔπορος, φιλέντολος.

   2 χαριτῶν Ma | νικη: η υμων υπερφυια cf. 17,9   3 ευτρεπην Π

Yesterday you raised up joy for your friends: today (you raise up) the joyful garlands of your victory. Divine Providence in its ordaining of things has made preparation; do not fail to keep God's commandments with regard to the poor and strangers. May you live free from pain, well off, loving God's commandments.

1. ἀνυψόω is the favorite verb used by the Greek Ben Sira to render the Semitic idioms for "to lift up" (the head, heart, voice, etc.). Cf. *P.Cair.Masp.* III 67279.27, II 67205.10; Nonnus *Paraphr.* 8.68, 16.43.

3. On θεία πρόνοια, cf. C. Parma, *Pronoia und Providentia* (Leiden 1971). Cf. *P.Cair.Masp.* I 67009.1, ἡ θεία πρόνοια καὶ ὁ φιλόχριστος ἡμῶν βασιλεύς.

4–5. Again the dominical commandments (cf. line 6), as in H17.3 and H10.14–15. The poor and the guest are one's neighbor par excellence. Cf. Dt. 10:19; Jer. 2:23.

6. φιλέντολος is used in Palladius *Hist.Laus.* PG 34.1217B = C. Butler, *Historia Lausiaca* (Oxford 1898; reprint Hildesheim 1967) 145, note on sections 6–8. Cf. Coptic ⲙⲁⲓϩⲏⲕⲉ, ⲙⲁⲓϣⲙⲙⲟ as above line 5 and in H10.14–15.

H17. Encomium on Count Colluthus the pagarch, *P.Cair.Masp.* I 67120 v F son of Apa Dios.

> ῏Ω παντάριστε τῷ λόγῳ πρυτανέων
> βουλῆς γερόντων καὶ νόμων εὐδοξίας,

χρυσ[ο]πύθμενος ῥίζης φιλεντόλου πλούτου,
συγκλητικοῦ γένους καλοῦ θεοφυλάκτου·
5 ὁ σὸς πατὴρ πάνλαμπρος ἐκ Διὸς πέλεν.
ἄνισος ἀρεταῖς παναρχόντων γόνος
Βίκτορος ἀειμνήστου ὅν οἱ νομοὶ μέλπον,
τύχης πανευφήμου πολιούχου Δίου·
ὑπερβολῆς τιμῆς φέρεις αἷμα καὶ μέλη.
10 Κόλλουθε νικηφόρε πανεξοχώτατε,
τιμᾷ τὸ θεῖον τοὔνομα σῆς κλήσεως.
οὐκ ἀμβλυνεῖ ἄστρον τὸ σὸν ποτ᾽ ἐκ θεοῦ
τὸ θεῖον, ὡς φιλεῖς ξένους καὶ πλησίους.
δότειρα χεῖρα τοῖς πᾶσι διανείμεις·
15 κἀμοὶ ἀόκνως εὐμενῶς χαρίζασθε
ἀμοιβὴν ἐκ θεοῦ καρπούμενοι πολύ.
μάλιστα δ᾽ εὐχαῖς οὐ πεπαύσομαι χεῖρα,
κάλλιστα διόλου θεῷ προσεννέπων,
πολυχρονικοὺς δεσπότας εἶναι ἡμῖν,
20 καὶ τοὺς φιλανθρώπους ἀδελφοὺς ἐνδόξους,
Καλλίνικον, Δωρόθεον ἀμφιβεβοημένους.
ζώοιτέ μοι τρίτατες ἀφθόνῳ βίῳ,
ἔπειτα καὶ Μάρκος σοφώτατος κριτής
σὺν σοφωτάτῳ Μάρκῳ πανενδόξῳ κριτῇ.

1 cf. 10 B 5 | παναξιας supra πρυτανεων Π   5 cf. titulum   6 de composito cf. 2,22   9 τιμη: cf. 16,2   11 υιος Απα Διου.   12 cf. 15,5   13 cf. 10,14   15 ευγενει pro ευμενως in margine dextro   16 πανυ et αει in m. dextro   17 deum invocantis est manus tollere   18 προσαναφερων in m. dextro   20ss cf. 13,20s   23s alter versus delendus

Most excellent in mind of officials, of senators and those who observe good judgment, of wealthy ancestry, with golden roots, loving God's commandments, of a fair senatorial house, guarded by God—your honored father came from God. You are a descendant unequaled in excellence of the high officials—Victor of everlasting memory, of whom poetry's numbers sing, and Dios, protector of cities, all-praiseworthy in his good fortune; you bear the blood and the repute of preëminent honor. O victorious and most highly exalted Colluthus, honor the divine name by which you are called. Your divine and God-given star will not become dim, because you love strangers and your neighbor. You hold out a giving hand to all; do not hesitate kindly to grant me the recompense from God I have fully earned. I shall not cease to lift up my hands in prayer, always addressing eloquent words to God, that my lords live long, they and their honorable and generous brothers, renowned Callinicus and Dorotheos. In the third place after them may you live a life free from envy, together with Mark, the most learned judge (together with learned Mark, the famous judge).

In this poem Dioscorus knits together many of the motifs he has used in other verses addressed to members of this family (cf. H13–H16).

1–4. These lines give a vivid description of just what a decurial official of a Late Roman city should be: intelligent, nobly born, pious, and of course generous—"of a fair, God-guarded senatorial house" like that of Hestia Polyolbos. Πρυτανεύς and βουλή are being used in a metaphorical sense; they are not evidence for a senate at Antinoë (see A. Bowman, *The town councils of Roman Egypt* [*ASP* 11, Toronto 1971]). The terms are classicizing renderings, in a somewhat Procopian or Agathian vein, of pagarch (allowing for the collegiality of the office) (cf. W. Liebeschuetz, "The origin of the office of pagarch," *BZ* 66 [1973] 38–46).

3. Underlying his use of this concept (cf. H5.40), did Dioscorus know of such Neoplatonic *tradita* as Proclus's comments on Hesiod's age of gold? (Cf. N. G. Wilson, *Scholars of Byzantium* [Baltimore 1983] 39.) The objects of his praise have "laid up treasures in heaven," being φιλέντολοι as well.

On the combination of golden ancestry and pious wealth, cf. also line 9, αἷμα καὶ μέλη.

5. Note the pun on Διός (cf. line 8).

7–8. Victor and Apa Dios cannot be exactly identified from the papyri. Cf. *P.Cair.Masp.* III 67279.14 and 24.

11. Again a reference to S. Colluthus, the patron saint of Antinoë (H13).

12–13. Here the personal star (cf. H15.5, and W. Gundel and H. G. Gundel, *Astrologumena* [Wiesbaden 1966] 236–244) is juxtaposed with the dominical precepts (ⲙⲁⲓϣⲙⲙⲟ, etc.).

<table>
<tr><td>To Colluthus.</td><td></td><td align="right">P.Cair.Masp. II 67187.</td></tr>
</table>

<pre>
[. .]πτε σὺ γ', Ἀρκαδίη, ζηλήσαο   τέκνον ἐμοῖο,
[Κο]λλοῦθον γλυκύμορφον, ἀρεῖ   ον ἀτ' υἵεα Μούσης
                                               πείσ[θ]η
[. . . .] ἀφραδίησι τεοῖς ναετῆρσι   ν ἐτύχθη
                                          [   ]το
['Αλκ]ινόοιο μύθοισι σὺν   [   ]ος ἰδέσθαι
5 [. . . . . .]ονος ἄμμιν ἔτελλεν [   ]. ν ἱκάνειν
   [. . . . . .]τολον πανάριστον αν   εκ . τλο[. . . . . . .]ε Νεῖλος
   [. . . . . . .]ωρα . ις [ἀτ]ίταλλε   [. . . . .]ς ἐνὶ κόλ[πω]
   [. . . . .]δεν κατερ   . . . [. . . . . . .]σε[τ]ο μελ[ίσσης(?)]
   [. . . .]οιως μεθέπει πα   [ναγάκλυ]τα(?) δῶρα μελίσση[s]
</pre>

The first nine lines preserved on the horizontal-fibers side of this papyrus, even more fragmentary today than in Maspero's time, contain the remains of verses apparently belonging to the Colluthus group, which will accordingly appear here. The remaining lines contain matter belonging to the Achilles-Polyxena ethopoiia (H26 and *P.Cair.Masp.* III 67353 v C), which will be considered later.

1. Apparently some sort of negative is to be restored, to give the sense "Do not you, Arcadia, envy my child, Colluthus the good-looking, warlike son of the Muse . . ." (Thebais *loquitur*). On Arcadia, see J. G. Keenan, "The provincial administration of Egyptian Arcadia," *Proc. XIV intl.congr. papyrol.* (London 1975) 189–194, and *Mus.Philol.Lond.* 2 (1977) 193–202.

4. "Alcinous's stories," a long-winded tale that would take too long to relate; proverbial in rhetoric, as Maspero pointed out. Cf. K. Tümpel, "Ἀλκίνου ἀπόλογος," *Philologus* 52 (1894) 523–533. Dioscorus may have got the notion from Aelius Aristides.

8–9. Cf. on H5.15. Not enough is left on the papyrus to support Maspero's restoration.

The next two poems may also be placed in the early part of Dioscorus's activity at Antinoë, as they have stylistic and prosopographical links with the epithalamium H24 and the encomium H5.

H7. Encomium on Domninus,   *P.Cair.Masp.* III 67316
cancellarius on the prefectural staff.

Εἰ μελοπο[ιὸς ἄ]ριστος ἐπ᾽ εὐνομίῃσιν ἀοιδῆς
ἵστατο μητιόων, γέρας ἡλίκον ὑμνοπολεύων
σῆς ἀρετῆς, παντάριστε, παναυγέος ἠδέ τ᾽ ἀρίστης,
τοῖον ἔπος κατέλεξον ἕως παρεμύθετο θυμός·
5 ὅ[τ]τι τέττιγξ πολύυμνος ἔχει δέμας ὁπλ[
νυκταδίῃ μελεδῶνι θεὸν κατ᾽ ὄρεσφι λιγαί[ν]ει.
κλυτὸς εὐκλείης βασιλεὺς θεὸ[ς ὕμ]νον ἀκούει
ρ. . . . . .]σ. . ραφι. . . . . . . πορα . . . ξον ἐνίψαι
ιδι . σλι . ν πανυ[. . . . . . μ]ῆτι[ς ἐ]πάρχων
10 τ. . . . .]ις ἐ[πέ]εσσι [τ]ε[ὸν κλέος ο]ὔποτ᾽ ὀ[λεῖται
η . . . . .]σων . ε. . ων καταμ. . . . . . . πα. . . . . .
ν. . . . . .]ωσε τάχα καλ. . . σαλ. . . . . ιος[
Δ[όμνινον] ἀμφιβο[ητ]ὸν ὁμών[υ]μος ομμ[
Ὀρφέα Καλλιόπης ἐνίκησας ἐτητυμί[ῃσιν,
15 μῦθον ἐπ᾽ ἐννεσίῃσι [τ]εὸν ποθέου[σιν ἐπά]ρχοι.
Νέστωρ οὐ λάθεν, ἀλλ[ά] σ[υ κριτ]ὴς ἄμμ[ι]ν ἐτύχθης,
ἱστάμενος πρόβολ[. . πανίκελος] ἔπλεο τοῖσδε
νόσφιν ἁλιφροσύν[ης
οὕτως ἀεὶ ζώ[οις ἀ]λυπώτατος, ἐκτὸς ἀνάγκης,
20 νηπιάχοισι τέκ[νοισιν, ἅμα] ζαθέῃ σέο νύμφῃ.
χεῖραν ἐμοὶ ἀτ[άνυσσον, ἐ]πεὶ ξένο[ς] εἰμὶ μογήσας,
ἐκ στυγερῶν κα[μάτω]ν, ἀδίκων κρίσ[ις] ἔνθα με ῥίπτει.

acrostichum: εις τον κ[ριτην vel κυριον] Δομνινον.   **5** cf. 5,15   **9** cf. 2,1
10 cf. 1 verso 7, ο]υποτ α[leg. Ma   **13** ομμασι λευσης Ma   **17** προβολος
vel προβολῳ   **18** Hsch. s.v. αλιφροσυνη· ικανη φρονησις, cf. ad XXIX 63
19 cf. 2,12   **20** cf. 2,30   **21** cf. 3,24   **22** cf. 5,19

If the best poet were to take a stand devising a song about good government, singing of honor in keeping with your excellence, O best of men, radiant with greatness, he would utter such a poem as to encourage my heart—like the songful cicada who has a chitinous body and sings in his nightly care even to the ears of God. Glorious God, the King of Glory, hears (my) hymn . . . craft of rulers . . . your glory will never perish . . . namesake of renowned Domninus. In truth you have outdone Orpheus son of Calliope, and nobles long to hear your story at their suggestion. Nestor was not without his fame; but you have arisen as a judge for us, standing as a bulwark; you are very like those (not) without good judgment. So may you live forever, without pain, free from need, with your little children and your divine wife. Stretch forth your hand to me, since I am a stranger and in distress, because of hateful troubles, where the judgment of the unjust has cast me.

1. The μελοποιὸς ἄριστος of course denotes Homer. Dioscorus, who owned *P.Cair.Masp.* II 67172–67173–67174, Homeric codex texts, was formed by the standard school curriculum as taught in Egypt until the Islamic period. This poem, addressed to a judge (see the acrostic lines 7–12 and line 16, if the restoration be correct), celebrates εὐνομία and deplores the ἀδίκων κρίσις that has troubled Dioscorus's past.

5–6. Again the Christianized image of the pastoral cicada (cf. H5.15), combining Menander Rhetor's device of modesty with a Callimachean or Anacreontic *topos* while giving the whole a Christian twist: θεόν as in *P.Berol.* 13894.18. Restore ὁπλ[ήεν ?

7. An echo, conceptually, of Ps. 24:7–10 (which is sung in the Coptic liturgy for Easter Vigil). See R. W. Daniel, "Christian hymn: P.Vindob. G. 40195 and P.Ryl.Copt. 33," *ZPE* 42 (1981) 71–77, esp. 74. Dioscorus is reworking the whole allusion by using a pair of synonyms, punningly, for δόξα. See also R. Taft, "Psalm 24 at the transfer of gifts in the Byzantine liturgy," in *The Word in the world: Essays in honor of F. L. Moriarty*, ed. R. J. Clifford and G. W. MacRae (Weston, Mass. 1973) 159–177.

13. Domninus cannot be exactly identified from the papyri; he appears to be the father of Paul (see following), the bridegroom of H24. The famous sixth-century Domninus was the city prefect at Constantinople in 566/7 (A. Cameron and A. Cameron, "The *Cycle* of Agathias," *JHS* 86 [1966] 21–22).

14. On the much-discussed figure of Orpheus in Late Antiquity, see A. Dupont-Sommer, ed., *Le mythe d'Orphée aux animaux et ses prolongements au judaïsme, au christianisme et à l'Islam* (Rome 1975). Compare the Coptic Museum reliefs (Zaloscer, *Kunst im christlichen Ägypten*, Taf. 18 and 23).[68]

68. Also cf. Volbach, *Elfenbeinarbeiten*, nos. 96 and 70.

H20. Encomium on Paul son of Domninus,   *P.Cair.Masp.* II 67185 v B
cancellarius on the prefectural staff.

Χαῖρ]ε πέπον, προφέριστε, τεὸν κλέος οὔποτ᾽ ὀλεῖται,
παν]τοίων ἐπέων πανεπάξιον οὔνομα ηὗρες.
ἀ[τρ]εκ[έ]ως Φαέθοντο[ς ἀπ]αστράπτει σέο μορφή.
ὑ]μνεῦσαι τὸν Ὅμ[ηρ]ον [. . . .]ιδας οὐ χρέα Μούσας,
5 λ[ώιόν] ἐστι σέθ[ε]ν π[ανα]οίδιμον οὔνομα μέλψαι,
ὅττι χάρις καὶ χάρμα καὶ εὐεπίης φίλον ἄνθος·
σὴν ἀρετὴν ποθ[έ]ο[υ]σιν ἀ[θ]άνα[τοι] ἠδέ τ[ε ἄ]νδρες.

acrostichum: χ(αιρε) Παυλος.— 1 cf. 1 verso 7 2 cf. 4 β 9 3 cf. 1 verso 9 4 ομηριδας sup. Ma e Nonn. D. 32,184, sed cf. 25,4 5 cf. Apollinar. Metaphr. 73,43 … τεον ουνομα μελψοι 5s cf. 1,5s 6s in marg. dextro scripti

Greetings, O bravest one, may your glory never fade; you bear a name worthy of eloquence of every kind. Truly your beauty flashes forth like that of Phaethon. I do not need Homer or the Muses to sing (of you); it is better (just) to hymn your name, renowned in song, as do Grace and Joy and the lovely flower of Eloquence; both men and gods long to see your excellence.

2. The name here is that of Saint Paul, the orator par excellence; cf. H. P. L'Orange, "Plotinus-Paul," in *Likeness and icon: Selected studies*, pp. 32–42. On the other hand, Chrysostom had regarded Paul as rather an unlettered, unskilled man whose rhetorical success was a miracle wrought by divine power and the intrinsic worth of the message he brought; *Jean Chrysostome: Panégyriques de S. Paul* (ed. A. Piédaguel, *SC* 300, Paris 1982) 202–209.

3. Did the figure of Phaethon also have a zodiacal connotation? See Nonnus's treatment of the myth in *Dion.* 38.90–434 for emphasis on his journey through the signs.

4. Dioscorus the *doctus poeta*, here altering his usual stance (cf. H14.1), is aware of Homer as the originator of rhetoric; Menander Rhetor 434.11 (ed. Russell and Wilson, with comment p. 347). On the Muses, cf. H12 B 3, H25.4, *P.Cair.Masp.* 67187.2, "der Musensohn."

6. Cf. H1.6, the encomium on Justin II; Dioscorus will also reuse the phrase χάρις καὶ χάρμα in iambics, in H11.6 and H3.13, the great encomium on Duke John. These qualities attest to the desirability of a proper classical education in a bureaucrat of the Thebaid. Cf. Wilson, *Scholars of Byzantium*, pp. 2–3, and F. S. Pedersen, "On professional qualifications for public posts in late antiquity," *Class.etMed.* 31 (1975) 161–213. The φίλον ἄνθος of εὐεπία is what distinguishes the prose of the *cancellarius*'s office.

H11. Encomium on unnamed officials.   *P.Cair.Masp.* III 67279 v

Θ[ήβη] πᾶσα χ[ό]ρευ[σον, εἰρήνην δέχου]·
οὐ γὰρ θεωρήσεις κακ[ουργικ]ὴν ἔτι,
πάντη δέος πέφυκεν ἀσπ[ίλου δ]ίκης
το]ῦ πανταρίστου καὶ διεσμ[ι]λιγμένου
5   νέου Σόλωνος λειπονε. εθιασαφη
δ[εῦρο] χ[άρις] καὶ [χ]άρμ[α] καὶ ἀνθολόφον
τοὺς εὐμενεῖς νικηφόρους στρατηλάτας
αἰὲν ἀγαλλε[. .
. ης οἱ νόμοι τρέμουσι πιστὰ φυλάττειν
10   . . . . η καὶ θέμετρα τοῦ Νείλου
[
[
ὁ] γράψας καὶ πάλαι λ[ι]χὰς [
καὶ σ[ο]ῦ χαράξει τοὺς χ[ρόνους διπλώ]ματι

    1–7 cf. 3,9–14   **4** cf. 10,4 | διεσμιλιγμενου = -λευμενου, cf. Schwyzer I
160.209   **10** cf. 3,6   **13s** cf. 5,38s | χαραξη Π

Let the whole Thebaid dance and welcome peace, for you shall not
behold evildoing any more; for fear of the spotless justice of the most
excellent and polished new Solon has sprung up everywhere . . . Come,
Grace and flower-crowned Joy, ever to honor the beneficent and victorious rulers . . . The laws stand in awe to guard (their) faithful judgments . . .
and the sources of the Nile . . . May He who in ancient times wrote (the
Tablets of the Law) write many years in your Book of Life.

3. Again ἄσπιλος, from the Catholic Epistles (James 1:27, 1 Tim. 6:14, 2
Pet. 3:14), qualifies δίκη.

4. διασμιλεύω is a rare word, found in Alexander Rhetor and the gram-
marian Pollux, and reused in the tenth century in *AP* 15.38. On the -γ- , see
F. T. Gignac, *Grammar of the Greek papyri of the Roman and Byzantine periods*
I (Milan 1976) 72–75. Cf. H10.4.

5. Cf. H5.59, and H3.12, 30. Could Dioscorus have known of Solon and
the Seven Sages from John Philoponus's comments on Aristotle's περὶ
φιλοσοφίας ? Cf. Cyril *In Julianum* I.12 (PG 76.521A).

6. ἀνθολόφος appears to be Dioscorus's own coinage.

9. Cf. Nonnus *Paraphr.* 1.199, 4.172.

10. On the sources of the Nile, especially in Neoplatonic/Alexandrian
commentary, see H13.3, with *P.Turner* 10. Nonnus's treatment of the "living water" in Jn. 4:10–14 (*Paraphr.* 4.43–69) has been linked to the Egyptian
notion of the life-giving, Osirian Nile by R. Kuiper, "De Nonno Evangelii

Johannei interprete," *Mnemosyne* 46 (1918) 246–247; cf. line 69, . . . οὐ χθονίου ποταμοῖο.

13. λιχάς, if correct, may be a very early witness for the meaning attested in Hesychius of "a hard thing like stone or pebble." For the scriptural figure, cf. H12 A 17–18; and differently in H5.38 (on lawgiving).

H19. Encomium on Hypatius,   *P.Cair.Masp.* II 67185 v A
excubitor on the prefectural staff.

Ὑ] . . . . σιν ἀίδιος ἔλλα[χες ἀλκ]ήν,
πα[ν]τοί[ων ἐπέω]ν πανεπά[ξιον οὔνομ]α εὗρες.
ἀ]τρεκέως, [προφέρι]στ᾽, ὑπατηίδ᾽ [ἐπίκ]λην ἀε[ί]ρεις
τῆ]ς π[ο]λ[υ]κ[α]λλίσ[τη]ς φιλομετ[ρίας] . . . . . . οἴστρου.
5 ἴσ]θι, φέριστε, πένησι βοηθόος, ὄφρα τὸ θεῖον
ὁ]πλοτέρη[ν γ]εράεσ[σ]ι φυλάσσεται ὑψόθι πάντων
σὴν ἀρετὴν θαλέθο[υσ]αν ἐπὶ χρόνον ἄσπετον εἶναι.
εἰ ὕπα[τον] Κρονίδης βα[σιληί]δος ἕζετο θῶκον,
{εἰ ταμίην ὑπά[τ]ων βασιληίδος εὐρύοπα Ζεύς}
10 μ]ᾶλ[λ]ον τεὴν σθενέεσκε [φ]ερώνυμον ἕξειν ἐπίκλην.
{ . . .]αχεν . α[.]λαι τ[ε]ὴν σθενέεσκεν ἐπίκλην εὑρειν.}

    acrostichum: Υπατιος.—   2 cf. 4 B 9   4 εμπλεος sup. Ma, 'poesis studio ardens' **8ss** cf. 1 verso 2s **11** ελλαχεν sup. Ma

. . . You, O everlasting, have brought us help, and you bear a name most worthy of every sort of eloquence. Precisely speaking, Your Excellency, you bear a consular name, being 'consul' in your love for poetry's beautiful numbers. Be a helper to the poor, O most brave, so God may guard from above with gifts of honor your young and thriving excellence for a countless time. If Zeus sat upon the consular seat of kingship (if far-seeing Zeus [established?] a housekeeper for kingship in the form of consuls), may God all the more be strong in keeping your name renowned. . . .

The title may also be restored as *exceptor* or possibly *exactor* (from εξκτ/ Pap.). *Exactor* seems not to be in use this late; for *exceptor*, cf. *P.Cair.Masp.* III 67312.5, *P.Lond.* V 1714.14 (ducal staff at Antinoë). For *excubitor*, cf. *SB* I 4890.1.

This poem is really an extended pun, playing on the recipient's name: lines 2–3, 8–9. For consuls in the Byzantine papyri, see R. S. Bagnall, A. Cameron, S. R. Schwartz, and K. A. Worp, *Consuls of the Later Roman Empire* (Atlanta, 1987) (cf. *P.Cair.Masp.* II 67178 v B 2).

4. No traces are any longer visible on the papyrus, but I should like to restore ὕπατος, reinforcing the pun (also cf. *P.Antin.* III 188.3).

H22. Epithalamium for Matthew.   *P.Lit.Lond.* 99
                                              + *P.Cair.Masp.* II 67180
                                                          + 67181

Νυμφίε, σ[εῖο γάμοι] χαρίτων πλήθουσι χ[ορε]ίης,
νυμφίε, σεῖο γάμοι μαλακοτρεφέων ῥοδοε[σσῶν,
νυμφίε, σεῖο γάμοι μελιηδέων ἐκ σταφυλ[άων·
νύμφης [λ]έκτρα [φέρεις π]αναριζήλ[ης Ἀριάδ]νης,
5   αἴσιος ἐκ γενετήρων εὐπατέρειαν ἐφ[εῦρες.
σήμερον ἐξαπίνης φάος ἔπλετο δώμασι τοῖ[σδε,
ὅττι νέος Μαθαῖος πολυφίλτατος ἔλλαχ[ε νύμ]φην.
σωφροσύνης τὸν ἔρωτα γαμοστολίης λ[ά]χες Ἥρης·
ὡς χρυσὸς χρυσῆς ἔτυχες, παν[αρ]είονες ἄμφω,
10 νύμφης ὀμφακόεντος εκ . . . . μελίσσης.
νυμφίε, κάμψον ἔρωτι τεὸν νόον· οὐράνιος Ζεύς
Εὐρώπης διὰ κάλλος ἀκούεται εἰσέτι ταῦρο[ς
καὶ Λήδης δι᾽ ἔρωτας ἀκούεται εἰσέτι κύκνος.
Εὐρώπην σὺ φέρεις εἰς οἰκίον, οὐκ ἐπὶ πό[ντον,
15 Λήδης λ[έκτρα φέρεις, ἀλλ᾽ ο]ὺ πτ[ερ]ύγεσσι κομ[ίζει]ς.
νυμφίε, μὴ . τ . . . . . . τεσ . . ουν . . · καὶ γὰρ Ἀπόλλω[ν
ἡδυβόλων πολύυμνος ἐδέξατο κέντρον ἐρώ[των·
Δάφνης γὰρ δι᾽ ἔρωτας ἀεὶ Δαφναῖος Ἀπόλλω[ν.
Δάφνην καὶ σὺ φέρεις, ἀλλ᾽ οὐ φεύγουσαν, ἄκοιτιν.
20 μυρία Φοῖβος ἔτευξε, καὶ οὐκ ἐτύχησεν ἐρώτων.
οὐ μετὰ δὴν ποθέων πολυφίλτατον ὄψεαι υἷα
ἡδέα παππάζοντα τεοῖς ἐπὶ γούνασιν ὄντα
εἰκόνα σὴν ποθέοντα καὶ ἱμείροντα τεκούσης·
οὐ γλυκὺς ἵμερος ἄλλος ἐπάξιος ἀμφ᾽ ὑμέ[ναιον.

iustum ordinem versuum 1–7, quem supra legis, poeta litteris δεγβα
significavit.—   **1–3** cf. 21,1   **4** cf. 21,3   **5** cf. 24,9s   **9** cf. 21,6
11 γαμψον Π   **19** cf. 21,14   **21** ου μετα δην cf. LVI 39   **21–23** cf. 23,17–
20; 24,22

Bridegroom, may your wedding be filled with the dancing of the
Graces, with gently nurtured roses, with honey-sweet grape clusters; you
are marrying a bride who is an enviable Ariadne, and fittingly you have
found her nobility of descent. Suddenly today a light has filled these our
houses, because dear young Matthew has taken a bride. May you have the
love of Wisdom, with Hera to bless your marriage; like gold you have
found your golden bride, both of you like heroes, she ripe as a honeycomb. . . . Bridegroom, bend your mind to love; Zeus himself in heaven,
because of Europa's beauty, is known to have become a bull; for love of
Leda he was esteemed a swan. Carry your Europa over the threshold, not
over the sea; go to bed with your Leda, but don't worry about wings. Even
revered Apollo has felt the sting of sweet-darting love, for out of his love
for Daphne Apollo is always known as god of the laurel. Take your

Daphne to wife, but she will not run away from you. Phoebus crafted
many things, but he was not successful in love. You will not have long to
wait until you see your dear children on your lap, prettily saying "Daddy,"
the lovely image of you and of their mother. This pleasant desire is worthy
to follow your wedding.

1. Dioscorus used this line at the opening of Count Callinicus's epithalamium, H21.

4. Also borrowed from H21 is the Ariadne figure, an image appropriate
both for a happy wedding and as a type of the soul united, after vicis-
situdes, to God.[69]

6. The image of light filling the houses echoes the scene in Nonnus
Paraphrasis 3.3–8, Nicodemus's night visit to Christ, when "they went into
the house, where there was a light," a scene painted like a de la Tour with
one candle. Here the light is bright, for rejoicing; compare the figure of
Phos in the Hestia Polyolbos tapestry at Dumbarton Oaks (Wessel, *Koptische Kunst*, pl. 132).

7. We cannot identify Matthew from the Antinoë/Aphrodito papyri;
clearly he is not one of the *coloni* in *P.Antin.* III 201.

8. For σωφροσύνης, cf. H12.9, and in the next epithalamium below,
H23.2. Dioscorus probably derived the figure of Hera, at the wedding of
Peleus and Thetis, from Colluthus *Rapt.Hel.* 25, 64, 88 (ed. P. Orsini, Paris
1972). Philosophers would think of Damascius's "Orphic" system linking
Hera, Hestia, and Demeter (Friedländer, *Documents of dying paganism*, pp.
12–13). For γαμοστολίης, cf. Musaeus 7, and K. Kost, *Musaios: Hero und
Leander* (Bonn 1971) 142–143.

9. Here a slightly abbreviated version of Dioscorus's line alluding to the
doctrine of affinity of like with like, as in H21.6. Παναρείων is a *hapax* for
our poet here.

10. For ὄμφαξ, cf. Triphiodorus 34 and the comments of B. Gerlaud, ed.
(Paris 1982) 108.

12–19. Dioscorus here begins to adorn his epithalamia with classical
images of the loves of the gods that are embodied in some of the best-
known works of Coptic art: Europa and the Bull, Leda and the Swan,
Apollo and Daphne.

12, 14. For Europa and the Bull, cf. the Coptic Museum relief, Zaloscer,
Kunst im christlichen Ägypten, Taf. 14; and Volbach, *Elfenbeinarbeiten*, no.
82, the Trier ivory. The upper register of the Trier plaque contains a repre-

---

69. Compare again the Ariadne on the Vienna textile (above n. 59), Wessel, *Coptic art*,
pl. 113.

sentation of the Dioscuri, who are of course associated in myth with Leda (the next image in the poem). Was Dioscorus, in using these myths, at all conscious of making a kind of self-referent pun on the associations of his own name? (Cf. Hanfmann, "The continuity of classical art," in Weitzmann, *Age of spirituality*, pp. 89–90; and N. Leipen, "Classical tradition in early Christian art: A textile fragment in the Royal Ontario Museum," in *Studies in textile history in memory of H. B. Burnham*, ed. V. Gervers [Toronto 1977] 168–177, on the Dioscuri.)[70] I have suggested elsewhere that Dioscorus's name may be a Hellenization of the name of the great Monophysite monk Shenoute ("son of God"), as well as an eponym of the great Monophysite culture hero, Patriarch Dioscorus I.[71]

13, 15. Two of perhaps the most famous works of Coptic art are the Leda and the Swan relief in the Coptic Museum and that in the Graeco-Roman Museum at Alexandria (Zaloscer, *Kunst im christlichen Ägypten*, Taf. 22, for the latter; Beckwith, *Coptic sculpture*, pl. 69, for the former; cf. also Beckwith, pl. 70, for another, fragmentary relief in Alexandria). These striking images have inspired speculation on Coptic sexuality since Strzygowski's *Koptische Kunst* (Vienna 1904) xvi, 33–35 (also in *BSAAlex* 5 [1902] 42–46). See Torp, "Leda Christiana," pp. 101–112. The position of J. Lauzière, "Le mythe de Léda dans l'art copte," *BSAC* 2 (1936) 38–46, might still be taken seriously.

These four artfully constructed lines, a pleasing transformation of a classical decorative conceit, amusingly contrast the loves of Olympian mythology, so omnipresent in the visual art of Dioscorus's period, with the realities of a sixth-century wedding (cf. the Projecta casket, combining the Toilet of Venus with *vivatis in Christo*). The charming contrasts of οὐκ ἐπὶ πόντον . . . οὐ πτερύγεσσι are followed by ἀλλ᾽ οὐ φεύγουσαν (line 19) (cf. H21.14, a Helen "of Troy" who will not run away).

18–19. To illustrate Dioscorus's imagery, there are well-known Coptic representations of Daphne (cf. H27): in the Coptic Museum (Zaloscer, *Kunst im christlichen Ägypten*, Taf. 19 and 20) and in the Louvre (Beckwith, *Coptic sculpture*, pl. 61). The nymph is usually shown grasping two exuberantly twining branches of laurel that frame her figure.[72]

20. Note the play on ἔτευξε . . . ἐτύχησεν.

---

70. Perhaps there are Egyptian associations with the very late Europa on the famous Veroli casket; see E. Simon, "Nonnos und das Elfenbeinkästchen aus Veroli," *JbDAI* 79 (1964) 279–336.

71. L. S. B. MacCoull, "Dioscorus and the dukes," *BS/EB* 14 (1988).

72. Compare also the Ravenna ivory, Volbach, *Elfenbeinarbeiten*, no. 80; and the "Shawl of Sabina" in the Louvre, (Weitzmann, *Age of spirituality*, no. 112), from Antinoë.

22. Cf. *P.Cair.Masp.* II 67179 r B (IV).

In this poem Dioscorus is quite closely following the prescriptions laid down by Menander Rhetor for an *epithalamios logos* (ed. Russell and Wilson, pp. 134–147, 309–323).

H23. Epithalamium for Isakios.						*P.Cair.Masp.* III 67318

Ἴστασο, Καλλιόπη, καὶ μέλπεο, μῆτερ ἀοιδῆς,
σεμνὸν ἀεὶ στίλβοντα γάμον πολυσώφρονος εὐνῆς,
ἀγλαίης σὺν ἔρωτι πεπληκότα δ᾽ ὀλβοσυνάων.
Κύπριδος οὐκ ἐνόησεν ἀεικέα δ᾽ ἔργα τελέσσαι,
5 ἱστὸν ἀναστῆσαι φιλαμάρτου Τυνδαρεώνης.
᾽Ωγυγίης γενεῆς ἱερὸν γένος ἐγγύθι Νείλου,
λεύσατε, πῶς μεθέπουσιν ὁ νυμφίος ἠδὲ καὶ νύμφη·
ἀκλινέως κατέμαρψαν ἐοικότε Βελλεροφόντῃ,
μήνην ἀμφιέπουσιν ἀγαλλομένην ὑμεναίοις
10 π]υροφόρου χαρίεντας ἐπ᾽ ἄνθεσιν αὔλακας αἴης.
ῥηιδίως Διόνυσον ἐνὶ στεφέεσσι καὶ Νεῖλον
ῥυσάμενος πολύτεκνον ἀεὶ θεὸς ἐγγυαλίξοι
οὐλομένης ἀπάνευθεν γάμον προφερέστατον ἄλλων.
τούνεκ᾽ ἀεὶ ζώοιτε καὶ ἄφθιτον ἐς χρόνον ἔλθοις
15 ἄφθονον εὐνομίης παναοίδιμον ἦδος ἀείρας
τοσσατίης ἀρετῆς, ἄμ᾽ ἀριζήλῃ σέο νύμφῃ.
ὤ]ριον, οὐ μετὰ δὴν ἐπὶ γούνασιν ὄψεαι υἷα,
νέκ[τα]ρος ἡδύτερον, πεποθημένον εἰς ἔο κάλλο[ς,
ὑμετέρων καμάτων πανεπάξιον ὀλβιστῆρα,
20 μῆτιν ἀερτάζοντα πανίκελον ὔμμι τοκεῦσι.
φεύγεο, βασκανίη, γάμον ἵλαον ἐκ θεοῦ τόνδε
᾽Ι[σα]κίου χα[ρ]ίεντος ἀμύμονος ἐκ γενετῆρος.
᾽Ισὰκ ὀμβριμόθυμος, ἐφεύραο νύμφην ἀρίστην,
ὡς χρυσὸς χ[ρ]ρυσῶν ἔτυχε καὶ ἄργυρος ἄργυρον εὗρεν.

acrostichum: Ισακιω λαμπρ[ρ]οτατω νυμφι[ι]ω.—   **8** cf. 21,6 et 5,24 **11s** sententia contracta sed non corrupta esse videtur; cf. 3,42–44; 5,25–28; 10 B 2s; 21,8–10; 25,6–11   **13** ουλομενη (nomen subst.) = malum, cf. κακουργικην 3,10   **14** cf. 2,12   **15** ηδος ex ητος cor. poeta   **16** cf. 5,12 et 2,30   **17–20** cf. 22,21–23   **21** cf. 12,3   **24** cf. 21,6 | ετυχε delendum?

Come, Calliope, mother of song, and sing the ever-shining and solemn marriage of this couple who lie together in wisdom, filled with the blessings of splendor and love. He did not know how to do the matchless acts of Aphrodite, to set up the web of sinful Helen. Holy people of Theban descent on the banks of the Nile, look how the bridegroom and the bride are coming; to judge impartially, they have surpassed Bellerophon in likeness; they have surrounded the joyful moon with wedding songs, in the furrows of the grain-bearing earth that rejoice with flowers. Easily protecting garlanded Dionysus and the Nile with his many children, may

God grant a noble marriage free from the destructive envy of others. So may you live forever and reach a boundless length of life, exalting the renowned delight of good government, free from envy, and of such excellence, with your admirable wife. Soon you shall see children on your lap, sweeter than nectar, loved for their beauty—a blessing that your troubles have merited, as you do honor to the ability of your forebears. Go away, evil eye; this marriage is graced by God, this marriage of joyful Isakios, son of a famous father. Isakios, strong of spirit, you have found your noble bride, as gold has embraced gold and silver has found silver.

On the acrostic, with lines 22–23, there is no way to tell if this Isakios is the same person as the Isakios mentioned in P.Vat.Copti Doresse (see MacCoull, "Prosopography of Aphrodito," 91–94).

1. Cf. H7.14, on Calliope, mother of Orpheus.

3. *Aglaia*, splendor, cf. H12 B 5, νυμφίον ἀγλαίης. The perfect characterization of the colorful visibility of Late Antique festivity, especially that of a wedding procession.

4. The subject of the verb is uncertain.

5. φιλάμαρτος is an understandable epithet to apply to faithless Helen; withal, it is a somewhat rare and odd word, found in Nilus of Ancyra and, in the seventh century, in the exegetical homilies of Antiochus the Monk.

6. Here Ogygia applies to Egyptian Thebes—a clever transference.

7. λεύσατε: a device of eagerness, pointing out the imminent approach of the wedding procession.

8. On Bellerophon, see comment on H24.11.

10. πυρόφορος is characteristic of Ptolemaic documentary usage; e.g., *SB* 4369, *PSI* 432.

11–12. The interwoven imagery of God, Dionysus and his train, and the old river god Nile is that of much of Coptic textile art. See Weitzmann, *Age of spirituality*, nos. 121, 123, 125, 136.

13. οὐλομένης: the Homeric echo would have been lost on no Egyptian schoolchild.

21. On the Evil Eye, cf. comment on H12.3; and on Abaskantos, see L. Robert in *Hellenica* 26 (*Rev. de philol.* [1944] 41–42; *Opera minora selecta* III [Amsterdam 1969] 1407–1408).

24. Once more Dioscorus uses the doctrine of affinity as a simile for the couple's perfect union.

The group of the next three poems, H4, H9, and H28, is contained on the horizontal-fibers side of *P.Cair.Masp.* I 67097. The sale of land on the vertical-fibers side mentions a "present fifth indiction," which must be A.D.

571; while the receipts on the horizontal-fibers side mention a seventh and coming eighth indiction—A.D. 573/4. Hence, the poems must fall between these two dates.

H4. Encomium on Duke Athanasius.   *P.Cair.Masp.* I 67097 v BC
                                                               (See Figure 9)

Δέχνυσο, πότνια Θήβ[η, ὃν ο]ὐκ ἐδάμ[ασ]σαν α . . . . . .
ν[αὶ] τὸν Ἀθανάσι[ον, κλει]τὸν ῥυτ[ῆρα] πο[λήων.
a   [οὐ χθὼν πᾶσα], θάλασσα [μό]λις πέλεν ἀξία ῥίζης
     κυδαλίμων πατέρων ἀπ[ὸ ῥί]ζης [ὀ]λβιστήρων,
5   Εὐστοχίου γε [σ]οτῆρος ἀτὰρ Κυρίλλου τε Κομήτου,
     ὧν βασιλεῖς τρομέουσι τὰ μήδεα πυκνὰ σοφίης.
     τέρπεό νυν, στρατίαρχε, τεὸς χρόνος οὔποτ' ὀλεῖται·
     ἐκ θεοῦ παμβασιλῆος ἐπεὶ θέμιν ἔλλαχες ἀλκήν,
     ἐκ θεοῦ παμβασιλῆος ἀοίδιμον οὔνομ' ἄειρες.
10 ο]ὕτως ἀεὶ ζώοις καὶ ἀμοίρατον ἐς χρόνον ἔλθοις
     σὺν τεκέεσσι φίλοισιν, ἐπ' αὐχένι δυσμενέεσσιν.
     θάλλε μοι, εἰσέτι θάλλεις ἕως ὅτε ψαύσῃς Ὀλύμπου,
     γῆς Φαρίης κρατέων ἠδ' Ἀρκαδίης μετὰ Θήβης,
     σὺν πόθῳ ἤτε φόβῳ τὰ θεμίστια πάντα νομεύων.
15 ὦ στρατίαρχε μέγιστε καὶ ὕπατε, πάτερ ἀνάκτων,
     χεῖραν ἐμοὶ ἀτάνυσσον ἐμὴν πενίην διασῶσαι.
     ἤ]λυθον οὐκ ὄλβον διζήμε[νο]ς οἷάπερ ἄλλοι,
     ἀλλὰ πόρον βιότοιο καὶ υἱήεσσιν ἐμοῖσι,
     μὴ [σ]φέα[ς] ὀλλυμένους ἀ[έκ]ων βλεφάροισι νοήσω.
20 . . . [. .]ν[. . .]μνη[. . .]ν διαμπ[ερὲ]ς ἤματα σεῖ[ο
     εκ[. .]ονα[. . . . . .]λιν[. . τ]ερπωλ[ὰς] ἰδ' ἑορτάς.
β   οὐ γὰρ ἔτι Βλεμύων γένος ὄψεαι, οὐ Σαρακηνῶν,
     οὐ τρόμον ἀνδροφόνου ληίστορος ὄμμασι λεύσ[ει]ς.
     πᾶ[σ]ι [γὰρ εἰρή]νη θεοίκελος ἤνθεε πάντη.
     σὸς τρόμος ἐκτὸς ἔλασσεν ἀεργέας ἔργα διῶξαι,
5   Καλλίνικόν τε Κόνωνα πενιχροτάτους π. ο[
     οὐ πέλεν, οὐ πέλεν ἄλλος ὁμοίιος Ἀθανασίῳ
     εὐρυτέρων ὑπάτων καὶ πατρικίων βασιλήων,
     ὧν γενεῆς τὸ πάροιθεν ἀοίδιμον οὔνομ' ἀκούω.
     παντοίων ἐπέων πανυπέρτατος ἔπλετο μοῦνος.

2 cf. 2,26   **3** litteris α et β (v. infra) mutationes poeta significat; cf. ad 1 *verso* 2|cf. 2,27   **4** cf. 6,2; 13,4   **7** cf. 1 *verso* 7   **10** cf. 2,12   **11** cf. 2,30 et 12,13   **12** cf. 2,29; 12 B 9   **13** cf. 2,2   **16** cf. 3,24 | λνειν supra σωσαι Π **17–19** cf. 6,24–26; 14,5s   β **3** cf. 5,32; 9,4   **4** σον δεος supra σος τρομος, νυξεν supra ελασσεν, νοησαι post διωξαι Π   **5** λιγωσθ.. supra -τατους Π **6** cf. 2,3   **7** των προτερων supra ευρυτερων Π   **9** cf. 6,17; 12,14; 19,2; 20,2

Lady Thebes, welcome one whom . . . have not overcome, I mean Athanasius, the famous saver of cities. The whole earth and the sea are hardly worthy of his family, sprung from renowned ancestors, from the stock of the blessed, Eustochius the savior and Cyril and Comes, before whom kings tremble as before the strong seed of wisdom. Rejoice now, Duke, your lifetime will never perish; you have got strength for justice from God, the King of all; from God the King of all you take your renowned name. So may you live forever and reach a boundless length of life, with your dear children, triumphing upon the necks of your enemies. Flourish and again flourish until you touch Heaven, ruling the land of Alexandria and Arcadia as well as the Thebaid, shepherding all your judgments in love and awe. O greatest and most high Duke, father of lords, stretch out your hand to me to relieve my poverty. I have not come like others, seeking riches, but seeking a means of living for my children as well, lest I see them with my eyes as they are perishing. . . . You shall not see the tribes of the Blemmyes or of the Saracens, nor shall you behold with your eyes fear of the destructive robber; for godlike peace has blossomed everywhere for all. Fear of you has kept the pernicious from having their way, namely that Callinicus and Conon oppress the poor. . . . Never, never was there anyone of far-famed consuls and noble kings like Athanasius, the famous name of whose ancestry I have long since heard. You alone are most highly exalted in eloquence of every kind.

1. Again Dioscorus personifies Lady Thebes; cf. H5.8, the encomium on Duke Callinicus; and HS10 r 9.

2. On Athanasius, cf. J. Maspero, "Etudes sur les papyrus d'Aphrodité, 2. Flavios Marianos, duc de Thébaïde," *BIFAO* 7 (1910) 97–119, and idem, "Les papyrus Beaugé," *BIFAO* 10 (1912) 131–157, esp. 143; MacCoull, "Dioscorus and the dukes."

On the concept of "saving cities," cf. my comments on H10 B 6, and on H28.16.

3. Cf. HS10 r 14; Viljamaa, *Greek encomiastic poetry*, p. 52.

5. On Cyril and Comes, cf. H9.8. A Eustochius cannot be identified from the papyri or from *PLRE* II.

6. We are reminded of the extra overtones attaching to this word (σοφίης), and plays on it, during the reign of Justin II and Sophia; Averil Cameron, "The empress Sophia," *Byzantion* 45 (1975) 5–21 (reprinted as no. 11 in her *Continuity and change in sixth-century Byzantium*) (and cf. eadem, "Notes on the Sophiae, the Sophianae and the harbour of Sophia," *Byzantion* 37 [1968] 11–20).

8–9. On παμβασιλεύς, cf. my comment on H6.23 (Egyptian liturgical usage).

9. His full name (from *P.Cair.Masp.* I 67002.1) was Fl. Triadios Marianos Michael Gabriel Constantine Theodore Martyrios Julian Athanasius—an impressive list of heavenly patrons for a nobleman (cf. MacCoull, "Dioscorus and the dukes"); cf. β line 8.

13. Φαρίης, the land of the Pharos, i.e., Alexandria and the Delta; a poetic hyperbole indicating that the duke's power and renown range widely outside his specific administrative sphere. Cf. H2.2; and E. Bernand, *Inscriptions métriques de l'Egypte gréco-romaine* (Paris 1969) 73.2 (of a Lycopolitan). Nonnus used it in his epigram on himself (*AP* IX 198).

β **1.** See E. Livrea, ed., *Blemyomachia* (*P.Berol.* 5003) (Meisenheim am Glan 1978) 11–15; L. S. B. MacCoull and L. Koenen, "Papyrus fragments from the monastery of Phoebammon," *Proc. XVI intl.congr.papyrol.* (Chico, Calif. 1981) 491–498; R. T. Updegraff, "A study of the Blemmyes" (Diss., Brandeis University 1978). It would appear that the codex containing the Blemmyomachia poem came, not from "a tomb" at Thebes (Livrea, p. 1), but from the monastery of Phoebammon, mentioned in *P.Cair.Masp.* III 67299.51, if this can be identified with the Theban house and not with one in the Antinoë area. On the campaign of Narses against the Blemmyes, under Justinian, cf. Livrea, p. 13 with n. 19 and the literature there cited. Antaeopolis had been sacked by the Blemmyes early in the sixth century, in connection with a notorious case of suspected paganism (Gnosticism?): *P.Cair.Masp.* I 67004.9 (petition to Duke Athanasius), cf. *P.Cair.Masp.* I 67009 x 18 (with Saracens on r 22). The inhabitants of the area could well hope for deliverance from a real threat.[73]

2, 4. For rhetoric along these lines, cf. *P.Cair.Masp.* I 67089 r B, analyzed by Bell, "An Egyptian village," pp. 27–28, esp. lines 6, 8–11.

5. Obviously this Callinicus is not the Duke praised by Dioscorus in H5 and elsewhere; this villain and his colleague Conon cannot be identified from the papyri but perhaps were extortionate pagarchs of a type with which Dioscorus was already all too familiar.

<table>
<tr><td>H9. Encomium on an unnamed duke
of the Thebaid.</td><td style="text-align:right">P.Cair.Masp. I 67097 v D</td></tr>
</table>

Θήβη πᾶσα χόρευσον, εἰρήνην δέχου·
οὐ γὰρ θεωρήσεις κακουργικὴν ἔτι,
οὐ βαρβάρων δέος, φιλοπραγμόνων κρίσιν.
πάντη γὰρ εἰρήνη θεόπνευστος ῥέει.
5 ὁ γὰρ στρατηγός, οὐ ξένος παρ[ί]σταται
. . . . ατιω[
. . . .]ς μέγας συνίστωρ †αθαμας ης,
ὁ τοῦ Κυρίλλου καὶ Κομήτου τῶν πάνυ,

73. Compare the testament (*P.Cair.Masp.* II 67151; see Chapter 3) in which the testator leaves money in his will to rescue prisoners of the Blemmyes; see H.-R. Hagemann, *Die Stellung der Piae Causae nach justinianischem Rechte* (Basel 1953) 65–70; R. T. Updegraff, "A study of the Blemmyes," (Diss., Brandeis University 1978) p. 152.

οἳ καὶ κυβερνῆται μέγιστοι πελα{σ}τικῶν.
10 εἴ τις δυνήσεται ἀριθμεῖν ἀστέρας
ἢ τοῖς κυάθοις τῆς θαλάττης ῥεύματα,
ναί που πάντως κἀγὼ δυνήσομαι μετρεῖν
τὰς ἀρετὰς σοῦ, δέσποτα. εἰ δὲ συνγνώμην ἔχω,
κέλευσον ὕδωρ ἐμβαλέσθαι τῷ [
15 ἡ γὰρ θάλαττα σῶν ἀρετῶν [πε]ριώσι[ος.
νίκη μεθ᾿ ὑμῶν εὐμενὴς ἔποιτ᾿ ἀεί
χρόνιος ἀμυθήτοις ἑορταῖς ἀφθόνως.
ἀεὶ κυβερνῶν ἀκριβῶς τὴν ὁλκάδα,
τὴν ἀστυμφέλικτον καλὴν ἐπαρχείαν,
20 τῷ σῷ ὄρεξον οἰκέτῃ ὄλβου χεῖρα.

1s cf. 3,9s   4 cf. 4β 3   7 Αθανασιος? Keyd   10–13 cf. 5,43–46   13 an δεσποτα delendum?   15 cf. 2,27; 6,15   16 cf. Menand. Epitr. fr. 11 (616)   20 cf. 5,62

Let the whole Thebaid dance and welcome peace; for you shall not behold evildoing any more, nor the terror of the barbarians, nor the judgment of the corrupt. For God-inspired peace is shed abroad everywhere. For the Duke has come, not as a stranger. . . . you are the great sharer, inflexible (?), successor in every way to Cyril and Comes, who were the great captains of their clients. If someone could number the stars, or measure out the sea's waves with a spoon, then I could measure your excellence, my lord. If I have your leave, order the water to dash against . . . For the sea of your greatness is immense. May generous victory ever follow you, living long and in plenty amidst indescribable festivity. May you ever steer the ship of state aright, the beautiful unshakable eparchy, and stretch out your hand of blessing to one of your household.

3. Cf. the previous poem, H4, β 1–4. For φιλοπράγμων, cf. Romanos, *Cantica*, ed. P. Maas and C. Trypanis (Oxford 1963–1970) 46 pr. I 1.

4. θεόπνευστος, cf. Nonnus *Paraphr.* 1.99, 2.89, 4.2, 10.136.

5. οὐ ξένος: this has been interpreted as expressing wonder at the Egyptian origin of the duke (E. R. Hardy, *The large estates of Byzantine Egypt* [New York 1932] 138; G. Rouillard, *L'administration civile de l'Egypte byzantine*[2] [Paris 1928] 187, 205 n. 4). But the reference is scriptural: Eph. 2:19, not ξένοι or πάροικοι, but συνπολῖται.

7. Maspero emended ἀδάμας, which makes sense and is explicable by the δ/θ interchange deriving from Coptic interference: Gignac, *Grammar of the Greek papyri* I, pp. 96–97; cf. 85–86.[74]

8. The repeated reference to Cyril and Comes, plus the import of line 3, might incline one to think of Athanasius as the recipient of this poem as well.

74. Cyril uses ἀδάμας of Christ; Lampe, *A patristic Greek lexicon*, s.v.

9. Compare line 18, and *P.Cair.Masp.* I 67089 r B1. Dioscorus might possibly have known Plato's *Phaedrus*; could he have been aware of Alcaeus 208? Specifically for κυβερνήτης, cf. Serapion of Thmuis, *Euchologion* 7.1 (ed. F. X. Funk, *Didascalia et constitutiones apostolorum* 2 [Paderborn 1905, reprint Turin 1959] 164); of Christ, οἰκόνομον καὶ κ. καὶ σωτῆρα.[75]

"The great captains of their clients": for an old-fashioned view of patronage and clientage in Late Antique Egypt (as in Hardy, *Large estates*, pp. 22–24, and Rouillard, *L'administration civile*, 9–15, 182–184), see A. H. M. Jones, *The Later Roman Empire* (Norman, Okla. 1964) 775–781. Justinian's Edict 13 was much more concerned with the collection of the grain *embole* than with attempting to regulate the relations of patrons and clients. For a revised view of the *oikos*, see J. Gascou, "Les grands domaines, la cité et l'Etat en Egypte byzantine (5ᵉ, 6ᵉ, et 7ᵉ s.)," *Trav.etMém.* 9 (1985) 1–90. The "great house" provided the state with *phoros*, revenue. The best way to see this world is to read the documentary papyri (in both Greek and Coptic), not to construct theories about "feudalization."[76]

Patronage in Late Antique Egypt is a subject that requires thorough reexamination. In such an agrarian realm, the individual producer's relation to each of four loci of power must be evaluated: to the central government, to the patron or landlord, to the church, and to the kindred. The areas of these four circles overlap in complex ways.

What was principally emphasized in earlier approaches to the subject was the double aspect of "privatization": first, the growth of a colonate in which immobility, attachment to the land, was originally a prime determinant, and the subsequent growth of a new definition of the social condition of the person; and second, the assumption by landowners of functions previously thought of as belonging to the imperial government at Constantinople and its agents. Every agricultural producer in Egypt grew some grain that went to feed the capital city, via the *aisia embole*, the "auspicious" *embole* or annual shipment. (Modern critics have seen the epithet as ironic; but Dioscorus, who used it often, took it directly from the text of Justinian's Edict 13:4.1, and the classically educated chancery writers were not being ironic.) The collection and shipment of this grain was seen to at the most basic local level; hence, the importance, where it existed, of the right of *autopragia*, or self-responsible collection, and the freedom from being col-

75. On Christ the κυβερνήτης in the Christian East, see R. Murray, *Symbols of church and kingdom* (Cambridge 1975) 249–253, cf. 168 n. 2.

76. See now P. Crone, *Roman, provincial, and Islamic law* (Cambridge, England, 1987); cf. L. S. B. MacCoull, "Notes on the social structure of late antique Aphrodito," *BSAC* 26 (1984) 73–75 with n. 21.

lected from twice over by the (imperial) pagarch. How farmer-producers became "clients" as opposed to, or as well as, simply tenants, renters, is the question.

Scholars have begun examining patronage with the term *coloni adscripticii* in the law codes; its Greek calque, ἐναπόγραφος γεωργός, is attested in the papyri from the 460s, and recent work has tried carefully to define its meaning.[77] (In fact, the Greek term and the development that preceded it may actually antedate the Latin.) The fifth century saw the growth of stability to an *idia* or place of origin in which a farmer was "enrolled."[78] This bookkeeping, in its turn, was done in order to facilitate the *embole*. In any case, colonate and clientage differ. The latter is a social contract; the former, a civil status relevant to tax liability. Being an adscript had to do with your relationship as a taxpayer to the central government, whereas having a patron involved you in a relationship of quasi-*paramone* ("being near by") with an *oikos* (a noble clan and its domain), an entity that furnished administrative capability on the spot.[79]

Churches and monasteries also functioned as landlords, especially through the medium of the heritable land lease or *emphyteusis*, with its provisions for improvement of the property (paralleling the entrepreneurial activities of estate clients who improved their lands with subcontracted labor). And underlying every other economic relationship in Egypt was the inescapable bond of physical kinship. The Christianization of Egypt had involved an effort to cut across the ties of the stiflingly close Egyptian extended family by substituting other ties, e.g., those of anachoresis and the "monastic family." By the sixth century, we see the conflicting claims of these two centers of power (e.g., the case of the novices Anoup and Julius, Chapter 2). In Late Antique Egypt, it was conceivably possible to be in the

77. Extremely helpful is the work of J.-M. Carrié, "Figures du 'colonat' dans les papyrus d'Egypte: lexique, contextes," *Atti XVII congr.intl.papirol.* (Naples 1984) 939–948, and his own work and the literature cited p. 939 n. 1. See also J. G. Keenan, "On law and society in Byzantine Egypt," *ZPE* 17 (1975) 237–250, and his study of social mobility in Egypt to appear in *ANRW*; also MacCoull, "Patronage and the social order in Coptic Egypt," *Egitto e storia antica* (conference, Bologna, September 1987).

78. See the list of *enapographoi* up to that time by J. G. Keenan, "The names Flavius and Aurelius as status designations," *ZPE* 11 (1973) 55–56, n. 96. They seem to be involved in transactions of renting irrigation machinery and of surety; idem, "On P.Oxy. XXVII 2479," *ZPE* 38 (1980) 246–248 (cf., in Coptic, P. Berol. 11349 in Chapter 2: hire of a *mechane* and field damage by unruly animals).

79. *Oikos* and *phoros* are elucidated by Gascou, "Les grands domaines, la cité et l'Etat en Egypte byzantine (5ᵉ, 6ᵉ, et 7ᵉ s.)," *Trav.etMém.* 9 (Paris 1985) 1–90. One hears this phenomenon attested to even today: "That man belongs to one of my villages," a Coptic nobleman will say.

position of owing an obligation—financial, social, or both—to your uncle
the monastic *oikonomos*, who was simultaneously the collector of your
farm's rent and the accountant of the grain collection for that indiction.

10. As well as using this as a poetic cliché (as in H5.43), Dioscorus is
possibly also alluding to Gen. 15:5 (and Hebr. 11:12), on the seed of Abraham.

17. Cf. the remarks of J. G. Keenan on the yearly calendar of Aphrodito
and Antinoë (in an article to appear)—the recurring round of ecclesiastical
and secular festivity that shaped one's world.

18. On the "ship of state" (Pl. *Rep.* 488A–E; Arist. *Polit.* 1276B), cf.
Cod.Just. III.1 14.1; Theodoret *De prov.* 2, 7 (PG 83.576AB, 676B–D). As
Dioscorus calls the ship ὁλκάς, a merchantman (cf. Nonnus *Dion.* 1.66), he
may be alluding to the grain fleet, for whose safe operation the Duke was
responsible.

19. ἀστυμφέλικτον, cf. Nonnus *Paraphr.* 3.84 (of faith), 10.1, 18.48 (of
Scripture prophecy). This line is a beautiful idealized term for a desired
style of rule, the place of safe borders. For the thought behind it, cf. Hebr.
12:28a.

H28. Anacreontic.   *P.Cair.Masp.* I 67097 v F
(See Figure 10)

ἀεὶ θέλω χορεύειν,
ἀεὶ θέλω λυρίζειν.
γεραρὴν λόγοις ἑορτὴν
ἀνα[βά]λλομαι λυρίζειν.

5 θέλγουσίν με αἱ Βά⟨κ⟩χαι
  α . . . υ[
  [
  [

  ὅταν πίννω τὸν οἶνον,
10 εὕδουσιν αἱ μέριμναι·
τί μοι πόνων, τί μοι γόων,
τί μοι μέλει μεριμνῶν;

  στρατηγὸν νέον ἔραμαι,
  ποθοβλήτην Ἡρακλέα,
15 δαμάζοντα τοὺς λέοντας·
ἀεὶ τὰς πόλεις σαῶσαι.

    carmina Anacreontei generis; cf. Cr l.c. 664–66.— 1 θελω supra χαιρω |
cf. Anacreont. 49,10 (R) παλιν θελω χορευειν   2 post 2 et 4 bini versus

excidisse videntur **5** leg. Cr **9–12** = Anacreont. 45,1–4 **12** μέριμναι Π
14 ποθόβλητον coni. Ma

> I want always to dance, I want always to play the lyre. I strike up my
> lyre to praise the solemn festival with my words. The Bacchae have cast a
> spell on me. . . . When I drink wine, my cares go to sleep. What do I care for
> pains and groans, what do I care for troubles? I love a young soldier, a
> Herakles with longing eyes, a lion tamer; ever one to save our cities.

For comments on this poem, see MacCoull, "Dioscorus and the dukes."
One can almost see what Dioscorus's young soldier would have looked
like: a figure in cataphract's mail, with the great dark eyes of an encaustic
portrait. This sixth-century *skolion* is unique in its way, using the universal
form of the drinking song (beginning with a straight classical borrowing) to
voice some of the deepest concerns of Byzantine Egyptian society. If the
verse as we have it was ever actually sung, its background would have
been one of the opulence necessary to the concept of the noble life as lived
by Coptic *dynatoi:* a summer palace or great villa, an Egyptian equivalent of
Qusayr Amrah. The patronage feasts of the great families of Antinoë (and
Aphrodito, and Oxyrhynchus) must have taken place in appropriate architectural surroundings (unfortunately not yet discovered by excavation),
accompanied by the Greek and Coptic equivalent of the lost art of the
Sasanian court dinner minstrels. It is telling that the most important deed
for which the νέος στρατηγός is praised is "saving the cities." Beautifying
and restoring one's city was the most honorable, honor-conferring, and
generally splendid thing a Late Antique nobleman could do. And this poem
seems to be the last drinking song to come out of Egypt (already sadly
noted by Crönert in *Gnomon* 2 [1926] 663–666). The Moslem conquest was
to put a damper on such pleasures, and the civilizing work of Nestor
Gianaclis, the Alexandrian Greek who single-handedly revived the Egyptian vineyards in the early twentieth century, was to be short-lived.

Dioscorus's source is Anacreontea 45 (ed. K. Preisendanz, Teubner,
Leipzig 1912), with echoes of 38 and 39. The parallels are laid out by
Crönert in *Gnomon* 2 (1926) 664–666.[80] Th. Nissen, *Die byzantinischen
Anakreonteen* (SB. Bayer.Akad.d.Wiss., Munich 1940) treats George Gram-
maticus and Sophronius, but does not mention Dioscorus (but cf. p. 16 on
the name Colluthus, so characteristic of the Antinoë region).

It has often been noticed that Dioscorus's Greek-Coptic glossary (H. I.
Bell and W. E. Crum, "A Greek-Coptic glossary," *Aegyptus* 6 [1925] 177–226)

80. See B. Baldwin, "Dioscorus of Aphrodito and the Anacreontea," *Museum Philo-
logicum Londiniense* 8 (1987) 13–14.

contains many words for wine and drinking-song terminology, most famously (*P.Lond.* V 1674v = 1821) lines 250–252 Ἀνακρέων ⲡⲙⲉⲑⲩⲥⲧⲏⲥ ⲉⲧϫⲟⲩ ⲡⲡⲟⲓⲏ[ⲧ]ⲏⲥ, "Anacreon, the drunkard that sings, the poet." Similarly, lines 245–249, 260–262. See Bell, "An Egyptian village," p. 30; and Baldwin, "Dioscorus of Aphrodito," pp. 327–331. For the Sasanian drinking song, see M. Boyce, "The Parthian *gosan* and the Iranian minstrel tradition," *JRAS* 3d ser. 68 (1957) 10–45.

5. For θέλγω, cf. Nonnus, *Paraphr.* 3.146, 10.97.

14. On ποθοβλήτην (noticed by Crönert in *Gnomon* 2 [1926] 664; Maspero's correction is unnecessary), cf. *P.Cair.Masp.* II 67184 r 10; Nonnus *Paraphr.* 9.124, *Dion.* 34.20. The sense is active, not passive.

The Herakles figure in Coptic art (cf. M. Simon, *Hercule et le christianisme* [Paris and Strasbourg 1955]) is a well-known one, especially assimilable to the figure(s) of David or Samson wrestling with lions. Examples are the Coptic Museum frieze (Zaloscer, *Kunst im christlichen Ägypten*, Taf. 52, 54); the Brooklyn Museum textile and bronze;[81] and the Sheikh Zoueïde mosaic (E. Bernand, *Inscriptions métriques de l'Egypte gréco-romaine* [Paris 1969] no. 122). In Dioscorus's own poetry, cf. H21.23; H2.21. Cf. Bernand no. 82.2 (4th c.): τὸν σοφὸν ἐν Μούσαις καὶ νέον Ἡρακλέα.

Also contained in *P.Cair.Masp.* I 67097v (below fr. F) is Dioscorus's *chairetismos* addressed to the emperor Justin II; for a full text and commentary, see L. S. B. MacCoull, "The imperial *chairetismos* of Dioscorus of Aphrodito," *JARCE* 18 (1981, appeared 1984) 43–46.

The following seven poems bear no evidence of their dates, either internal or external. They are assumed to belong to Dioscorus's Antinoë period, sometime between A.D. 566 and 573.

Poem on a monastic profession.   *P.Cair.Masp.* II 67182
(See Figure 10)

☧ Πῇ πόθεν Ἀδρι[α]νοῖο τέō(υ) γενετ[ῆ]ρ[ο]ς ἀρί[στ]ō(υ)
εὐσεβί[η]ς ἀλύτοιο δικαιοσύνη δε[. .]θεσμ[ο]ί
ὃς χρόνον ἀστυμφέλικτον ἀρεῖον . . . . . αλη . . . ν
ἐξετέλεσσεν ἀέθλον ὅσον βίον [ἀ]γγελιῶνα.
5 Ἀκτεανοὺς μὴ θραύσας, ἀπεχ[θ]αίρων ἐπὶ μύθοις,
        κάλλιστε
γείνεο καὶ σ[υ],μέγιστε, βοηθὸς ἄμμιν ὀπάων.

81. Textiles: D. Thompson, *Coptic textiles in the Brooklyn Museum* (Brooklyn 1971) no. 22 (pp. 54–55); bronze: Brooklyn Museum, *Late Egyptian and Coptic art* (Brooklyn 1943) pl. 25.

> How and whence, from Hadrian, your excellent father, came justice and
> the bonds of indissoluble piety, (for you) who (go to) a better, an unshak-
> able life, having achieved such a prize as the angelic life? Without ruining
> the poor, as your enemies might say, may you too, O greatest (fairest) one,
> become a helper and comrade to us.

This poem celebrates the entrance of a young man of Antinoë into the
monastic life.

1. It is uncertain whether "Hadrian" is actually the aspirant's father's
name or is a poetic way of designating, as forebear, the founder of Antinoë.
For Hadrians at Antinoë/Aphrodito, cf. Hadrian son of Abraham, soldier,
originally from Antaeopolis, in *P.Lond.* V 1671.5, 1844, *P.Flor.* III 280.12,
P.Cair.Masp. I 67052.4, a contemporary of Dioscorus's father Apollos;
Hadrian the priest, *P.Flor.* III 297.315 (cf. Abba Hadrian in *SPP* XX 248.3,
from Antinoë); Hadrian the goldsmith, *P.Flor.* III 297.126. A Count Hadrian
is mentioned in *PSI* VII 836.3 (no provenance); *P.Lond.* V 1761 is from the
Hermopolite, while 1788 and 1802 also have no provenance. In *SB* I 1896,
one Konnos son of Hadrian inscribed his name in the Valley of the Kings, at
an unknown date. Could this "son of Hadrian" be thus a contemporary of
Dioscorus himself, entering a monastery in his forties?

2. Cf. H6.6 (where θέσμοι can be restored at the end of the line); and
εὐσεβία will recur in H3.69 and *P.Cair.Masp.* II 67184 r B 4 (cf. H1.r 12).

3. Cf. H9.19 and Nonnus *Paraphr.* 3.84, 10.1, 18.48. Robert was wrong
(*Comptes rendus de l'Académie de Belles-Lettres* [1971] 597–619) to state that
this word is never used in a Christian context.

4. The classic locution for the monastic life is of course the βίος ἀγγελικός; see K. S. Frank, ΑΓΓΕΛΙΚΟΣ ΒΙΟΣ. *Begriffsanalytische u. Begriffs-
geschichtliche Untersuchung zum "Engelgleichen Leben" im frühen Mönchtum*
(Münster 1964). Compare the Vatican ostracon (unpublished) no. 19901,
ⲣ ϩⲁⲑⲏ ⲙⲉⲛ ⲙ̄ⲡⲁϣⲁϫⲉ ⲛ̄ⲉⲗⲁⲭ / (ⲓⲥⲧⲟⲥ) †ⲁⲥⲡⲁⲍⲉ ⲁⲩⲱ †ⲡⲣⲟⲥⲕⲩⲛⲉⲓ
ⲙ̄ⲡⲉⲧⲛ̄ⲁⲅⲅⲉⲗⲟⲥ ⲛ̄ⲁⲅⲁⲑⲟⲥ ⲙ̄ⲛ̄ⲡⲉⲧⲛ̄ⲥⲟⲟⲩϩ ⲉϩⲟⲩⲛ ⲛ̄ⲕⲟⲓⲛⲱⲛⲓⲕ[ⲁ ⲉⲧϣ-
ⲟⲟⲡ ⲙ̄ⲛ̄ⲛⲁⲅⲅⲉⲗⲟⲥ ("Before my humblest discourse I greet and do obei-
sance to your good angel and those in the angelic congregation"). (I am
grateful to Dr. Rosario Pintaudi and Professor P. J. Sijpesteijn for allowing
me to see a photograph of this text.) Angelic continence was to be striven
for (Chrysostom *De virg.* 11.1).

5. Perhaps a reference to the criticism of *anachoresis* as a way of
evading civic and patronal responsibilities; see Brown, *Making of late antiquity*, pp. 85–86, 93–94. (Could there have been an Egyptian Rutilius Nama-
tianus? Zosimus puns in derogatory fashion on notions of "poverty" in his
antimonk remarks in *Hist.nov.* 5.23.)

6. An allusion to the "second birth" of monastic profession, and to the role of the ascetic as friend and intercessor.

On entrances into the monastic life at Aphrodito/Antinoë, see the Coptic transactions written by Dioscorus in *P.Cair.Masp.* II 67176r, published in L. S. B. MacCoull, "A Coptic cession of land by Dioscurus of Aphrodito," *II intl. congr. coptic studies* (Rome 1985) 159–166; and *P.Cair. Masp.* III 67353r, reproduced in Chapter 2. These transactions record a cession of land and an arbitration made by the family of Julius son of Sarapammon, Anoup son of Apollo, and their mother Mesiane, before the two men enter the monastic life at Dioscorus's family's second house, the monastery of Pharoou. (Cf. M. Krause, "Zur Möglichkeit von Besitz im apotaktischen Mönchtum Ägyptens," *II intl.congr.copt.stud.* [Rome 1985] 121–134.) Could this poem have conceivably been addressed to either Anoup or Julius? The cession in 67176 is dated 28 October 569; the verso (with an *apokeryxis* draft) of 67353 is dated 12 November 569. No sure identification can, however, be made.

Encomium (epithalamium?) on Zacharias   *P.Cair.Masp.* II 67184
the *silentiarius*.

<pre>
(B)   . . . οι . . . . [χ]ρόνον. υ. . . . . [ε]σσιν
      [Ο]ὕ[τω]ς [ἀ]ε[ὶ ζήσεις, καὶ τέον κ]λέο[ς] ο[ὕπο]τ᾽ ὀλε[ῖτ]αι
      α . . . . ν[. . .]ν ἀκούεις,
      ἐκ γέν[νη]ς ἅτε θάλλ[ει]ς ε[ὐσε]βίης φρονεούσης·
                                                  πιστᾶος
5   ὡς γενέτηρ ἐφύλασσε θ[έ]μιτ[ος] θέσφατα παντός.
      Σὴν ἀρετὴν ποθέουσιν ἀθάνατοι [ἠδέ τ]ε ἄνδρες
      ἐκ σέο μειλιχίοις . . . ρη . . . . . υθοτ . . ειαις
      Λωίον ἐστὶ σέθεν παναοίδιμον οὔνομα μέλψαι
                            η . . . α   . ει . ειν
      ἔκτοθεν αὐτὸν ῞Ομηρον ἐπὶ χρ[ό]νον ἀκ[ο]ύσαι μολπῆς.
10   Νύμφιον ἄλλον ἴδον σε, ποθοβληέντα [γ]ε (?) πάντων,
      τῆς π[ολυκαλ]λίσ[τη]ς ἐ[γκ]υμόνα καλλιοπίης,
      [ἴ]κελ[ο]ν ῾Ηρακλῆϊ μένος καὶ θάρσος [ἰδέ]σθαι.
      ῎Αρεος ἐν πραπίδεσσι νεοῖς ἐνίκησας ἀέ[θλ]ους,
      ῥίμφα νόθους ἐδά[μ]ασσας ἐναντίον α . . . . λ . . . ν
15   [Τοσσα]τ[ί]ην σοφίην πόθεν ἔλλαχες, [ἀν]δρῶν ἄριστ[ος];
      ῞Ω γένος ἀφρά[σ]τοιο νοὸς κα . ν. ο . . . .
      . . . . . . υμετ[ερ]ῆς . . . . οσον παναθη[. . . . .
</pre>

Verso.

<pre>
                   ερσαιον
ρ . . . . ες ὁμόφρονος εὐρπατερέιης
</pre>

Τ[ούνε]κ' ἀεὶ [ζ]ῷοις καὶ ἀπείρατον ἐς χρόνον ἐλθοῖς   πυριζε[
σὺν τεκ[έεσσι φι]λοῖσι (sic), ἄμα ζαθέα σέο νύμφῃ.   στρυγιζ[
. . . . λ. . . . ε . ν ἐ[νί]κ[η]σες [ἀ]έ[θλ]ιος, ἐκτὸς ἀέ[λ]λω[ν].
5 Θάλλε μοι, εἰσέτι θάλλε, ξένον πα[ ]θεοντ' ἀτι[τάλλω]ν, τ[. .]καλ[λ
ὡς κεν ἴδω καὶ ἐγὼ πεφιλημένα νή[πι]α τέκνα.
        λυκαβαν. μ . . . θοντα τελεσσ[αι]
Ἐν χ[θ]ονὶ παμβασιλῆος ὅλον χρ[όνον] . . . .
[Ἤλυθον οὐκ] ὄλβον διζ[ή]μεν[ος οἱάπερ ἄλλοι],
ἀλλ[ὰ πόρον βιότοιο καὶ υἱήεσσιν ἐμοῖσι],
10 μὴ σφέ[ας ὀλλυμένους ἀέκων βλεφάροισι νοήσω].

  So may you live forever, and your glory shall never fade. . . . just as you flourish, being from a stock that bears piety in mind; as your father guarded the divine decrees of right and faith. Gods and men long for your excellence, from you in gracious . . . It is better to sing your all-praise-worthy name, let alone to hear Homer himself for a time of song. I have seen you as another bridegroom, looked at with longing by everyone, big with the loveliness of a most beautiful voice, resembling Herakles in strength and bold to look upon. You have surpassed the combats of Ares in your most recent deeds, having quickly vanquished the bastards. . . . Whence have you got such great wisdom, O best of men? O descendant of inexpressible . . . of like-minded nobility. So may you live forever and reach a boundless length of life, with your dear children and your divine wife. . . . Running for the prize, you have won, free from storms. Flourish and again flourish, cherishing the stranger, so I too may see my dear little children. (Having) spent a whole year in the land of the Emperor, I have come, not like others, seeking riches, but rather seeking a livelihood for my sons, lest I see them with my own eyes when they are perishing.

  The papyrus originally bore a list of the names of the four Aphroditans who went to Constantinople in 551: Dioscorus, Senouthos (representing Kyros), Apollos, and Callinicus. Dioscorus seems to have kept the papyrus and reused it for poetic work fairly soon after his return. Cf. *P.Cair.Masp.* I 67032.9–14.

  5. θέσφατα, cf. Nonnus *Paraphr.* 5.154, 7.160 (of Scripture prophecy). Read Dioscorus's own correction, πίστα(ος) = πίστεως.

  This verse proclaims once again that defense of the faith is the first job of a late Roman official and the prime ornament of a family tree.

  6ff. Crönert in *Gnomon* 2 (1926) 659–660 noticed the acrostic of *silentiarius*, and connected it with the ζαχαρ initials of (67315) H5.20–24 to identify one Zacharias the *silentiarius* as the recipient. The title *silentiarius* is otherwise not found at Antinoë or Aphrodito.

  9. Dioscorus's praise of Homer; cf. H20.4; H12 B 4.

  10. ποθοβλήεντα, cf. H28.14, here passive, not active, in sense.

  14. Who "the bastards" may have been is not known.

16. Cf. H6.1.

v7. If this line refers to Dioscorus's trip to Constantinople, perhaps the poem might thus be dated early, to soon after his return and possibly before his move to Antinoë. But the allusion is not a specific one.

Birthday poem.   *P.Cair.Masp.* II 67178

Νεῖλον

    † Σεῖο γενεθλίαδος ῥοδοε[ιδέ]ες ἔστεψ[α]ν ὧραι,
    καὶ χρονίοις νιφάδε[σ]σι νέ[φη] ποτίζειν χθόνα πᾶσαν·
5 [τ]ερπ[ω]λὴν ἀσκ[οῦσι]ν ἀ[εὶ κατ]ὰ γαῖαν ἐγείρειν.
    [Θ]άλλε [μ]οι, εἰσέτι θάλλεις εὐδμήτοισι μελάθροις,
    σὺν τεκέεσσι φίλοισιν, ἀριζήλῃ σέο νύμφῃ.
    'Ες χρόνον ἄ[φ]θιτον ἔ[λ]θοις ἐν πρυτάνοισιν ἀνώγων,
    ὡς σπόρος αυ..τε..σ.α. [β]έβ[ρι]θος ἄνθος ἀρούρης
10 φύσας ἀριπρ[ε]πέα κρατερὸν λόχον ἠδὲ καὶ ξανθὸν
    τοῖον σ.σ.......ἤργρατον γόνον ἔλλ[α]χε κιρρὸν
    με..ε σῖτον [ἔτικ]τεν ἀεὶ ξανθὸν εὐρέα γαῖα.
    Τούνεκά [μιν καλ]έω σε φερέσβιον ἀγρονομήων·
    ἀγρόνομο[ι γελόωσι]ν ἐπ' ἐλπίδι γαῖαν ὀχεῦει[ν]
15 α........ π[ο]λύαινος ἀεὶ σ[.....
        ]ἀρισ[τ]όγ.[
    τ[.....
    [πιτ]νόεσσα τελεσσ.......ιην πολ[υ]κάρπου
    [....]οσα...........[χα]ριεντι (?) Φαῶφι
    [........ χ]άριν..ἔρας ἔλλαχες ἐγγύ[θι]....
20 [.............................]
    Οὐ χθὼν πᾶσα ǀ, θάλασσα ǀ μόλις πέλεν ǀ ἄξια ῥίζης.

B

εὐρὺν

    Ζώοιτέ μοι ὕπατ[οι], ǀ παναπείρονα ǀ ἐς χρόνον ἔλθοις,

      τες

    σὴν Θήβην ἰθύνον ǀ ἅμα δρηστῆρσιν ἀρίστοι,
    Καλλινίκῳ γεράρῳ κ[α]ὶ ǀ Δ[ω]ρο[θέῳ προφερίστ]οι[ς] (?)
5 .ατα [.................... Δωρ[ο]θέοιο
    [..........] φορέον[τος] ǀ ἀεὶ στέφος, ὄμματα νίκ[ης (?)].
    Οὕτω σέο δρηστῆρες ὁμώνυμοι ǀ σῶν ἀρετάων·
    νίκην ἀμφιέπεις, περικάλλεα μῆ ǀ τιν ἄρι[στος],
    [ἀ]κλινέω[ς], κ[άλλι]στε, κατ' ὀρφναίην ǀ.........

The rosy Hours crowned your birthday, and the clouds watered the whole earth with timely showers; they practice ever to arouse delight along the Nile (throughout the land). Flourish and again flourish in your well-built halls, with your dear children and your admirable wife. May you reach an imperishable time, giving commands among the councilors, like seed heavy with . . . , the flower of the field, having brought forth a splendid, strong, fair-haired offspring; like the . . . has got tawny fruit, (so) the wide earth has always given birth to the fair grain. Wherefore I call you the farmers' lifesaver: the farmers laugh with hope to make their land fertile . . . ever much-praised . . . pine-wooded . . . rich in crops . . . in smiling Phaophi. . . . The whole earth and the sea are hardly worthy of your noble descent. Long live the *consulares;* may you reach an all-boundless length of life, guiding your Thebaid aright, together with your excellent co-workers, old Callinicus and Dorotheos, the outstanding ones, . . . ever bearing the crown, the eyes of victory. So your colleagues are named like their virtues: you keep company with Victory, the beautiful skill of the best (?), and, fairest one, you unswervingly (hold fast?) against the darkness. . . .

3. Cf. H25.3.

4. A literary reference, literally true only in the coastal strip of Egypt and parts of the Delta, but reminiscent of Ps. 64:10–12.

5. The Nile Flood, triggered by the rains in Abyssinia; cf. H10 B 1, the inundation.

8. Cf. H17.1–2 with comments.

9. An echo of Ps. 64:14, with Cant. 2:1.

10–12. ξάνθον . . . κῖρρον: cf. Dioscorus's glossary, *P.Lond.* V 1821.213.

13. φερέσβιον: cf. H1.1.

18. As the wine harvest usually took place in Thoth (September), Phaophi (October) marked the beginning of pressing the grapes for wine making—a pleasing image.

B1. In Dioscorus's poetry, cf. H4.3, and HS10 r 14.

2. On *consulares,* see now R. S. Bagnall, A. Cameron, S. R. Schwartz, and K. A. Worp, *Consuls of the Later Roman Empire* (Atlanta 1987).

4. The mention of Callinicus and Dorotheos ties this poem together with H21, H5, H13, H14, and H17. As Callinicus is called γεραρός, he may be past his term of office.

6. ὄμματα νίκης: "the apple of Victory's eye."

8. Perhaps restore ἀρί[στων.

9. A verb with the meaning "oppose" must have been lost here. A poignant foreshadowing of what was to happen to the polite culture of Dioscorus's world after the catastrophe of 641 and its aftermath.

The games of ancient Greece. *P.Cair.Masp.* II 67188.6–10

Τέσσ[α]ρες ἀγῶνες ἐν ῾Ε[λλ]άδι, τέσσαρες ἱροί,
οἱ δύο μὲν θνητῶν, οἱ δ[ύο δ]' ἀ[θα]νάτων·
Ζηνός, Λητ[ο]ίδα[ο], Παλ[α]ί[μο]νος, Ἀρχεμόροιο.

$$\overset{\delta\epsilon}{\overset{\cdot}{\mathring{a}}\theta\lambda a\,[\tau]\hat{\omega}\nu\,\kappa\acute{o}\tau\iota\nu o\varsigma,\,\mu\mathring{\eta}\lambda[a],\,\sigma\acute{\epsilon}\lambda\iota[\nu]a,\,\pi\acute{\iota}\tau\upsilon\varsigma,}$$
$$10\quad {}^{\prime}\mathrm{O}\lambda[\acute{\upsilon}]\mu[\pi]\iota a,\,\Pi\acute{\upsilon}\theta\iota a,\,{}^{\prime\prime}\mathrm{I}\sigma\theta[\mu]\iota a,\,[\mathrm{N}]\epsilon\mu\acute{\epsilon}a.$$

Four games there were in Hellas, four sacred events: two of men, two of gods. They were (the games) of Zeus, of Apollo, of Palaemon, and of Archemoros. Their prizes were the wild olive, the bay, the wild celery, and the pine: the Olympian, Pythian, Isthmian, and Nemean games.

9. For pine as the Nemean garland, and the rest, cf. Plutarch *Quaest. Conviv.* 676F; Euphorion, fr. 84 (Powell and B. A. Van Groningen, *Euphorion* [Amsterdam 1977] 153–156); Callimachus fr. 59 (Pfeiffer). An interesting witness to Dioscorus's knowledge of Hellenistic poetry.

10. The games are mentioned in the official, traditional order. The names of the tutelary god or hero and of the prize also occur in the same, corresponding order.

Dioscorus may have been prompted to compose this epigram, not only as a classical mnemonic, but also by awareness that the Olympian Games had been celebrated at Antioch as recently as A.D. 507 (and the circumstances of their cancellation in A.D. 520; Malalas 396.4–9, and esp. 417.5–8). Dating by Olympiads continued to be used in the work of Monophysite historians: the Chronicon Paschale, Jacob of Edessa, Elias of Nisibis, and even Michael the Syrian and the Armenian Samuel of Ani (cf. V. Grumel, *La chronologie* [Paris 1958] 211–212). Could Dioscorus also have been inspired by a small self-referent pun, inasmuch as the Dioscuri were presidents of the Olympic Games (Pind. *Ol.* 3.35; D. L. Page, *Further Greek epigrams* [Cambridge 1981] 35)?

Encomium? *P.Cair.Masp.* III 67338

$${}^{\prime}\mathrm{A}\nu\tau a\hat{\iota}o\varsigma\,\tau o\lambda\upsilon\pi\ldots\sigma\iota\,\pi o\lambda\upsilon\delta\acute{a}\kappa[\tau\upsilon\lambda o\varsigma]$$

$$\acute{o}\tau\tau\iota\,\chi\rho\acute{\upsilon}\sigma o\nu\,\mathring{a}\pi\epsilon\acute{\iota}\rho o\nu a\,\kappa o\iota\nu o\beta\acute{\iota}o\iota\sigma\iota\nu\,\acute{\epsilon}\theta[\eta\kappa\epsilon\varsigma]$$
$$\theta\epsilon\sigma\pi\epsilon\sigma\acute{\iota}o\upsilon^{\tau\epsilon}\,\Sigma\epsilon\nu o\acute{\upsilon}\theta o\upsilon\,\Sigma a\beta o\rho\acute{\iota}o\upsilon\,\mu\epsilon\lambda\eta[$$

$${}^{\prime}\mathrm{E}\xi\,\acute{\iota}\epsilon\rho\mathring{\eta}\varsigma\,\mathring{a}\nu o\rho o\acute{\upsilon}\sigma a\varsigma\,\mathring{a}\nu a\iota\mu\acute{a}\kappa\tau o\iota o\,\theta\upsilon\acute{\epsilon}\lambda\lambda\eta\varsigma$$

This papyrus is not, even today, quite so damaged as Maspero made it out to be. After the line beginning ᾽Ανταῖος, the following can be read:

$$\ldots\lambda\epsilon\nu\tau o^{\upsilon}\ldots\ldots\ldots\ldots a\rho\epsilon\tau\acute{\eta}\nu$$
$$\ldots\ldots\eta\epsilon\nu\,\epsilon\upsilon\rho a\ldots\ldots\ldots\ldots$$

and after the line beginning θεσπεσίου can be read:

$$a\mu\eta\tau\eta\varsigma\ldots\ldots\eta\nu\,\pi a\rho o\varsigma\ldots\ldots$$

There are traces of one line above Ἐξ ἱερῆς (this is not a beginning line, as Maspero asserted). Below it can be read:

                . . . . ν εταθη
                . . . . σοιο καί ατρε^θ
                . . . . στι ἀρχεβίη.
                . . . . . . χαλεπού πολυ . . . . ος

[Fold line]
                . . . ιου . . ζης πεφα . . ημεν . . . μύθου θεοῖο
                                ]παμβασιλέος
                           εἰς ἡμᾶς . . . .

As Maspero noticed, the reference is to the eponymous hero of Antaeopolis. (Cf. the Antaeus statue in the Cairo Museum: J. G. Milne, *A history of Egypt under Roman rule*[3] [London 1924] 243.) Antaeus had probably been identified with some form of ancient Egyptian divinity (Wernicke in *RE* I.2340, citing *ZÄS* 20 [1882] 135ff.). πολυδάκτυλος is an Aristotelian word, from the *HA* and *PA*; why it should be applied to the giant of Libya by our poet is unclear.

Maspero also assumed that the Senouthos mentioned by Dioscorus as titulary of a monastery is the great Shenoute of Atripe; I see no reason to doubt this. The monastery of Apa Saborios (Sabouerios) at Aphrodito is known also from *P.Cair.Masp.* I 67002 III 20; 67080.6. "You have settled limitless gold upon the monasteries of Shenoute and Saborios" appears to be praise for a local donor.

The third fragment is the least clear. μύθου θεοῖο and παμβασιλέος would appear to put it in a Christian frame of reference. (μῦθος is Nonnus's favorite word for a Dominical utterance in the *Paraphrasis*.) "You rose up out of the holy, bloodless storm" (fr. 1) may well refer to the storm on the Sea of Galilee, stilled by Christ (I owe this thought to Dr. O. P. Nicholson); cf. Mk. 4:37–41.

How this poem coheres is still to be explained. Perhaps Dioscorus was praising a magnate of Antaeopolis whose distinguished piety was manifested in large donations to (non-Chalcedonian) monastic foundations.

H27. *Ethopoiia* on Apollo with   *P.Cair.Masp.* II 67188v
Hyacinthus and Daphne

    Ἀπόλλω[ν ῾Υ]α[κί]νθο[υ καὶ] Δάφν[η]s ἐπὶ τὸ αὐτὸ
      ε[ἰs] φ[υτὸν] γενομέ[νων.

    ῾Υμεῖs, ὦ ῾Υά]κινθε καὶ α[ὐ]τή, πότνια Δάφν[η,
    ἐλπὶs ἐμῆs κραδίηs, μέγα χαίρετε. καὶ γὰρ [᾽Απ]όλλων

†ἐμετων κατ[ὰ] μέσ⟨σ⟩ον ἐπαρμένος εἰς φυτὸν εἶναι,
ὄφρα κεν ἀνεπάφοισι συναντήσαιμι καὶ αὐτός.
5   τί πλέον ἤθελον ἄλλο, τί δὲ ἤθελον ἠὲ νοῆσαι
δεξ[ιτ]ερὰν Ὑάκινθον, ὁμοῦ λαιῆσι δὲ Δάφνην;

versus restit. Cr l.c. 658s.   2 αλλης leg. Ma, εμης coni. Cr   3 αινέω ὧν κατα coni. Cr   5 cf. Nonn. D. 47,446

To you, Hyacinth, and you, lady Daphne, hope of my heart, many greetings. Apollo too stands between you, grown into a plant, so I too may be with you without doing you harm. What more could I want, what more could I imagine than Hyacinth at my right, and Daphne on my left?

On Apollo and Daphne in Dioscorus's poetry, cf. H22.18–19, with the visual parallels there cited, including the "Shawl of Sabina" in the Louvre and the Coptic Museum and Louvre reliefs. In fact, this piece sounds like an *ekphrasis* of a work of art, one unlike the Ravenna ivory (Volbach, *Elfenbeinarbeiten*, no. 80) showing Apollo with only one of his loves, but a symmetrical composition depicting the god between two plants, the hyacinth and the laurel. For such a composition in Nonnus, see W. Fauth, *Eidos poikilon: Zur Thematik der Metamorphose u. zum Prinzip der Wandlung aus dem Gegensatz in den* Dionysiaka *des Nonnos von Panopolis* (*Hypomnemata* 66) (Göttingen 1981) 18, cf. 144–157. Compare also George Grammaticus *Anacr.* 4 (ed. T. Bergk, Leipzig 1878). For the Christianization of the Daphne myth, see Torp, "Leda Christiana," 103.

3. ἐμὲ τῶν κ.τ.λ.

In the back of Dioscorus's mind may also have been a pun on the name of his father Apollos. Perhaps such a work of art adorned the walls of the house in which Dioscorus grew up in Aphrodito.

H26. *Ethopoiia* on Achilles and Polyxena.   *P.Cair.Masp.* III 67316v

Τίνας ἂν εἴπῃ λόγους Ἀχιλλεὺς ἀποθανὼν διὰ τὴν Πολυξένην

Ἄρτι πόθος θανάτοιο φίλον τέκος ἐξεφαάνθη
ἱμείρων φιλότητα καὶ ἱμείρω[ν] κακὸν ἔ[ξ]ειν.
ἀτρεκέως Ἄιδης Τρώων ἀλόχοισι λοχ[ε]ύει
πή ποθεν Αἰακίδην Πολυξείνης κάλλει θάπτειν.
5   καλλικόμων ὁ πόθος μετ[α]μόρφετο Ἄρεος αἰχμή
θη . οιτετ . . . [. . . . .] . . . . κ . . . . νιαλ . .
Τρῶες κἂν θανό[ντ]ε[s] . . . . π . . θη.

ad argumentum cf. XXVI, XXXVII et Cr l.c. 658.—   1 post ποθος aut post θανατοιο interpungendum   3 cf. Hsch. s.v. λοχευοντες· ενεδρευοντες

Just now the longing for death, my child, sprang up in me, dearest of dreams and worst of dreams at once. Surely it is Death that has quickened the Trojans' wives, how to bury Achilles because of Polyxena's beauty. The fair-haired ones' longing has been transformed by the spearpoint of War . . .

On this subject, cf. Heitsch XXXVII, *P.Flor.* 390 (fifth century?), and, in Dioscorus's own work, *P.Cair.Masp.* II 67187.10–18 (below); cf. *P.Cair.Masp.* III 67353 v C, preserving only the title, not the text, of an *ethopoiia* entitled "What Achilles would have said when asking Thetis for his armor." Last words were a favorite form of school exercise, especially those of a mythological character. Dioscorus probably learned the Achilles–Polyxena story from Quintus Smyrnaeus 14.213–215, 240–241, 257–328, and he very likely knew the work of his countryman Triphiodorus (403–404; 686–687). The love story of the hero and the Trojan girl is related by Malalas, 130.6–131.21, including Achilles' death scene.

1. On πόθος, see H24.8, with note on Alexander's πόθος. Cf. line 5. The punctuation of this line is my own suggestion.

3. Note the play on words.

5. Dioscorus will reuse Ἄρεος αἰχμή in H3.49, the encomium on Duke John. Here read αἰχμῇ.

In *P.Cair.Masp.* II 67187.10–18, after the encomium on Colluthus, Dioscorus also treated this subject. The text follows.

```
10  [         ]πω. . ειων Τρῶσι τοῦ ᾿Αχιλλέως θάνατ     [ος . . ]λλες Πο[λυ]ξένης
    [- ˘      ]αιεν Τρώεσσιν ἀρηγόνες εἰσὶ θε          αἶναι
    [- ˘ ˘ - ]ρομον ἄλλον ὁμόστολον ὡς ᾿Α             χιλλῆα
    [- ˘ ˘ - ]ν νεκύεσσιν ἐπάξατε δύσμορον            ἄστυ
    [- ˘      ]ἀειπλάνεον πεποθημ[έ]νον               ἴφθιμον εἶλεν
15  [- ˘ ˘ - ]ν γ[ρ]αφίδεσσι σὺν ἀσπίσι δεῦρο δομεντ. ς
    [         ]. . . . . . . . . . . . . τευχεα χερσὶν ἀεί[ρω]ν.
    [Τυμβον ἐ]νὶ σκοπίη πανεπόψιον ἔρξατε δεῦρο

                   a
    [ως μορ]ον Αικιδᾱο πολύστονον ἄφθιτον εἶναι.
```

(What) the death of Achilles and (the sacrifice) of Polyxena (would have meant?) to the Trojans. . . . The goddesses are helpers to the Trojans . . . another the same as Achilles . . . shatter the ill-fated city, (filled?) with corpses . . . (Death?) has taken the ever-wandering, longed-for, strong one . . . here with wrought shields . . . raising up the walls with (his) hands. Come and build on a peak the tomb that shall be visible everywhere, so that the lamentable doom of Achilles may be imperishable.

12. Cf. Pamprepius 4.39–40, on Miltiades.

16. Maspero cited Nonnus *Dion.* 47.679 as a parallel to the end of the line.

It may be that Dioscorus had yet another poetic model. His countryman, Christodorus of Coptos, had written an *ekphrasis* on the classical statues in the gymnasium of Zeuxippus at Constantinople (*AP* II). The works of art no longer existed after the fire of A.D. 532, so Dioscorus could not have seen them during his trip to the capital in 551; but in the world of late Egyptian poets, he might well have read Christodorus's work either before or after his journey. Lines 196–205 are part of an epigram (the whole is *AP* II.192–208) on two adjoining statues of Pyrrhus and Polyxena. Dioscorus was hardly at a loss for examples to draw on for the Death of Achilles/Polyxena story. Christodorus may have been one more of them.

Heitsch II S 10. Encomium on an unnamed   *P.Berol.* 9799
duke of the Thebaid.

recto

. . .

```
               ]νασ[
               κ]ρητῆ[ρ]α κεράσ[σ
               ]τρομον ἤθελε . . [
               ]αν ἐμὴ δ' ἐβιήσατο . . [
5    . . . . . . . . . . ] . . . . [ . ]ε καὶ οὐκ ὑπόειξεν ἀν[.
     . . . . . . . . . . ] . . . ν[ . . . ], ὀπάονι δ' εἴκαθεν ε[
     . . . . . . . . . ]ετω [πά]λιν Ἄρεα νόσφιν Ὀλύμ[που
     . . . . . . . . . . ] ἀπόλ[οιτ]ο πάλιν μελίης μελεδ[αίνων.
     Θ[ήβ]η μὴ τρομέοις, οὐκ ὄρχαμος ἄλλος ἀμ[είνων·
10   κ[οί]ρανος Αἰγυπτίων ἔτι κήδεται ἀχνυμε[ν. . . . . ,
     ο]ὔ[πω] γηραλέοιο λιτὰς ἠρνήσατο Νείλ[ου.
     Πέρσα[ι] ἀναπνεύσωσι Θεμιστοκλῆα φυγόν[τες.
     ἔμπαλιν ὀτρύνων σε νέμειν ἔτι πείσματα Θ[ηβῶν
     γράμματά σο[ι] προίαλλεν ἄναξ χθονὸς ἠδὲ [θαλάσσης.
15   τί πλέον ἠνήσω σε, τὸν ἤνεσε θεσπεσίη [ὄψ;
     δ[εί]ξας δ' ἀθανάτοιο χαράγματα παμβασι[λῆος
     χάρμα πό[ρ]ες ναετῆσι δι' ἄστεος ἵππον ἐλ[αύνων.
     σῆς σπρατ[ιῆ]ς δὲ φάλαγξ χλαινηφόρος ἤθελ[ε
     Θή]βης μὲν προκέλευθ[ος . . . . . . . . . . . . . . ]εθ[
20   φα]ιδροτέ[ρ]ω . [ . . . ]ω[
     ἐξ]είης δ' αλ. . [
     χ]ερσὶν ἄνω πρ[
     θ]αλπομένων ε[
     εὐ]φήμοι[ς] ἐ[π]έεσ[σιν
25   . . ]μεναρ . σ. αλ[
```

. .]εγγεσεχ . . . [
χ]θιζὸν εν . . . [
. . .]μ . . . ν . δε[
[
30   . .]. ερ[
. .]αστεν . . . σατα[
. .]εοιμιν . . . η. [
. .]λαιν[. . . .] . .

             . . .

           verso

. . . .] . . . [.]σα . [
35   . . . . .] . μνικ[.]ν[.] . . . [
. . . . .] πέμπε βέλ[ε]μνα μι . . . [
. . . . .] οσειουτε[.]κιν . σε εξα[. .]οπο[
. . . π]έμπε βέλεμνα γόων τ. [. .] . α . . [
. . . . .]εποπλο. αε βιησαμ[έ]νωι τ[. . . . . .]ασ[. .]ν
40   ἐντρο]παλιζόμενος καὶ εὔσκοπ[α] τ[όξα] τιτα[ίν]ων
καὶ βέλ]ος εἰς σκοπὸν ἧκε τὸ δεύτε[ρ]ον . . . . ο . . .
. . . . .] . οἰστεύεσκεν ἢ ἀντία τόξα [τίται]νε[ν
. . . . .]ον οιστευεσκκαιη . λυκεικ[. . . . . .]ουμ[
εὐστο]χίη, τὰ δὲ ν. [. . . .] πεπηγότα δού[ρατα] ες[
45   . . . . .]ενος δ' εφ . . . . . περισκέπτῳ ἐ[νὶ] χώρῳ
. . . . .]ας Αὐσονίων αἰώνιον ὅρκον . . αλ[
. . . . .] . . [. . . . .]μα[. . .] τ. [.]ισ . . . [

          (vacat)

. . . having mixed a wine cup . . . wished . . . my . . . was overpowered . . .
and did not give way . . . yielded to his comrade . . . Ares again far from
Olympus . . . again perished, though he had a care for his spear. . . . Fear
not, Thebes, there is no better leader; the chief of the Egyptians still cares
for those in trouble. Nor shall he deny the pleas of old Nile. (Even) the
Persians stop for breath fleeing from (this) Themistocles. Rousing you for
your part to manage the stays of the Thebaid, the lord of earth and sea has
sent out a letter to you. How shall I further praise you, whom the divine
voice has praised? You have received the inscriptions of the immortal King
of all, and you have bestowed joy on the inhabitants as you drive your
horse through the city. The mantle-wearing phalanx of your army has
wished to . . . the forerunner of Thebes. . . . more radiant . . . in order . . .
with lifted hands . . . warm . . . in pleasing words . . . yesterday's . . . throw
javelins . . . (who) keeps turning round and drawing his unerringly aimed
bow . . . and he sent a second missile at the target . . . shot arrows or drew
opposing bows . . . by good aim . . . firmly planted spears . . . in the admired
land . . . the eternal oath of the Latins . . .

In the matter of attributing this work to Dioscorus, I am grateful to Dr. G. Poethke of the Staatliche Museen zu Berlin (DDR) for a photograph of the papyrus.

7. On Ares in Coptic art, cf. e.g., the seated Ares at Dumbarton Oaks (Beckwith, *Coptic sculpture*, pl. 17).

9. μὴ τρομέοις is a favorite opening for a line by Dioscorus, as Heitsch noted; cf. H 1 v 7, H24.16, H3.35. (The rest of Heitsch's note is, however, to be disregarded; the parallels do not hold.) On ὄρχαμος, cf. Nonnus *Paraphr.* 18.163, 19.2, 197, 21.105.

10. Cf. H2.1; H1 r 17, v 2–3. Cf. H3.77 for a fuller treatment of this idea. Read ἀχνυμέ[νοισιν.

11. Again the personification of the river god, as in H5.25–26 and elsewhere.

12. An amusing reworking of a theme from classical history. The duke of the Thebaid is being compared with Themistocles, the defender of Athens at Salamis. (Had Dioscorus read Thucydides at school? Or was such an expression proverbial?) Could the reference be to Justin II's defense of the Armenians in his correspondence with Khusrow of Persia? (F. Dölger, *Regesten der Kaiserurkunden des oströmischen Reiches* [Munich and Berlin 1924], Justinos II nos. 22–23, citing Michael the Syrian [10.1; 2.282–283]).

13. πείσματα, the cables of the ship of state of the Thebaid. Cf. H9.18.

14. The phrase ἄναξ χθονὸς ἠδὲ θαλάσσης was noticed by Viljamaa (*Greek encomiastic poetry*, p. 52) as being characteristic of Dioscorus; cf. H1 v 5. Notice the parallelism between γράμματα here and χαράγματα in line 16. Cf. below, H3.33–34, 85.

15. On θεσπεσίη ὄψ for the imperial voice, cf. H1 v 9, ὀμφῆς (unemended).

16. Here χαράγματα παμβασιλῆος has a double meaning: both the imperial decree appointing the duke to his office, and the decrees of God, which the duke must uphold (cf. H 6).

17. A vivid picture of the duke's *adventus* in his official carriage.

18. Read στρατιῆς. J. Maspero's *Organisation militaire de l'Egypte byzantine* (Paris 1912) will be replaced by the forthcoming work of Dr. J.-M. Carrié.

19. For προκέλευθος, cf. Nonnus *Paraphr.* 1.22, 111, 10.14, 12.166, 14.7.

22. In a note on H17.17, Heitsch noted the parallel with the *orantes* on Coptic stelae.

46. An unusual phrase, in which we see Dioscorus's lawyer's mind at work. For the αἰώνιον ὅρκον, cf. *P.Cair.Masp.* II 67154.28–31, an oath by the

Trinity and the victory of Justinian; 67243 B 18–19, by the Trinity and διαμονή of Justin and Sophia. Perhaps this phrase, in poetry though it be, is evidence that it is not necessarily the case that the ἔθιμος ʿΡωμαίοις ὅρκος "verschwindet mit dem 3. Jahrhundert" (Seidl, *Der Eid* 2, p. 30). (Αὐσόνιοι are otherwise found, only much earlier, in *SB* 4313.16.)

This collection of verses is an odd assortment; it seems to be an encomium of a type perfectly well known from Dioscorus's pen (lines 9 to perhaps 27), sandwiched in between two lots of scrappy Homeric battle narrations (lines 1–8 and roughly 28–47). Are the Homeric combats intended to describe the duke's own campaigns? The first and last thirds of the papyrus are too fragmentary to reconstruct such a coherence.

Dioscorus returned from Antinoë to Aphrodito in A.D. 573 (*P.Cair. Masp.* I 67096 [cf. P. J. Sijpesteijn and K. A. Worp, "Chronological notes," *ZPE* 26 (1977) 279], I 67121). Back in his native town, he composed his last two preserved poems, both addressed to John, duke of the Thebaid from 573–576: the first, more of a sketch or overture; the second, his longest and grandest work. These two final poems recapitulate the themes and weave together all the threads of Dioscorus's contribution to the literature of his society.

H2. Encomium on Duke John.   *P.Cair.Masp.* I 67055 v
A.D. 574–576.

<pre>
     ῏Ω κλυτὲ κοιρανίης πα[ν] . λ . . . α μῆ[τις] ἀνάκτων,
     Θήβης καὶ Φαρίης γέρας . . . . μελίσσης.
     οὐ πέλεν, οὐ πέλεν ἄλλος ὁμοίιος ὕμμι γενέθλη.
     ἐν χθονὶ παμβασιλῆος . . . . η ἔπλεο μοῦνος,
5   . . . .] . . . . π[άν]τα διώκων·
     το]ύνε[κά σε προίαλλεν] ἄνα[ξ] στρατίαρχον ἀμύμων
     πήματ' ἀ]ποπτύει[ν . . . . τ]ῶν ναετήρων.
     οὕτως ἄμμιν] ἵκα[νες
     . . . . . ον . . . . εις . [. . . .
10   [. . . . .] . . . . [νο]μεύειν
     πή[μ]α[τ'] ἀποπτύ[ειν] ἀδίκων . . ρη . [. . . . .]ταξ[.]ι
     οὕτως ἀεὶ ζώοις καὶ ἀμοίρυτον ἐς χ[ρό]ν[ον] ἔλθοις
     Θήβης ὡς στρατίαρχος ἔχων κλ[έο]ς ἠνορεάων.
     [ἵλαθι μοι τρομέ]ον[τ]ι, τεὸν κλ[έο]ς ὄφρ[α] λιγαίνω.
15   ἔμπλεος ἐς πλόον ἦλθον ἀμετρήτων ἀρετάων.
     ζωγράφον ἀμφιβόητον ἐπίπνοον εἰκόνα πῆξαι
     ἀτρεκέως ἐθέλω πολυήρατον εἶδος ὑφαίνειν
     χάρματι λαμπετόοντ' ἀ[μ]αρύ[γ]ματα οἷα Σελήνη.
     ἀκλινέως ἐ[νίκ]ησας Ἀχιλλέα καὶ Διομήδην,
20   ῥηιδίως καὶ Ἄρηα πανίκελα Βελλερο[φό]ντῃ.
</pre>

τοὔνεκα μὴν καλέω σε πανάλκιμον Ἡρακλῆα,
ὃς ῥα καμὼν πόρε πᾶσιν ἐλευθ[ερ]ίης παναρωγήν.
ἄστεα κουρίζων διελήλυθες οὐ κατὰ κόσμον.
Θήβη τειχιόεσσα, καὶ ἐν κονίῃσι πεσοῦσα
25 ὀρθώθης πολὺ μᾶλλον, ἀείρεο δ' ἄχρις Ὀλύμπου,
χρύσεον ἄνδρα φέρουσα, τέον ῥυτῆρα πόληων.
οὐ χθὼν πᾶσα, [θ]άλασ[σ]α μόλις πέλεν ἄξια ῥίζης
τοῦ πολυκυδήεντος Ἰωάννου στρατιάρχου.
θάλλε μοι, εἴσετι θάλλοις, πατρίκιε κλέος,
30 σὺν τεκέεσσι φίλοισιν, ἀριζήλῃ σέο νύμφῃ.

1 cf. 5,13; 6,16; 13,7   2 cf. 4,13; 5,30 | μελισσης αλλο θαλασσης Π, cf. ad 1 verso 2   3 cf. 3,39; 4 β 6; 5,6; 6,9; 13,5; Nonn. Met. i 52   4 cf. 3,40; 5,4; 6,23; 13,6; 4 β 9   6s cf. 5,7s   7 cf. 11; 3,82s   7s et 11s variationes? cf. ad 1 verso 2   8 cf. 3,46; 5,18; 13,11   12 αμοιρυτον = αμηρυτον? cf. 4,10; 5,3; 13,18; 23,14   14s cf. 5,14; 21,24s   15 cf. 5,5   16–20 cf. 5,20–24; 21,17–19.22s; acrostichum Ζαχαρ(ιας) cognov. Cr   19 cf. 3,48   20 cf. 24,11   21s cf. 5,9s | μιν Π   22 de composito (παν-) cf. 13,3.17; 15,3; 17,6   23 cf. 3,38 | cf. 1,10   24s cf. 14,3 (3,58)   25 cf. 12B 9   27 cf. 4,3   29 cf. 4,12; 5,3; 12B 9 | θαλλεις semper Π   30 cf. 3,52; 4,11; 13,19; 23,16; Nonn. D. 2,594; passim

O renowned . . . of sovereignty, craft of rulers, honor of the Thebaid and Alexandria . . . Never, never was there anyone like you in noble descent. In the land of the Emperor you alone were . . . And so the noble lord has appointed you Duke, to turn away the inhabitants' troubles. So you come to us. . . . So may you live forever and reach a boundless length of life, as Duke of the Thebaid, having the glory of noble deeds. Be gracious to me in my awe of you, so I may sing your glory. I came sailing on my voyage, inspired by your measureless excellence. I wish a famous painter would accurately depict your lifelike image, with his craft to work your beloved likeness, whose bright beams flash with joy like the moon. To judge impartially, you have surpassed Achilles and Diomedes, and easily outdone Ares and Bellerophon, so like him. Therefore I call you all-brave Herakles, whose efforts bring the universal help of freedom to all. You have come as *curator* of our cities, and not just in a worldly sense. Walls of Thebes, though you have been trodden into the dust, you are far more set upright, you are raised up to heaven, bearing the golden one, the savior of cities. The whole earth and the sea are hardly worthy of the noble lineage of the most glorious Duke John. May you flourish and again flourish, high-born glory, with your dear children and your admirable wife.

2. Cf. H4.13; again a metonymy for Alexandria. Here is one place where the papyrus reading is difficult to coax into giving sense. "Another (honor) of the sea" might refer to the duke's being sent from the capital; for μελίσσης, cf. H5.15.

5. Perhaps "prosecuting all malefactions" or the like.

7. Cf. line 11; perhaps they are alternate versions, as noticed by Heitsch.

13. ἠνορέων, a Pindaric (*Nem.* 3.20) as well as Homeric word, favored by Nonnus (*Dion.* 3.223, 21.138, 30.193, 35.323, 37.178, and elsewhere).

15. This line, already used of Duke Callinicus (H5.15), is marked by its assonance, alliteration, and play on words. The specific reference is probably to the Duke's Nile boat (M. Merzagora, "La navigazione in Egitto nell'età greco-romana," *Aegyptus* 10 [1929] 117; *P.Cair.Masp.* II 67136).

16ff. This is the third time Dioscorus has used this passage in an encomium. For ἀμφιβόητος, cf. Nonnus *Dion.* 26.141, 45.44 (active, not passive); not in the *Paraphrasis*. Again cf. Mango, "Antique statuary," pp. 64–67, and the papers of L'Orange and Marrou cited in the comment on H24.8. As usual, what is desired is an ἐπίπνοον εἰκόνα. Note ὑφαίνειν: the artist is admired for his skill at bringing off something complex (cf. G. Mathew, *Byzantine aesthetics* [London 1963] 76–77).

18. In the image he depicts in this line, is Dioscorus influenced by the traditional Eastern idea of beauty, that of a face like the full moon?

20–22. Dioscorus is fond of compounds in παν- ; see *P.Cair.Masp.* II p. 260 and III p. 259.

23. ἄστεα κουρίζων: not only "training up," but also a pun on the title *curator civitatis*; another instance of how Dioscorus's words, as art and as cultural and legal documents, are a source for the penetration of late Roman official language into the Greek of Egypt (S. Daris, *Il lessico latino nel greco d'Egitto* [Barcelona 1971]).

οὐ κατὰ κόσμον (cf. H1 r 10): a reminiscence, applied in the sphere of (imperial or) provincial government, of John 14:27, 15:19, 17:14–15(–16); to be thought of together with Nonnus *Paraphr.* 14.105, 15.73–74, 17.50, 53 (verse 16 does not seem to have underlain Nonnus's text).

24. Hundred-gated Thebes is again personified, in similar circumstances to those of H14.3.

26. One is reminded of the Late Roman fondness for golden or gilded statues; see Alan Cameron, *Porphyrius the charioteer* (Oxford 1973) 216–222. ῥυτῆρα πόληων recalls H10.6, H28.16, with P. R. L. Brown in Weitzmann, *Age of spirituality*, p. 19; Cameron, "*Pap.Ant.* III.115," pp. 126–127.

28. Heitsch's text is misprinted: read στρατιάρχου.

The expected desirable combination of personal beauty, illustrious ancestry, and just dealing adorns this official and reflects on what he is to try to accomplish in an Egypt tensely concerned with both theological correctness and ecclesiastical peace.

H3. Encomium on John,
duke of the Thebaid.
A.D. 574–576.

P.Berol. 10580 +
P.Cair.Masp. III 67317
= *BKT* V.1.117–126

[Ὦ θεῖον ὄντως καὶ ἀκριβῶς χρυ]σοῦν γένος,
[γουνάζομαί σε δεσπότην τῶν] δεσποτῶν,
[γουνάζομαί σε προστάτην τῶν] προστατῶν
. . . . .] καθεστ[　　　　　　　　]οσαγεφ. ς
5　το πανταρισ[το　　　　　　　　]μενων
Θ]ήβης τὰ τείχ[η καὶ θέμεθλα τ]οῦ Νείλου
τ]ύχης αμαρα[　　　　　　　　] μορφεας
ὅ]θεν κιβωτοῦ τ[　　　　　　]ηδαλιν.
Θ]ήβη πᾶσα χόρ[ευσον, εἰρήν]ην δέχου·
10　οὐ] γὰρ θεωρήσει[ς] κα[κουργικ]ὴν ἔτι,
πάντῃ δέος π[έφ]υ[κεν ἀσπίλ]ου δίκης
νέο[υ] Σ[ό]λων[ο]ς λ[ει]πον[. . . . . . σ]αφαι.
δ]εῦρο χάρις κα[ὶ] χάρμ[α καὶ] ἀνθολόφον
τ]οὺς εὐμενεῖς ἀνι[κήτους] εναουνγε . . ιν
15　τὸν εὐτυχέστε[ρον κλυτ]ὸν ἡγεμόνα,
ἄρχο[ντ]α πά[ν]των [δικαιότατ]ον πάνυ,
τὸν ἀμφιδ[έ]ξιον β[ραβευτὴ]ν ἐπὶ μόνον
καὶ μισοπόνηρον [. . . . . . .]α τῆς εὐδοξίας
νίκαις ἀμιμήτοις τε[διεσμιλευ]μένον.
20　τοῦ κατὰ παλαίτατον [εὐ]μενοῦς πάλιν
φ[έ]ροντ᾽ ἀνατλάν[τας . . . .]νις . . . . . . αν
χαί]ρων χορείης εἰς [μυριάμφορ]ον χρόνον
ἄλ[υπ]ον [ἄφ]θον[ο]ς π[. . . .]ν . . . .
χεῖραν ἐμ[οὶ] ἀ[τάνυσσον ἐμὴν] πενίην ἀπολύειν
25　χεῖραν ἐ[μ]οὶ ἀ[τ]ά[νυσσον　　　]ιασπ . . . . ς
οἴκτι⟨σ⟩τον ὄφρ[α] λι[γαίνω . . .
μοῦσα [θ]εορρή[των ἐτ]έρην [δ]ρόσ[ο]ν [ε]ὐεπιάων
ἄμμι νέης μέ[λπου]σα δίδ[ου] τινὰ κ[α]ρπὸν ἀοιδῆς,
τὸν νέον ἡγεμόνα προφερέστατον ὑμνοπολεύειν
30　τῆς χρυσοστεφάνοιο νοήμ[ονο]ς υἱέα Δίκης
καὶ Σαραπάμμωνος ὀβρ[ιμω]τάτου, Ἄ[μ]μονα Νείλου,
τὸν κλυτὸν Ἰωάννην ἴκελ[ον] ἔ[παρ]χο[ν ἀν]άκ[τ]ων.
ὡς γενετὴρ δεδάηκε τὰ νεύματα [πα]μβ[α]σιλῆος
ἄ]μμι καὶ ἐν γραφίδεσσι χ[αρ]άγματα χερσὶ τινάσσει.
35　τούνεκα μὴ τρομέει στάθ[μα]ις τὰ πά[ν]τα νομ[ε]ύειν·
ἐ]γγύθ[ι] κοιρανικ[οῦ σ]έθεν ο[ὔ]νομα λ[ά]μψεν [᾽Ολ]ύμπου,
Αἰγύπτου Φαέθων νέος, [ὡς] π[ά]ρος ἐν χθονὶ [ἄ]λλῃ,
ἄστεα κ[ου]ρίζων διε[λ]ή[λ]υθες
οὐ πέλεν, οὐ πέλεν ἄλλ[ος ὁμοίιος ὕ]μμι γενέθλῃ
40　ἐν χθονὶ παμβασιλῆος, ἀεὶ δὲ παροῦσαν ἀρωγήν
ἀχράντου Τριάδος μον[ο]ειδ[έ]ος ἔ[λ]λαχε δῶρον.
ἐκ σέθεν ἡγητείρας ἀ[θ]έσφατον [ἔ]πλετο ὕδωρ,

Νεῖλος ἀρουραβά[τ]ης ἐπεθ[ύ]σατο δ' αὔλακι γαίης.
Διόνυσός τις ἔης φιλο[τε]ρ[πέσι]ν οἶνον ὀπάζων.
45 ὡς [π]έ[λεν ἀ]γρονόμοισι [. .]α[. . . .] . [. .]ενοτοκλ . ,
οὕτως ἄ[μμ]ιν ἵκανες [.] . [. . .] . [. . . . π]αναρωγός.
σῖτον ε[. . . . . . .]φη[. . . . . .]σ[. . .]λεας κατ' ἀλωάς.
ῥηιδίω[ς ἐνίκ]ησας Ἀχ[ιλλέα κ]αὶ [Διο]μήδην,
αἰχμὴ Ἐ[ν]υαλίοιο πα[. . . . .] ἄμβροτε[ν] ἄφνω,
50 καὶ γὰ[ρ . .]κατέπεφ[νες . . . .]σας οὐ κατὰ κόσμον.
τωοισαι . . θρεπτήρια [. . . . .]ε[. .]λήων
σὺν τεκέεσσι φίλοισιν, [ἀριζή]λῃ [σέο] νύμφῃ.
πρός τε θεοῦ μεγάλοιο καὶ ἀθανάτου βασιλῆος
κλῦ]θι πονειομένων Παφ[ίης χ]θ[ονὸ]ς ἐνναετήρων.
55 . . . .]υι . [. . .]τετ[. . . . .]ηλθε . [. .] . ν
. . . . . δυσμενέας χρυσοδέκτ[ας . . .]ατο πάτρης.
θ . . . . νανδρε[. . . .] ἐλευθ[ερ . . .] ἠδὲ μιαίνων
τ . . δε χαμαὶ τύπτ[ησ]ε ποσι . α . νια δήσατο δεσμοῖς,
αἰκιζέν τ' ἀλόχους . ροα κερδαλεόφρον' ἐόντα.
60 ἡμέας ἔτρεψεν [δὲ ὑπὸ] ζυγὸν αἰκίαις αἰσχραῖς,
αἱρεῖ πέντε κέρατα νομίσματος ὡς χρυσοδέκτης,
ἀμφιλαφῆ προσέ[θη]κε νέην ἐπὶ κώτικι μοῖραν.
μὴ χρυσόν περ ἔχων σφετερίσσατο σῖτον ὁμοίως
δόρπου δευομένων· ἀνομοίων ἐκ γενετήρων
65 ὁ πρὶν [ἐ]ὼν τὸ [π]άρ[ος γε] πένη[ς] μέγας ὄλβιος ὤφθη.
ἀ[λ]λότρ[ι]ον κα[τ'] ἀ[γρὸν] ἐκτή[σ]ατ[ο] κέρδος ἀλιτρόν.
τ[ο]ύνε[κ]α τὸν δεκαλυτον ασ . λυτ[ο]ν παραρῖψαι
. . . . . .]ης ἀπέε[ι]πε[. .]ηθρυλ[. .] δότε τ' ἄλλῳ
εὐσ]εβ[ί]ης ἀλύτου μεμε[λ]ημ[έν]οι τῶν ναετήρων.
70 ἔ]σχετ' ἂν ὑμεῖ[ς .]αι . ιτεον κλέος ἠνορεάων
ὑμετέρων περ απο . . υσες . . . ἀλέγιζε μελάθρων.
ὡς γὰρ [χ]ὴν καθ' ἔτος τ[ις] ἐμὸν σπόρον ἔρχεται ἄφνω
δυσσεβέων νέος ἄλλος ἐπίτροπος ἠδὲ βοηθός
Βίκτωρ αὐγουσθάλ[ι]ς [ὅ] τ' υἱονὸς ἠδέ γε Κῦρος
75 αὐτοκασίγνητος τὰ[ς ἀ]λωὰς ἀφαιρῆσ[α]σθαι.
μὴ φόρον εὐσεβίη[ς βασ]ιληίδος ὄφλω ἐκείνοις.
ὀξέα τόνδ' ἐδίδου κ[α]κογείτοσ[ι]ν, οὕνεκα κεῖνται
ἐν Φθέλᾳ γῇ δια . νοαπρος μοῖραν ἐπισπεῖν.
καί νύ κεν αὖτις [ἐμ]ὸν σπόρον οἰόμενοί κ' ἀθερίζειν
80 ὥσπερ [τὸ] πρότε[ρον] δύω λυκάβαντας ἀδίκως,
⟨   ⟩
τούνε[κα γ]ουνάζομ[α]ί [σ]ε, πανάλκιμον Ἡρακλῆα,
πή[ματ' ἀ]ποπτοιεῖν Βλεμύων γένους, ἤτοι βοηθόν,
πήμα[τ' ἀ]ποπτοιεῖν Βλεμύων γένους, ὥς κεν ἐφεύρω
ἄργυρ[ον ἐ]κτίσειν, βασ[ι]λήιον ὃν φόρον οἴσω.
⟨   ⟩
85 ψῆ[φο]ν ἐνὶ γραφίδεσ[σι] καὶ ἀστυφέλικτον ἀνωγήν,
μηκ[έτι] δυσμενέας [τ]ὰς ἀλωὰς ἀφαιρήσασθαι.
χρήσ[τη]ς γάρ με διώ[κει] καὶ οὐκέτι φαίνομαι πάτρη

σπερμοβόλων ἐπίηρα διὰ προτέλε[ι]αν τῶν χρυσῶν.
πρός τ᾽ ἑὰ τέκνα φίλα γλυκερὴν φάσιν ἔκδοτε δούλῃ,
90 χάρματι νοστῆσαι πά[λ]ι⟨ν⟩ ἣν ἐπὶ πατρίδα γαῖαν,
εὐχωλὴν ἀπέραντ[ον ὑ]πὲρ σέο πάντοτ᾽ ἐνίψαι.

1–3 cf. 5,40–42 |]στιν pro]σουν leg. Sch-Wi   5 cf. 3,19; 5,47; 10,4; 11,4
6 cf. 11,10, ubi θεμετρα   9–11 cf. 5,53–55; 9,1s.4; 10,1–3; 11,1–3 | θεωρησης
semper Π   12–14 cf. 5,59; 11,5–7; cf. etiam 1,6   19 cf. 10,4; 11,4   22 = P.
Cairo Cat. I 67097 F 29; Aristoph. Th. 981, Pax 521   23 παντευτυχεστατος
sup. Cr   24 cf. 4,16; 12B 14; cf. etiam 6,28; 13,14; v. M. Leumann, Homer.
Wörter 36ss   27 sup. P. Friedländer cl. AP I 19,3; cf. XXX 31 et Claudian.
Gigantom. 7s   34 cf. 5,38; 8,4; BKT V 1 p. 115 v. 16s δειξας δ᾽ αθανατοιο
χαραγματα παμβασιληος χαρμα πορες ναετῃσι δι᾽ αστεος ιππον ελαυνων.
35 μη = ου Wi (?)   36 Ολυμπους Π   37 cf. 14,1   38 cf. 2,23 | ν[ει]αζων
ατε[.]η[. . . . .] σανθ[Sch-Wi   39s cf. 2,3s   40 cf. Claudian. Gigantom. 6
41 cf. 6,8, sed etiam e.g. 19,8 | ακραντου Π, cor. Ke   42s cf. 10 B 2s; 21,8 |
⟨εις⟩ κτητειρας add. leg. Sch-Wi, sed cf. 5,25s   45s cf. 5,17s   46 cf. 2,8
47 αυσταλεας vel διψαλεας sup. Wi   48 cf. 2,19   50 cf. 1,10   51 τῳ σοι
αει coni. P. Friedländer   52 cf. 2,30   54 πονιωμενων Π, cf. 13,14
57 ανδρεσσιν ελευθεροις? Sch-Wi   59 αλοχου{ς} χροα? Sch-Wi   62 codex
64 an post ομοιως interpungendum?   65 ωφθι Π   67s τονδε ακλαυτον
ασυλητον παραριψαι Ιωαννης απεειπε coni. Sch   69 cf. 6,6 | μεμελυμενοι Π
76 ευσεβεης et οφλων Π   78 praefectus Augustalis Blemmyis stipendium
solvit, quam pecuniam ab incolis exigit.   **post 80** (et 84) lacunam statuit
Wi   81 cf. 2,21   82 cf. 2,7 | βοηθων Π, coni. Wi   85 αστυμφελικτον
ανωγειν Π   87 Aegyptus ipsa loquitur   88 επιηρα 'quantum ad colonos
pertinet'; cf. 12 B 16   89 = θ᾽ ἑὰ   90s 'λειπει το ωστε' Wi

O descendant of a divine and really golden line, I entreat you, lord of
lords, I entreat you, patron of patrons, . . . the walls of Thebes and the
sources of the Nile. . . . Let the whole Thebaid dance and welcome peace;
for it shall not behold evildoing any more since fear of the spotless justice
of the new Solon has sprung up everywhere. . . . Come, Grace and flower-
crowned Joy, to . . . the bountiful and unconquered . . . , the fortunate and
famous Duke, the most just ruler of all, who alone is the impartial judge
who hates evil, skillfully shaped by the inimitable victories of glory. He
does not bring back benefits (only) in the old way, having borne. . . . Dance
for joy for a time full of celebration, without pain or envy. . . . Stretch forth
your hand to me to relieve my poverty, stretch forth your hand to me in
compassion so I may sing. . . . O Muse, shed on me the new-fallen dew of
divine eloquence, singing the harvest of a new theme of song, to compose
songs of praise for the most excellent new Duke, son of golden-crowned
and wise Justice and of strong Sarapammon, the Ammon of the Nile,
renowned John, who is as the chief of lords. Like a father he has taught us
the commands of the Emperor, and brandishes his proclamations in his
hands that have written them. So do not be afraid to manage all things
with a true rule; your name shines near to sovereign heaven, new

Phaethon of Egypt, the way it used to in another land: you have come as *curator* of our cities. Never, never was there anyone like you in noble descent in the realm of the Emperor; you have brought as a gift the ever-present help of the undefiled Trinity, single in essence. Under your leadership there has flowed forth the water that surpasses words, the Nile that covers Egypt's fields, that is poured out as an offering in the furrows of the earth. You come as a Dionysus giving your fellow revelers wine as their companion. As to the farmers, . . . so you come to us with every aid, . . . grain on our threshing floors. You have easily surpassed Achilles and Diomedes, the spearpoint of War . . . and not just in a worldly sense . . . nourishing . . . with your dear children and your admirable wife. By the mighty God, the eternal King, hear the suffering inhabitants of the land of Aphrodito. Wicked tax collectors . . . have shamefully beaten (men) to the ground and bound them in chains, torturing even women in their greed for gain. He has put us under the yoke with shameful torments, grasping at five keratia per solidus in his capacity as a tax collector; he has added on a new Doom in the huge Book. When he did not have money, he appropriated grain, like one without food. The one who formerly came from a dissimilar origin, and then was poor, seemed greatly blessed; but it was on someone else's land that he made his sinful profit. And so in addition . . . having been concerned with the firm piety of the inhabitants. You bring the glory of your noble deeds . . . caring for our households. As the wild goose returns every year, who of the impious will come upon my descendants to appropriate their threshing floors (their properties) now that Victor the *augustalis* is our prefect and helper, and his grandson, and Cyrus his own brother? May I not incur at their hands tax responsibility for the imperial piety. Give a hard time to those bad neighbors, because of whom . . . lie in wait to rule our fate even in the land of Phthla. And now, since right now they are concerned to dispossess my descendants, like the two years before, in their injustice, on their account I beseech you, brave Herakles, drive away our sufferings at the hands of the tribes of the Blemmyes, and help us, (drive away our sufferings from the tribes of the Blemmyes,) so I can find a way to pay the money in full for the imperial tax which I shall bear. Number among your writings too an unshakable command, so that wicked men do not appropriate our property. For my creditors are after me (Egypt), and I no longer seem the land of sowers that renders good service, because of previous payments of money. And grant your servant the sweet words her dear children say, to come home again in joy to their motherland, ever to exalt your boundless good will.

This poem, Dioscorus's *chef d'oeuvre* and his most extensive poetic statement about his world, is on the subject of justice. It is close to being a fair copy, written in Dioscorus's most careful Coptic-style slanted uncial hand, with only two cases of alternate versions of lines (24–25, 82–83) and without interlinear corrections. It has attracted comment since Schubart and Wilamowitz (*BKT* V, Berlin 1907), whose identification of John with the *praefectus praetorio Orientis* of Edict 13 was corrected by J. Maspero, "Un papyrus littéraire d' Ἀφροδίτης κώμη," *BZ* 19 (1910) 1–6. Cameron, *"Pap. Ant.* III.115," pp. 125–127 also discusses this poem. It is time to consider its text from a point of view that does not speak of poetry's having "sunk to the level of Dioscorus" (Cameron, p. 127).

For (probable) depictions of the Duke of the Thebaid in Coptic art, cf. the ivory rider in Aachen (Volbach, *Elfenbeinarbeiten*, no. 77, Taf. 44) and the corresponding standing warrior (Beckwith, *Coptic sculpture*, pl. 107), together with the equestrian figure in the Walters Art Gallery (Volbach, *Elfenbeinarbeiten*, no. 86b, Taf. 47).

1. Cf. H5.40 with the parallels given in the note thereto.

6. Cf. H2.24 and H11.10, here combined, with note on H13.3, on the sources of the Nile in Olympiodorus's commentary on the *Meteora*. A perennial myth, and a source of fantasy and wonder, as well as matter for the speculative Alexandrian scientist.

8. On κιβωτοῦ, cf. H1 v 8 (applied there to Justin II), on the Ark of the Covenant; and L. S. B. MacCoull, "The panegyric on Justin II by Dioscorus of Aphrodito," *Byzantion* 54 (1984) 575–585.

16. (Cf. 11): the statement of the theme, justice.

18. μισοπόνηρον: cf. φιλέντολος, H16.6; and, on the juxtaposition, Ps. 44:8.

19. διεσμιλευμένον: cf. H10.4, H11.4. Platonic metaphors of the shaping of statues would have been not unfamiliar to Dioscorus's audience (e.g., Roger A. Pack, *The Greek and Latin literary texts from Greco-Roman Egypt*[2] [Ann Arbor 1965] 1386–1426).

22. This is the last line of Dioscorus's imperial *chairetismos, P.Cair. Masp.* I 67097 v F 27, published by MacCoull, "Imperial *chairetismos*," pp. 43–46. It is not discussed by B. Baldwin, "Dioscorus of Aphrodito and the circus factions," *ZPE* 42 (1981) 285–286.

27. Wilamowitz (in *BKT* V) already noticed the Christian emphasis (θεορρήτων) in this invocation to the Muse.

29. Cf. H23.13. προφερέστατος is not in Hornickel.

30. I agree with Cameron (*"Pap.Ant.* III.115," p. 127) that "son of Justice" is an epithet designating the duke by poetic personification, not a statement that the duke's actual mother was a woman called Dike (as Wilamowitz in *BKT* V). This is the *genos* in the panegyric.[82]

---

82. So, too, E. H. Kantorowicz, "ΣΥΝΘΡΟΝΟΣ ΔΙΚΗΙ," in his *Selected Studies* (Locust Valley 1965) 1. Compare ΔΙΚΑΙΟΣΥΝΗ at el-Bagawat: Bock, *Matériaux pour servir à*

31. Ammon, the horned god of Thebes, was also, according to the Siwa legend, the real father of Alexander. The association would have been alive to Dioscorus. Could there be an identification with the Sarapammon, Constantinopolitan senator (with such a characteristically Egyptian name), of *SB* 9453 (*PLRE* II p. 977)?

νοήμων . . . ὀβριμώτατος are a pair of qualities that spell out what the background of the duke, the "son of Justice," is required to be: intelligence and strength, both put at the service of justice.

33. An echo of the refrains in Ps. 118 LXX (e.g., v. 12) (Sahidic ⲇⲓⲕⲁⲓ-ⲱⲙⲁ). Justin II had succumbed to madness, but his efforts at reconciliation were still alive in Egypt: Averil Cameron, "The early religious policies of Justin II," *SCH* 13 (1976) 51–67. The duke is hailed not so much as a bearer of the capital's religious policy but as an honest administrator with good Constantinopolitan ideas of how to get things done.

34. ἐν γραφίδεσσι does not mean, as against Cameron in *Porphyrius the charioteer*, p. 219, with n. 1, "in a painting," at least not exclusively and above all not here. Nor is it just a poetic cliché, Nonnian ecphrastic use notwithstanding. It means "documents," the written instruments emanating from the ducal chancery; cf. the comment on line 85, ἐνὶ γραφίδεσσι. Here in this line is Dioscorus's (the lawyer's) whole experience of the governing of Egypt by written proclamations, written instruments; the meshing of the Justinianic codified law with the Hellenistic-Coptic inheritance of customary law; the notion, repeated in Coptic documentary phraseology, of the producibility of written evidence in court.

35. νομεύειν: here and elsewhere in Dioscorus, cf. Nonnus *Paraphr.* 10.49, 13.14.

36. John means "God is gracious"; cf. H18.3, and Milne in *P.Lit.Lond.* p. 78.

37. Dioscorus uses the shining figure of Phaethon here for the last time; cf. H14.1, H24.5 with note. The inference drawn from the second half of this line is that John has already held high office in another province, and is now reassigned to Egypt (*BKT* V p. 123). (Compare the way the recipient of Heitsch S10 [line 12] has been thought to have served in a Persian campaign; A. Körte in *Archiv* 5 [1913] 540.)

38. Cf. H2.23.

40. A deliberate echo of Ps. 45:1 LXX.

41. On this line and its parallel in H6.8 (Dioscorus's first and last

---

l'archéologie de l'Egypte chrétienne (St. Petersburg 1901), pl. 15. From epigraphy, compare the *synthronos Dike* in Louis Robert, *Hellenica* 4 (1948) 24–27.

poems), see MacCoull, "A Trinitarian formula," pp. 103–110, and "μονοειδής," pp. 61–64. This is the core of this poem, which is a poem about
Justice. In the 570s, Dioscorus may have been well aware of the controversy
surrounding the Trinitarian and Christological doctrines of his old teacher,
John Philoponus of Alexandria (see MacCoull, "Dioscorus of Aphrodito
and John Philoponus," pp. 163–168), well enough to address a verse letter
to him (*P.Berol.* 13894), assuring him of his continued respect. Trinitarian
thought in the 570s was being shaken by this Tritheist controversy. Dioscorus reasserts the vital importance of Trinitarian faith in his praise of the
new administrator who is to alleviate the terrible evils recently suffered by
Aphrodito (so graphically described in lines 55–66, 87–88). The gift (δῶρον)
brought by the Duke is this most precious of all gifts. The source of just
government is right faith.

43. For Νεῖλος ἀρουροβάτης (as in H5.26), so evocative of Dioscorus's
genius loci, cf. Cyril *In Isa.* 11.15–16 (*PG* 70.337B). R. Keydell drew the
parallel to H10 B 3 in "Zwei Stücke griechisch-ägyptischer Poesie," *Hermes*
69 (1934) 424–425. Compare also *P.Turner* 10, esp. 1–2, 8, 12, 15, 22; and C.
Römer in *P.Köln* IV 172, p. 45.

44. Dioscorus's last Dionysiac thiasos: it could be illustrated by such
works of Coptic art as the Metropolitan tapestry, Dionysus holding grapes
(Weitzmann, *Age of spirituality*, no. 121), or the Boston tapestry, Dionysus
with wineskin (ibid., no. 123). The vintage festival would take place after
the Nile flood (M. Schnebel, *Landwirtschaft im hellenistischen Ägypten* [*MB*
7, Munich 1925] 281–285).

49. Cf. H26.5, ῎Αρεος αἰχμή.

50. See comment on H2.23.

54. Cf. H8.2 with comment.

56ff. These lines are a bitter indictment of the dark side of Dioscorus's
world: contrasting Egypt's woes with the prosperity to be brought by the
new regime of Duke John.

59. On violence to religious and women, cf. *P.Cair.Masp.* I 67002 III 2–3.

60. The subject of the (singular) verb is not specified but must be
another of the exortionate pagarchs of Dioscorus's extensive experience.

61. Heitsch's text is misprinted (correct text in *BKT* V): read πέντε.

62. This is a vivid image of the inescapable tax book looming over
every Egyptian taxpayer. For the δημόσιος κῶδιξ or Domesday Book of land
taxes at Aphrodito, see *P.Michael.* 40.25, 41.23, 42 A 19 (A.D. 566); L. Papini,
"Notes on the formulary of some Coptic documentary papyri from Middle
Egypt," *BSAC* 25 (1983) 83–89; *P.Lond.* V 1686.18; P.Vat.Copti Doresse 1, 5.
Cf. ἀνακωδίκευσις (the loan-form here used for the Justinianic legal codification) in Malalas 448.6 (on A.D. 529); R. Scott, "Malalas and Justinian's

codification," in *Byzantine papers*, ed. E. Jeffreys and M. Jeffreys (Canberra 1981) 12–31.

64. The villain's origins are of course base: a stock theme of invective.

66. ἀλλότριον ... ἀλιτρόν: note the punning assonance and alliteration.

69. The theme restated: the root of justice is εὐσεβία.

72. On the image of the wild goose, cf. *BKT* V.1 p. 124 ("ägyptisch"). The flight of geese, as painted at the monastic site of Bawit, marked the changing seasons. The Egyptian wild goose or χηναλώπηξ symbolized to Egyptians the love of offspring; according to Horapollon,[83] the hieroglyphic for "son" was the picture of a wild goose, a bird also sacred to the Nile (Olck in *RE* 7.712). A secondary theme of Dioscorus in this poem is his concern for his children's inheritance (lines 72, 79); as indeed so often in his appeals for help (H6.25–26, H4.18–19, and elsewhere).

74. Victor the *augustalis* is not to be identified with Victor the *hegemon* of H10. Cf. H17.7? Cyrus cannot be identified from the papyri.

76. On the meaning of φόρος, see now Gascou, "Les grands domaines," pp. 1–90; and cf. line 84 below, βασιλήιον φόρον. The reference to the "imperial piety" here may be one of the few places Dioscorus alludes to the conflict between the official Chalcedonian faith of Constantinople and the adherence of most Egyptians to the non-Chalcedonianism of Patriarch Dioscorus I. Just exactly where on the doctrinal fence Dioscorus sat is difficult to determine. If Aphrodito had been under the direct patronage of the empress Theodora (*P.Cair.Masp.* III 67283), this may be evidence for its having been non-Chalcedonian in its basic stance and sympathies, at least as far as the majority of its inhabitants were concerned. But there is no hard evidence. We do not know which of the very numerous religious buildings at Aphrodito belonged to which doctrinal persuasion. What happened on a Sunday morning at Aphrodito is hard to conjecture: did most people walk to the non-Chalcedonian churches, with a minority attending Chalcedonian liturgy? The papyri do not tell us.

78. Phthla was identified by Maspero, "Papyrus littéraire," pp. 1–6. See *P.Cair.Masp.* I 67002. 14, 17; II 67134, 67135; III 67319, 67326, 67327; *P.Lond.* V 1660, 1665, 1666, 1677, 1686, 1689, 1702. See J. G. Keenan, "Village shepherds and social tension in Byzantine Egypt," *YCS* 28 (1985) 245–259.

80. Do the two years refer to Dioscorus's last two years at Antinoë (i.e., A.D. 571–573), during which more "injustices" had occurred at Aphrodito?

---

83. J. Maspero's material presented in "Horapollon et la fin du paganisme égyptien," *BIFAO* 11 (1914) 163–195, is discussed by Karren, "Damascius' Life of Isidore," pp. xx–xxi, 15–21.

82–83. On the Blemmyes, cf. comment on H4 β 1.

85. For the meaning of ἐν γραφίδεσσι, see comment on line 34. On ἀστυφέλικτον, cf. H9.19 with comments.

87ff. The poem closes with the affecting *prosopopoiia* of Egypt herself speaking, contrasting her fruitful and beautiful past with her present sufferings. On personifications of Egypt, cf., e.g., the ivory pyxis in Wiesbaden (sixth century: Volbach, *Elfenbeinarbeiten*, no. 105, p. 75, and Taf. 56); and cf. E. H. Kantorowicz, "The 'king's advent,'" in *Selected studies* (Locust Valley, N.Y. 1965) 57, for personifications of Egypt in representations of the Flight into Egypt. (Also a favorite subject was the fall of the old Egyptian idols at the approach of the infant savior.[84]) A bold and deeply felt poetic device wrought by a poet of Egyptian consciousness.

88. προτέλεια: cf. *P.Flor.* III 296.47 (from Aphrodito).

90. νοστῆσαι: perhaps a reference to those who had had to travel abroad owing to financial troubles, like Dioscorus himself.

91. ἐνίψαι: cf. Nonnus *Paraphr.* 1.17, 204, 8.168, 9.77, 87, 110, 116, 120, 12.194, 16.40, and many other occurrences.

Egypt concludes her appeal to the duke by invoking his εὐχολή, a quality that also fosters his sense of justice. To reiterate, this is a poem about justice, as it is seen to be evolving in the specific circumstances of sixth-century Egyptian society. We may think of that other Egyptian work, the (ps.-Apollinarian) *Metaphrasis Psalmorum*, Προθεωρία, 36–39:

οὐκ ἀίεις, ὡς πρόσθε τεὸς Δαυῖδος ἀμύμων
πνεύματι θεσπίζων Αἰγύπτιον ἔκφατο λαὸν
πρῶτα δικαιοσύνης ἱκέτην ἔμεν, εἶπέ τε χεῖρας
Αἰθίοπας πρώτιστον ὀρέξασθαι βασιλῆι;

This poem is also Dioscorus's most carefully and classically constructed *logos prosphonetikos*, following the rules of Menander Rhetor (ed. Russell and Wilson, pp. 164–171, 327–330). Our poet praises the duke's wisdom and administrative ability (line 29, cf. Menander 415.29 [with p. 329]), his background in another post (line 37), his civic activity (line 38), his

---

84. The legend of the fall of the idols was already widespread in fifth-century Egypt (cf. Sozomen *HE* 5.21)—e.g., in the homily of Theophilus of Alexandria; see M. Simon, "Les écrits de Théophile d'Alexandrie," *Muséon* 52 (1939) 43–44, and M. Guidi, "La omelia di Teofilo di Alessandria sul Monte Coscam," *Rend.Acc.Lincei* ser. 5, 26 (1917) 381–390. It is commemorated in the Synaxarion on 24 Pachons; edited by I. Forget, *CSCO* 90.134–135. (This transmission took place in Arabic.) The later homily on the Flight into Egypt by Zacharias of Sakha, ca. 700, does not mention it; G. Giamberardini, *Il culto mariano in Egitto* II (Jerusalem 1973) 37–42. The ps.Mt is a late, Western growth, but from old roots. (Rilke: "platzten alle Götzen wie verraten . . ." [*Marienleben*, no. 8: "Rast auf der Flucht in Ägypten"]).

Trinitarian faith (line 41). The duke's virtue of temperance is exalted in his being compared with Diomedes (line 48, cf. Menander 416.20). The land he is to rule, Aphrodito, is lauded (lines 54, 90), and this praise is interwoven with that of the duke's courage in standing up for his subjects. The *synkrisis*, or final comparison, comes in the appeal put in the mouth of a personified Egypt herself. This involved and inclusive construction results in a memorable poetic production.

Dioscorus's last preserved venture into poetry, H3, produced a work that is deeply rooted in his own circumstances, deeply critical of what he sees as the ills of his society, and highly reflective of his own values and beliefs. It is a work of the *genius loci* (the Nile, the personification of Egypt), in which his own native Christian sentiments and his inherited education blend to produce a moment of happy opulence, a cry of outrage, and a vision of the better life all at once. This moment of vision is clothed in a language resonant with echoes of the syntax of his native Coptic speech, of the poetic foundations of the school curriculum, and of the carefully learned legal language (e.g., synonyms) of his public profession. It is imbued throughout with the quality of being steeped in the Scriptures, through the ubiquity of the Coptic liturgy and fathers. Dioscorus's work is the work of a man who prayed the Psalms after he had read the poets.

The Egyptian culture of Dioscorus's day was concerned with an ὀρθὴ πίστις that spoke to the realities of one's personal predicament, not with the logomachy beloved of church historians. In the verbal and syntactical coloration of this work of a lawyer turned poet can be seen the co-inherence of the totality of his cultural concerns. In the words of Heidegger, "das denkende Dichten ist in der Wahrheit die Topologie des Seins."

· IV ·

THE CULTURE OF DIOSCORUS

*that the Mediterranean
interpretation of the humanist
disciplines shall prevail*

Dumbarton Oaks inscription

To understand the world of Dioscorus of Aphrodito, we must make an effort to identify just what was the coherence—the co-inherence—of all the aspects of his culture. We must for a moment seek to socialize ourselves into the expectations of the culture, in order to try to categorize and describe what it was that makes for the uniqueness of the Coptic world of Late Antiquity, the strength of its *genius loci* from landscape to specific forms of Christianity. To understand Dioscorus's world, one must become, if only for a moment, that old-fashioned creature, an unabashed believer in the *Zeitgeist*—something you can see in the carved wooden furniture ornament from Aphrodito, in Dioscorus's handwriting (that same hand writing Greek, Coptic, Latin), in a carved ivory comb and an inscription on stone from Antinoë, in a niche from Bahnasa, in the way a contract from Dioscorus's archive looks in its layout and feel. There is a definite consonance among major happenings in the culture.[1] One must also be prepared to subscribe to the perhaps somewhat old-fashioned methodology of presenting an individual figure as "a microcosm of his world"—if only because of the accident of physical preservation that has given us his papers. Starting from this one figure, we must look at the condition of learning and the law

---

1. The phrase is from E. R. Miner, H. Odagiri, and R. E. Morrell, *The Princeton companion to classical Japanese literature* (Princeton 1985) 17.

in post-Chalcedonian Egypt; at the social function of classical learning in Coptic culture; and at the characteristic concepts, the cognitive style, that informed the world of that time and place.

The world into which Dioscorus was born lay at the point of intersection of many worlds: the world of Justinian and Constantinople, the sphere of Syria and Palestine, the rough society of Merovingian Gaul, and the troubled world of Byzantino-Gothic Italy. It was a world in which the old Roman structured territory of *metropoleis* and *chora* had largely shifted into a pattern of large landholdings, those of great noble families and of monasteries and churches. It was a world in which the two old cohabiting strains, Egyptian and Greek, which had variously interacted since Ptolemaic times,[2] had evolved an equilibrium—really a blend—that gave rise to brilliantly original art forms, in which the inherited Mediterranean education was used by every social group, with exuberant results; in which the old separatism and status seeking had enlarged their scope toward a productive fusion. It was a world beginning to be polarized between Chalcedonian and non-Chalcedonian[3] ways of mapping unseen reality; and it was a way of realizing human possibilities that was to perish forever.

Every fiber of Dioscorus's life belonged to and in the world of Egyptian Christianity, which informed every aspect of late Roman society with its own special flavor. The church of Alexandria was dominant, while the churches of the nome capitals and villages, the urban and rural monasteries, stood out in the physical landscape and forged powerful economic and emotional ties with the people. The landscape of the Antaeopolite nome was a friendly patchwork of hospices and holy men. Nestorius had died in Egyptian exile, and so too would Severus of Antioch (while Patriarch Dioscorus I had spun out the sad end of his life in Gangra, out of sight of the Nile and the sea). Even the neighborhood stylite was not unknown in the local scenery.[4] Egyptian Christianity, having at once resolutely set its face against what was left of Pharaonic religion and made its own kind of accommodation with classical-pagan cultural furniture, had given its own new texture to every aspect and detail of learning and letters. A whole new Greek language continued to be created in Egypt, salted with Christian

2. For the earlier period, see R. S. Bagnall, "Egypt, the Ptolemies and the Greek world," *BES* 3 (1981) 5–21.

3. D. W. Johnson, "The 'monophysitization' of the Copts," paper at the American Academy of Religion/Society of Biblical Literature, December 1984; cf. idem, "Anti-Chalcedonian polemics in Coptic texts, 451–641," in *The Roots of Egyptian Christianity*, ed. B. Pearson and J. Goehring (Philadelphia 1986) 216–234.

4. *P.Turner* 54, from Antinoë; cf. A. Leroy-Molinghen, "Mention d'un stylite dans un papyrus grec," *Byzantion* 51 (1981) 635.

theological and Roman bureaucratic technical terms, even with the odd
borrowing from Coptic (ⲧⲱⲛⲉ from ⲧⲱⲛⲟⲩ)—flexible, often highly para-
tactic, spiced with vivid abstract nouns. Classical poetry had flowered in
the twin aspects of Nonnus, in biblical paraphrase[5] and evangelical drama,
in panegyric and celebration of local heroes. A bold new spirit was at work.

Dioscorus belonged by origin and formation to the late Roman world
of the Mediterranean *koine*. One may infer that his great-grandfather
Psimanobet (fl. ca. 460+?), even if a monoglot Copt, at least moved on an
educational and cultural level consistent with society's expectations; he
had named his own son Dioscorus (a calque of ϣⲉⲛⲟⲩⲧⲉ?—the poet
Dioscorus's brother was called Sinouthios). Dioscorus's father Apollos, a
traveled landowner and *protocometes* turned monk, had moved up from
Aurelius to Flavius. By the fourth generation, we can see in the lawyer and
man of letters at the ducal court the persistence of immemorial Mediterranean values of shrewdness, keeping the wheels oiled, and the pre-
eminence of clan. Dioscorus grew up in the bright flat landscape of the
Antaeopolite, accustomed to the privilege that clothed the first family of his
town. From his early education he had, of course, Homer and the drama;
and from the fashionable currents of reading of his time, Nonnus and the
Egyptian "wandering poets." His imagination naturally saw Dionysos in
the local setting; his mind was stocked with the "inherited conglomerate" of
the curriculum. From his legal training, he had the necessary Latin, a
command of technical vocabulary, and a feeling for the interpenetration
and mutual effects of the law of Old Rome, New Rome, and the traditional
chora. Education at Alexandria gave him facility with rhetorical figures and
the Philoponian blend of Aristotelian patterned thought and Platonic
sensitivity. Thus equipped, Dioscorus made his entrance upon the stage of
great events at Constantinople.

It was to a capital city alive with administrative intricacy and urgent
theological controversy that the young squire traveled. The city and court
were, in 551, two years away from hosting the great pageant of an ecu-
menical council,[6] an effort to keep Egypt (and Syria) sweet. Dioscorus came
bearing the burdens and problems of his hometown,[7] a town that had long
looked directly to the imperial court and had present ties of patronage to

5. See now M. Roberts, *Biblical epic and rhetorical paraphrase in late antiquity*
(Liverpool 1985), mostly on Latin material, but see pp. 198–223 on the stylistic combination
of aesthetics and devotion.

6. Cf. Averil Cameron, "Cassiodorus deflated," *JRS* 71 (1981) 184–185.

7. G. Geraci, "Dioskoros e l'autopragia di Aphrodito," *Actes XVᵉ congr.intl.papyrol.* 4
(Brussels 1979) 195–204; G. Poethke, "Metrocomiae und Autopragie in Ägypten," *Graeco-
Coptica*, ed. P. Nagel (Halle 1984) 37–44.

Theodora herself. Impelled by the changing nature of *autopragia*, drawn perhaps by the pervasive presence of the great Fl. Strategius of Oxyrhynchus, he would have found the atmosphere charged with energy. We can only speculate about what impression the domes and sights of Justinian's city made on Dioscorus's mind and senses.[8] But the traces of his journey are reflected in his documentary style and in his poetry: echoes of the chancery language he shared with John Lydus, of the theological correspondence of his old teacher, Philoponus, with the emperor; the gracious commemorations made permanent in diptychs, and the grave ubiquity of the glittering imperial image. At Antinoë in his law practice and writing, at Aphrodito administering his father's foundation, one may be sure the influence of his travels lived on in his consciousness.

Dioscorus worked as an encomiastic poet, a panegyrist. When he is mentioned in literary histories at all, it is as a *Gelegenheitsdichter*, a sort of producer of greeting-card verses, with apologies for what a past critical mentality thought of as exaggerated flattery. In the present climate of research, such judgments are seen through and set aside. Dioscorus lived in a praise culture, a world of high visibility where the praise of local officials and dynasts answered to a deep need of the society. The scribe incarnated learning; good government brought a good harvest; the palazzo of the great family, hung with tapestry and bright with color and carving, was the stage on which was publicly enacted the ceremonial that gave meaning to everyday life. In this Mediterranean world where all of life was lived outdoors in the courtyard and face to face, where the person had to be seen and proclaimed to possess his special attributes, the springs of Dioscorus's poems are easy to find.[9] They tell us, as artifacts of Byzantine-Coptic culture, much about both the recipients and the writer. They shared that exuberantly extroverted mentality in which relationships from friendship to tax paying[10] are externalized in gesture, color, shape. (We can sense a little of its quality in the academic procession or the law court.)

The poems also are a unique lens through which we can watch the process of poetic composition at work, in the high style. As Dioscorus substitutes words, juggles formulas, borrows from himself, there is visible

8. Cf. J. G. Keenan, 'Aurelius Apollos and the Aphrodite village elite,' *Atti XVII congr.intl.papirol.* (Naples 1984) 957–963.

9. L. S. B. MacCoull, 'Dioscorus and the dukes: an aspect of Coptic Hellenism in the sixth century,' *BS/EB* (1988).

10. Is it significant that he wrote more poems to lay officials than to ecclesiastics? Compare later discussion.

on the very surface of the papyrus—in that hand with the instantly recognizable scalene alpha—the same transforming operation being done on the classics that brought the inherited civilized paraphernalia to their latest high polish.

Dioscorus's *Fachprosa* in both languages opens yet another window onto the originality and depth of his culture. You turn the pages of *P.Cair.Masp.* or *P.Lond.* expecting vistas of boring legal gabble, of empty servility, and the luminous phrase, the rasping or melting or glittering epithet, the compound abstract noun with a surprise lurking in its heart come singing off the page: the healing hand of the imperial power—and the plague and blight brought on by endemic corruption; the departed souls that long and faint for Christ's appearing to harrow hell; the old singing toper of a Greek school text; the hosts of Midian and the ramping lion, familiar as figures in a tapestry; above all, the landscape, overspread with grain and vines and white churches. Even the lawyer's device of paired near-synonyms takes wing in Dioscorus's hands and becomes a kind of mathematical-logic game, a template for constructing more and more well-formed definitions. To watch a lawyer at work, in an Egyptian provincial capital of the sixth century, is to put a finger on the very pulse of that culture; settling disputes, watching over the transfer of land and its products, smoothing over possible incipient cracks in the fabric of society, he deploys his prose in the patterns needed by his society. His immediacy and the authenticity of feeling shine like Egyptian sunlight through the lattices of the institutionalized requirements of documentary form. Dioscorus saw causality in more than just the reduction of the world to specific relationships. At the same time, his prose writing reflects how in touch he was with even small happenings in his environment. Dioscorus predicated his work on justice—where it mattered, he did not compromise.

Not all the loose ends had by any means been tied up in sixth-century religious culture. It is indicative of something—of the nature of our evidence, if little else—that it is hard for the scholar to reconstruct Dioscorus's personal piety. One cannot even say with the hard-and-fast certainty of labeling by hindsight which side of the confessional fence, Chalcedonian or non-Chalcedonian, he came down on. (Cyrillian seems the best label.) There is no easy classification rule that equates "Greek-speaking" and "classically educated" with "upper class and Chalcedonian." (One of the Apions went to the capital and accepted communion with the "imperial party"; did the rest of his family remain on speaking terms with him? Was there tension on his return visits to Oxyrhynchus? And yet much of the phenomenon of "Coptic hatred of the Byzantines"—Byzantines per se, not Chalcedonians, who were hated at the grass roots—is the creation of later historians.)

But neither is it possible glibly to put Dioscorus down as "just a Copt" and thence to extract Monophysite doctrine from his writings, when it simply is not explicitly there. We cannot even find out from the sources whether Aphrodito had a patron saint; whether it stood in a special relation to one holy figure like the patronal figure of S. Colluthus at Antinoë.[11] To whom did Aphroditans, of varying social levels, turn at moments of crisis? Not even the list of dedications of churches and monasteries[12] gives us a ready answer. But we can see that Dioscorus had an immediate and fruitful relationship with local piety, especially monastic piety and the veneration of holy men—his poems on the βίος ἀγγελικός and on St. Senas show how he was moved to create imaginative encomia on religious figures, both of his own time and of history.

We have seen how all of his language is imbued with the Bible and the liturgy. If vocabulary borrowings and rhetorical echoes are any indication, he was well acquainted with the works of Cyril—probably also in Coptic, mostly lost to us. The happy unity of classical and Christian imagery in his documentary phraseology and in his poetry testifies to the high level of civilization attained by the Coptic leisured class during its period of optimum development.

This Coptic leisured class was at home simultaneously in the worlds of what we divisively label as classical and as Coptic culture; it is not at all certain that they perceived them as contrasting sharply with one another. In fact, what comes out of the texts and the visual art is the compatibility, not the contrast. The fifth century, marked by the domination of Shenoute and his line of succession as prolific Coptic writers and highly visible ecclesiastical leaders, had been a period of high achievement in Coptic culture; the late sixth, late in Dioscorus's lifetime, was to see another such period of flowering.[13]

Dioscorus's family and clients had ties with the White Monastery, and

11. Cf. L. Papini, "Due biglietti oracolari cristiani," *Trenta testi greci*, ed. M. Manfredi (Florence 1983) 68–70; and "Biglietti oracolari in copto dalla Necropoli Nord di Antinoe," in *II intl.congr.copt.stud.* (Rome 1985) 245–256. Perhaps the Virgin comes closest to being Aphrodito's patron.

12. See now S. Timm, *Das christlich-koptische Ägypten in arabischer Zeit* III (Wiesbaden 1985) 1438–1461.

13. See the remarks of T. Orlandi on the period of Patriarch Damian (after 578) in "Coptic literature," in *Egyptian Christianity*, ed. Pearson and Goehring, pp. 75–77; and now

he most probably would have been acquainted with Shenoute's many-sided philosophical and expository output. (The theme of the obligations of the *dynatoi* would have been close to Dioscorus's heart.) We know that Coptic hagiography was part of the furnishings of his mind. Very likely Coptic homiletic was as well. (Were Pachomians and Shenouteans famous as guest preachers in the leading churches of the river cities?) In the last decade or two of Dioscorus's life, the reign of Patriarch Damian, himself a theologian,[14] gave rise to a fresh outburst of Coptic literary activity in the cities of the cultural heartland not far from Aphrodito (Hermopolis/Ashmunein, Lycopolis/Assiut, Hypselis/Shotep). The way these writers make use of classical Greek rhetoric[15] has much in common with the way Dioscorus constructed a legal document, or composed as a *doctus poeta*.

Creative activity in Coptic in the later sixth century also took place in Middle Egypt, in the Heracleopolite nome (north of Oxyrhynchus), and in the Delta itself. Next to the panegyrics of Constantine of Lycopolis[16] and John of Hermopolis, we have the work of Stephen of Heracleopolis, whose panegyric on the Monophysite archimandrite Apollo, who fled from the Pachomian headquarters of Pbow owing to an attempted Chalcedonian takeover, is a good witness to ecclesiastical propaganda at mid-century.[17] And John of Parallos, who in the late sixth century inveighed against the popularity of heretical texts,[18] transmits the names of five of those "blasphemous books," of which four (the *Preaching of John*, the *Laughter of the Apostles*, the *Teachings of Adam*, and the *Counsels of the Savior*) sound like nothing so much as "Nag Hammadi" Gnostic tractates. We already know

---

C. D. G. Müller, "Damian, Papst und Patriarch von Alexandrien," *Oriens Christianus* 70 (1986) 118–142 (based on narrative sources, not papyri).

14. The Coptic text of his synodal letter is given in W. E. Crum and H. G. Evelyn White, *The monastery of Epiphanius* 2 (New York 1926) 148–152 (English translation, pp. 332–337).

15. See the forthcoming dissertation of M. Blanchard of Catholic University on Shenoute as a classical rhetorician.

16. For Constantine of Assiut, see T. Orlandi in *CSCO* 350 (Scr.copt. 38; Louvain 1974), esp. viii–xv, xvii–xix; R.-G. Coquin, "Saint Constantin, évêque d'Asyūt," *SOCC* 16 (1981) 151–170; G. Godron in *PO* 35.4 (Turnhout 1970), 508–669. The description of an imperial messenger at a shrine feast, bearing ϭⲁⲓ ⲛ̄ⲓⲡϩⲛⲓⲕⲟⲛ, in late sixth-century Upper Egypt in MS Morgan M587 f.42ʳ is striking.

17. Published by K. H. Kuhn in *CSCO* 394–395 (Scr.copt. 39–40; Louvain 1978).

18. See A. van Lantschoot, "Fragments coptes d'une homélie de Jean de Parallos contre les livres hérétiques," *Miscellanea Mercati* 1 (Vatican City 1946) 296–326. We can identify the "Investiture of Michael" as the text published by C. D. G. Muller in *CSCO* 225–226 (Scr.copt. 31–32; Louvain 1960).

that Dioscorus was acquainted with Gnostic material, possibly transmitted through the Pbow-Atripe/Panopolis-Aphrodito connection.[19] Texts of this type seem to have maintained an underground life in Dioscorus's own time and place. Elements of both the mainstream and the covert Coptic culture can thus be seen to have contributed to his formation.

The culture carried on in the Coptic language was, of course, not exclusively religious. Coptic was the vehicle of everyday letters, taxation, and lawsuits as much as of sermons and saints' lives. It is an accident of preservation that most extant Coptic documentary papyri are from the seventh century and later. But what little of the Coptic material from sixth-century Aphrodito[20] has been permitted to survive, such as scraps of Dioscorus's correspondence with the Apa Apollos monastic community of which he was overseer, brings into view the *realia* of this world with even greater clarity. Even a contract or a letter composed in Coptic could not help being filled with classical content.

Classical learning, its forms and substances and attributes, its textures and flavors and atmosphere, played a strongly positive social role in Egypt during the sixth and early seventh centuries. The period was, in spite of the "Melkite-Monophysite" tension at Alexandria and the protracted vacancy in the non-Chalcedonian patriarchate, a moment of equilibrium, a long summer. The land, ever the basis of life in Egypt, had been subject to variously evolving forms of tenure and of disposition of its products, from the older Roman organization to the late fifth-century world of the great estates.[21] Dioscorus was securely settled into a way of life that was naturally at home with the bits and pieces of classical cultural furniture—in clothing and the omnipresent architectural ornament, in polite modes of address and the figures of epithalamia. (The Coptic language itself, interwoven with one-third Greek loanwords like raisins in a pudding, has no trace of feeling them as foreign bodies. They are simply there.) And Chris-

19. L. S. B. MacCoull, "*P.Cair.Masp.* II 67188ᵛ1–5: Dioscorus's 'gnostica'," *Tyche* 2 (Vienna 1987), 95–97.

20. L. S. B. MacCoull, "The Coptic archive of Dioscorus of Aphrodito," *Cd'E* 56 (1981) 185–193, and eadem, "A Coptic cession of land by Dioscorus of Aphrodito," *II intl.congr.copt.stud.* (Rome 1985) 159–166; L. Papini, "Notes on the formulary of some Coptic documentary papyri from Middle Egypt," *BSAC* 25 (1983) 83–89, eadem, "Annotazioni sul formulario giuridico di documenti copti del VI secolo," *Atti XVII congr.intl.papirol.* (Naples 1984) 767–776. There is Coptic material among the lot numbered Egyptian Museum S.R. 3733, though the authorities take pains to conceal the existence of Coptic antiquities.

21. J. Gascou, "Les grands domaines, la cité de l'Etat en Egypte byzantine (5ᵉ, 6ᵉ, et 7ᵉ s.)," *Trav.etMém.* 9 (Paris 1985) 1–90.

tianity, a distinctive and passionately held Christianity, was domiciled in the thoughts and hearts of a majority of Egyptians,[22] giving them another rich repertoire of cultural forms, and transfiguring the classics they had learned in school. Together these great traditions gave Coptic culture a whole kit of conceptual tools with which to map out and make sense of the world.

Yet we can see from hindsight that somehow one bonding ingredient in the whole colloid did not quite jell. What that was still defies explanation. A quest for the historical roots of a kind of anti-intellectualism,[23] a devaluing of learning in Coptic culture, is a matter of high priority. The Byzantine province of Egypt had everything: an infrastructure of schools, positions, human talent—a set of routes by which one could rise to the top. In the very career of Dioscorus we have a classic case of the high standing and rewards that accrued to the jurist/poet, the learned man par excellence. How then was it possible that learning never became a holy act in Coptic culture as it so definitely did in the other high cultures of the Christian Orient? The consequences of this unarticulated, almost unperceived, attitude deep under the surface of the culture were to prove disastrous.

22. Earlier scholars, by a curiously inverted standard, suffered from a desire to defend at all costs whatever survivals of paganism they could find. This methodology has not proved useful. The question is still debated as to why Christianity struck such very deep and tenacious root in Egypt. The old facile "explanation," that the "native Copts," long despised by the Greek ruling class, "nationalistically" latched onto the new faith as a way of reasserting their identity, as a promise of radical hope for the hopeless, is a creation of romantic historians, and can in no way be extracted from the sources. Also unproductive is the old notion that "the Monophysite heresy" was an expression of "Egyptian nationalism"—disproved by A. H. M. Jones—and its corollary, that somehow "the Monophysite mind" was more congenial to Egypt and Syria, and helped facilitate the Moslem conquest. Serious work with the sources can dispel these tired and harmful clichés from our historiography.

23. Cf. J. Timbie, "Dualism, orthodoxy, and the thought of the monks of Upper Egypt" (Diss., University of Pennsylvania 1979) 216–224, 227–233; L. S. B. MacCoull, "Three cultures under Arab rule: The fate of Coptic," *BSAC* 27 (1984) 61–70, and eadem, "The strange death of Coptic culture," London Colloquium on Late Antiquity and Early Islam (June 1986). The "distrust-of-Hellenic-learning" syndrome is common enough in Eastern monasticism; but that is not the issue here. The fact remains that, in spite of high achievement, Coptic culture never engendered an atmosphere in which excellence— ἀρετή—felt completely natural. One is left somehow with the feeling that all of the accomplishments were made in the face of heavy odds—and that when the odds tipped yet more heavily, something broke down irrecoverably. For an example of the old-fashioned type of synthesis I am seeking to correct, cf. P. du Bourguet, *The art of the Copts,* trans. C. Hay-Shaw (New York 1967) 9–34: an overview with which I disagree at many points. Easy explanations of "subject status" and "poverty" will not do (they are still

What, then, is the cognitive style characteristic of Coptic culture in its classical phase? And how does that cognitive style manifest itself, reverberate, throughout the forms of institutions, art, thought, and life that flourished in Egypt between about 475 and (at the very latest) 750? What is the unity underlying all the productions of this culture that instantly leaps to the mind? Why would one never mistake a Coptic artifact for an object of any other place or time? What, indeed, are the special values implied by "being Coptic"? Through Dioscorus we can try to formulate answers to these questions.

Dioscorus was bilingual. The Coptic language is a transmuting prism through which to see the world; Coptophony gives one a new set of eyes and ears.[24] The language is rich in syntactic categories that are not at all familiar or naturally to be expected.[25] It is clear by now that we cannot impose Indo-European linguistic categories onto the Coptic language;[26] such a mediated understanding seriously distorts our grasp of how the language works. In Coptic our familiar notions of noun and verb, object and predicate, transitive and intransitive, do not apply. The Coptic world is one of a very exactly and subtly detailed directionality in three dimensions, in which direction and movement are signaled by an extremely rich "spatial relations network" of markers.[27] The language is well fitted to deploy clauses in delicate logical arrangement;[28] in documents the use of a Second Tense marks the "dispositive" function of the written instrument,[29] a function central to the activity of Dioscorus the jurist. The whole way thoughts are constructed in Coptic is done by operations of what is now understood as a "modifier," a concept that cuts across things we think of under labels like mood and attribution. Genders, their weight carried in the pronoun/article, are shuffled about in predication; tenses behave in all sorts of

---

repeated by Johnson, above note 3). If there was a basic distrust of ἀρετή, and there seems to have been, it remains unexplained.

24. I am also an unashamed neo-Whorfian. See J. A. Fishman, "A systematization of the Whorfian hypothesis," in *Culture and cognition*, ed. J. W. Berry and P. R. Dasen (London 1974) 61–85.

25. H. J. Polotsky, "Coptic," in *Current trends in linguistics* 6, ed. T. Sebeok (The Hague and Paris 1970) 563.

26. My remarks here are based on the brilliant study of A. Shisha-Halevy, *Coptic grammatical categories* (Rome 1986): a fiendishly difficult but most illuminating work that will totally remake our thinking about the self-perception of the Coptic mentality and of how the workings of the language shape the Coptic mind.

27. Ibid., p. 35.

28. Ibid. p. 47; cf. p. 156, "a topic-prominent language."

29. Ibid. pp. 79–80 with p. 80 n. 92.

ways and fulfill all sorts of functions; the notion of "taking an object"
operates quite variously; emphasis is built right into the bones of sentences.
The concretizing nature of the language goes deep, as half a century of
etymological research has made plain. Concrete results are expected from
imperatives in a kind of reverse *do-ut-des* syndrome.[30] The Coptic language
should be seen as being inhabited not by words but by "syntagms"—
patterns of ordered categories.[31]

These categories determine perception, classification,[32] and logic in
ways subtly different from the classical. The very categories of self-awareness are individual. Coptic epistemology is rich in the two verbal concepts
ⲥⲱⲟⲩⲛ/ⲉⲓⲙⲉ, corresponding to *savoir/connaître* or *wissen/kennen*, the ety-
mologies of which go back to Egyptian determinatives with "eye" and
"hand," respectively. Even the basic purpose-particle ⲭⲉⲕⲁⲁⲥ comes from
the juxtaposition of two roots meaning "to say" and "to put."[33] A society
bilingual in Coptic with its ancient yet innovative freshness, and Greek
with its "either/or" logical clarity of deployment, drank at two nourishing
cultural springs and saw causality in a whole new way. Analytic and
synthetic go into the same compound.

A patterned language—a patterned visual art. All of the clichés applied
in the description of Coptic art fall short of the underlying unity. (And now
that so many works formerly accepted as type pieces are having their
authenticity called into question,[34] we have a less firm database than was
thought.) Abstract, linear, hard-edged; popular, impoverished, provincial;

30. Polotsky, "Coptic," 568.

31. Shisha-Halevy, *Coptic grammatical categories*, p. 164.

32. Look at Dioscorus's Greek-Coptic glossary (cf. L. S. B. MacCoull, "Further notes
on the Greek-Coptic glossary of Dioscorus of Aphrodito," *Glotta* 64 [1986] 253–257), and its
Late Antique categories of classification. Profoundly rooted in its environment, this bare list
comes across almost like a genre painting, with nature, wildlife, the Nile, irrigation, and the
everyday craftsmen and workers of Egypt seen going about their business in their
landscape—a landscape with the occasional Dionysiac figure or drunken poet thrown in.
Dioscorus was very likely compiling this list of "all trades, their gear and tackle and trim"
in order to work the Greek names of implements, if they would scan, into dedicatory
epigrams. None has, alas, survived.

33. R. Kasser and W. Vycichl, *Dictionnaire étymologique de la langue copte* (Leuven
1983) 201–202, 62–63, 325.

34. Thanks to the important work of G. Vikan, e.g., his "The so-called 'Sheikh Ibada'
group of early Coptic sculptures," *Third BSC Abstracts* (New York 1977) 15–16; and
Questions of authenticity among the arts of Byzantium (Washington, D.C. 1981). It is possible
that many fakes, later purchased by the unsuspecting, were perpetrated in the late 1950s
and early 1960s, at the time of the great expropriations, with a view to discrediting the
"Coptic heritage" that might have become a cultural movement. Vikan has shown that
many sculptures the public thinks of as typically Coptic are not ancient, but modern
reworkings of pieces of old stone.

light-and-shade contrast, flatness, "symbolist" deformation, the great staring eyes: all are clichés[35] that miss what the observer's eye seizes upon. Also misguided is the notion that Coptic art expresses some sort of age-of-anxiety syndrome and hence appeals to the "modern" sensibility.[36] This is a creation, or projection, of romantic dilettanti, and need not detain scholars. Look instead at a basket capital from the region of Antinoë and see, in its joyous transformation of classical forms, a parallel to the exuberance of rhetorical figure, the elaborately contrasted constructions, in Dioscorian prose. The underlying unity in the classic phase of this culture would seem to be a positive reëvaluation of classical form vivified by autochthonous content—as though the energy and the chemicals of the Nilotic sap have changed the very shapes of the leaves in that vine scroll seen on the Antinoë praetorium or Shenoute's monastery. But this too would seem a cliché. The flavor, the texture, the almost shattering visualness of the works produced by Coptic culture in its high phase are full of an awareness that the really enjoyable part of classics is not just what you learned in school; it is the piquancy of using just the right classical term in a context that makes the perceiver exclaim "So *that* is what it really means!" When Shenoute uses ⲤⲨⲚⲦⲈⲖⲈⲒⲀ or ⲠⲀⲢⲀⲪⲨⲤⲒⲤ, when Dioscorus uses $\mu\nu\rho\iota\acute{a}\mu\phi\circ\rho\circs$ or even $\dot{a}\rho\gamma\nu\rho\acute{o}\pi\epsilon\zeta a$, one's reaction is sheer delight.

The essence remains hard to seize and formulate. It can best be apprehended by turning over the leaves of the British Museum's or John Rylands's Coptic papyri, the legal documents from Jeme, or running the eye down plates of the sixth-century Coptic documents from Aphrodito. Practicality of mind, yes; a consciousness, helped by that Mediterranean awareness of the presence of the dead, of the transience of all things, the terrifying nearness of the boundaries ("zwischen Strom und Gestein") where everything can break down. A combination of toughness and delicacy; a sense of the nearby breathing of the unseen world. A sparkle of perennial,

---

35. The same words are used in talking about Syrian or Visigothic or Merovingian artifacts that would never for a moment be confused with Coptic.

36. E.g., *BSAC* 19 (1967/68) 227–290. Coptic art has too long been the province of amateurs. And the phenomenon of patronage has not yet been studied in the domain of Coptic art (of the classical period). This is because the field has been under the domination of those whose earlier-day equivalents were themselves patrons. One now speaks of a paradigm shift in the study of Byzantine art, from emphasis on style to emphasis on patronage. But unfortunately Coptic art has not caught up; in this field, still all too often a playground for those who cannot read the Coptic language, the writers of studies of objects still as often as not stand in the position of those who collect fashionable objects and jot down their impressions of them. Only recently has the field of Coptic art begun to be the object of serious study by qualified professionals.

ineradicable classicism, interwoven with a rough-textured, grainy astrin-gency. In Coptic letters we see at work the mind of the society Dioscorus embodied. In the tones of feeling that pervade Coptic culture as it flour-ished from the mid-fourth to the mid-seventh century, and even a little after, we sense why it was a culture founded on and structured around praise. Before Heian Japan, before Romantic Vienna, Coptic Egypt—the first expressionist society—confronted transitoriness ("so leben wir und nehmen immer Abschied") with a heartfelt affirmation of the perceived details of life. Dioscorus's simile of the cicada was apt: he sang in the noonday, and did not ask questions.

To all this there is a chilling postscript: it is that there is no postscript. This was a culture that was to die without a *Nachleben*. Nothing could be more wrong than proleptically to cast a shadow over its bright colors and vibrant life; its happy connectivity; and its universe of strong, original forms. But the fact remains that it died, and it alone of all the flourishing cultures of the Christian Orient died out totally. The rich and multiform culture of Byzantine-Coptic Egypt found a mode of survival for another hundred years or so after the Moslem conquest. At first, administrative structures were (for purely practical reasons) preserved; some Greek was used, outside of the liturgy; the "inherited conglomerate" remained *au fond* intelligible. But after the ninth to tenth centuries, in wrenching contrast to what happened in Mesopotamia, Armenia, and other regions of the east Mediterranean, the Coptic language and all the values it carried began its irreversible dying. We do not know why; and we do not know, as his-torians and students, whether that way of being human can ever become viable again.

CHRONOLOGY

Before 514	Death of Dioscorus the elder (the poet's grandfather)
514	Apollos and Besarion *protocometai* of Aphrodito
518	Accession of Justin I
ca. 520	Birth of Dioscorus of Aphrodito
523	Apollos probably *riparius* of Aphrodito
527	Accession of Justinian
529	John Philoponus, *De aeternitate mundi*
532	Nika Riots at Constantinople
533	Promulgation of *Digest*
535	Apollos again probably *riparius*
536	Theodosius I, non-Chalcedonian Patriarch of Alexandria
538	Apollos founds his own monastery, of Apa Apollos; Severus of Antioch dies in Egypt
539	Probable reorganization of Egypt by Justinian's Edict 13
541	Apollos travels to Constantinople with local delegation
542	Plague
543	First dated document written by Dioscorus of Aphrodito
546/7	Death of Apollos
548	Death of Theodora
551	Dioscorus travels to Constantinople; Justinian publishes *De recta fide;* earthquake at Berytus
553	Dioscorus returns to Aphrodito from Constantinople; is *protocometes*

560   John Philoponus, *De opificio mundi*

565   Accession of Justin II

566   Dioscorus moves to Antinoë, works as notary and poet;
       death of Patriarch Theodosius in Constantinople

573   Dioscorus returns to Aphrodito

574   Dioscorus *curator* of monastery of Apa Apollos; madness of
       Justin II

578   Damian Patriarch of Alexandria

582   Accession of Maurice; revolt of Three Brothers in Lower
       Egypt

585   Last dated document from archive of Dioscorus

BIBLIOGRAPHY

This bibliography contains the main works cited in the footnotes and annotations.

Greek papyri are cited according to J. F. Oates, R. S. Bagnall, W. H. Willis, and K. A. Worp, *Checklist of editions of Greek papyri and ostraca,* 3rd ed. (*BASP* Supplement 4; Atlanta 1985).

Coptic papyri are cited according to A. A. Schiller, "Checklist of Coptic documents and letters," *BASP* 13 (1976) 99–123.

PRINCIPAL SOURCES:

Greek:	*P.Cair.Masp.* I, II, III	*P.Mich.* XIII
	P.Lond. V	*P.Vatic.Aphrod.*
	P.Flor. III	*P.Hamb.* III 230–234
	P.Freer	

Coptic: BM, CO, KRU, Ryl, ST, VC; Bal; P.Vat.Copti Doresse

SECONDARY WORKS:

Antonini, L., "Le chiese cristiane nell'Egitto dal IV al IX secolo," *Aegyptus* 20 (1940) 129–208.

Bagnall, R. S., and K. A. Worp, *The chronological systems of Byzantine Egypt* (Zutphen 1978).

———, *Regnal formulas in Byzantine Egypt* (Missoula, Mont. 1979).

Barison, P., "Ricerche sui monasteri dell'Egitto bizantino ed arabo," *Aegyptus* 18 (1938) 29–148.

Becker, C. H., "Arabische Papyri des Aphroditofundes," *Z.Assyriol.* 20 (1906) 68–104.

Beckwith, J., *Coptic sculpture* (London 1963).

Bell, H. I., "The Aphrodito papyri," *JHS* 28 (1908) 97–120.

————, "An Egyptian village in the age of Justinian," *JHS* 64 (1944) 21–36.

Bell, H. I., and W. E. Crum, "A Greek-Coptic glossary," *Aegyptus* 6 (1925) 177–226.

Bowersock, G. W., "Poets and patronage in Byzantine Egypt," Dumbarton Oaks lecture, 8 May 1986. Unpublished.

Bowman, A., *Egypt after the Pharaohs* (London 1986), esp. 156–164.

Browne, G. M., "Harpocration panegyrista," *Ill.Cl.Stud.* 2 (1977) 184–196.

Cameron, Alan, "Wandering poets: A literary movement in Byzantine Egypt," *Historia* 14 (1965) 470–509.

————, "*Pap.Ant.* III.115 and the iambic prologue in late Greek poetry," *CQ* 64 (1970) 119–129.

————, "The empress and the poet," *YCS* 27 (1982) 217–289.

Cameron, Alan, and Averil Cameron, "The *Cycle* of Agathias," *JHS* 86 (1966) 6–25.

Cameron, Averil, "The empress Sophia," *Byzantion* 45 (1975) 5–21.

————, "The early religious policies of Justin II," *SCH* 13 (1976) 51–67.

Carrié, J.-M., "Figures du 'colonat' dans les papyrus d'Egypte: Lexique, contextes," *XVII Congresso internazionale di papirologia* III (Naples 1984) 939–948.

Casanova, G., "La peste nella documentazione greca d'Egitto," *XVII Congresso internazionale di papirologia* III (Naples 1984) 949–956.

Colman, R. V., "Reason and unreason in early medieval law," *J.Interdisc.Hist.* 4 (1974) 571–591.

Daris, S., *Il lessico latino nel greco d'Egitto* (Barcelona 1971).

Drew-Bear, M., *Le nome Hermopolite* (Missoula, Mont. 1979).

du Bourguet, P., *The art of the Copts* (New York 1967).

Garitte, G., "Rufus de Shotep," *Muséon* 69 (1956) 11–33.

Gascou, J., "Les grands domaines, la cité et l'Etat en Egypte byzantine (5e, 6e, et 7e s.)," *Trav.etMém.* 9 (Paris 1985) 1–90.

Gascou, J., and L. S. B. MacCoull, "Le cadastre d'Aphroditô," *Trav. et Mém.* 10 (Paris 1988) 103–158.

Geraci, G., "Dioskoros e l'autopragia di Aphrodito," *XVe congrès international de papyrologie* IV (Brussels 1979) 195–205.

Geremek, H., "Les πολιτευόμενοι égyptiens sont-ils identiques aux βουλευταί?," *Anagennesis* 1 (1981) 231–247.

Gignac, F. T., *Grammar of the Greek papyri of the Roman and Byzantine periods* I–II (Milan 1976–1981).

Girgis, V., *Prosopografia e Aphroditopolis* (Berlin 1938).

Golega, J., *Der homerische Psalter* (Ettal 1960).

Hagedorn, D., and M. Weber, "Die griechisch-koptische Rezension der Menander-sentenzen," *ZPE* 3 (1968) 15–50.

Hardy, E. R., *The large estates of Byzantine Egypt* (New York 1932).

Hartigan, K., "Julian the Egyptian," *Eranos* 63 (1975) 43–54.

Heuser, G., *Die Personennamen der Kopten* (Leipzig 1929). Indexed by W. Brunsch in *Enchoria* 12 (1984) 119–153.

Horn, J., "Latino-Coptica," *XVII Congresso internazionale di papirologia* III (Naples 1984) 1361–1376.

Hunt, L.-A., "Coptic art," *Dictionary of the Middle Ages* 3 (New York 1983) 585–593.

Hurst, A., et al., *La vision de Dorothéos* (*P.Bodmer* 29; Geneva 1984).

Johnson, D. W., ed., *The panegyric on Macarius of Tkow* (CSCO 415–416; Louvain 1980).

————, "Anti-Chalcedonian polemics in Coptic texts, 451–641," in *The roots of Egyptian Christianity*, ed. B. Pearson/J. Goehring (Philadelphia 1986) 216–234.

Karren, S. L., "Near Eastern culture and Hellenic paideia in Damascius' Life of Isidore" (Diss., University of Wisconsin 1978).

Keenan, J. G., "The provincial administration of Egyptian Arcadia," *XIV International Congress of Papyrology* (London 1975) 189–194.

————, "On law and society in Byzantine Egypt," *ZPE* 17 (1975) 237–250.

————, "The case of Flavia Christodote," *ZPE* 29 (1978) 191–209.

————, "Aurelius Phoebammon, son of Triadelphus, a Byzantine Egyptian land entrepreneur," *BASP* 17 (1980) 145–154.

————, "The Aphrodite papyri and village life in Byzantine Egypt," *BSAC* 26 (1984) 51–63.

————, "Aurelius Apollos and the Aphrodite village elite," *XVII Congresso internazionale di papirologia* III (Naples 1984) 957–963.

————, "Village shepherds and social tension in Byzantine Egypt," *YCS* 28 (1985) 245–259.

————, "Notes on absentee landlordism at Aphrodito," *BASP* 22 (1986) 137–169.

Koenen, L., et al., *The Cairo codex of Menander* (London 1978).

Kuhn, K. H., ed., *Panegyric on Apollo* (CSCO 394–395; Louvain 1978).

Liebeschuetz, W., "The origin of the office of the pagarch," *BZ* 66 (1973) 38–46.

Livrea, E., "Pamprepio ed il P.Vindob. 29788A–C," *ZPE* 25 (1977) 121–134.

————, ed., *Blemyomachia* (Meisenheim 1978).

————, ed., *Pamprepii carmina* (Leipzig 1979).

————, "*P.Oxy.* 2946 e la constitutio textus di Trifiodoro," *ZPE* 33 (1979) 57–74.

————, ed., *Musaeus* (Leipzig 1982).

————, "Towards a new edition of Nonnus' Paraphrase of St. John's Gospel," *XVII International Byzantine Congress Abstracts* (Washington, D.C. 1986) 198–199.

McCail, R. C., "P.Gr.Vindob. 29788C: Hexameter encomium on an unnamed emperor," *JHS* 98 (1978) 38–63.

MacCoull, L. S. B., "Dioscorus and the dukes," *Second BSC Abstracts* (Madison 1976) 3–4. (Second version to appear in *Byzantine Studies/Etudes byzantines*.)

————, "The Coptic archive of Dioscorus of Aphrodito," *Cd'E* 56 (1981) 185–193.

————, "Documentary texts from Aphrodito in the Coptic Museum," *SOCC* 16 (1981) 199–206.

————, "The imperial *chairetismos* of Dioscorus of Aphrodito," *JARCE* 18 (1981) 43–46.

————, "Papyrus fragments from the monastery of Phoebammon," *XVI International Congress of Papyrology* (Chico, Calif. 1981) 491–498.

————, "A Trinitarian formula in Dioscorus of Aphrodito," *BSAC* 24 (1982) 103–110.

————, "μονοειδής in Dioscorus of Aphrodito: an addendum," *BSAC* 25 (1983) 61–64.

————, "Additions to the prosopography of Aphrodito from the Coptic documents," *BSAC* 25 (1983) 91–94.

———, "Coptic sources: A problem in the sociology of knowledge," *BSAC* 26 (1984) 1–7.

———, "Notes on the social structure of late antique Aphrodito," *BSAC* 26 (1984) 65–77.

———, "The panegyric on Justin II by Dioscorus of Aphrodito," *Byzantion* 54 (1984) 575–585.

———, "An ecclesiastical letter from Antinoë," *Muséon* 97 (1984) 187–195.

———, "A Coptic cession of land by Dioscorus of Aphrodito," *II International Congress of Coptic Studies* (Rome 1985) 159–166.

———, "Missing pieces of the Dioscorus archive," *Eleventh BSC Abstracts* (Toronto 1985) 30. (To appear in *Chronique d'Egypte*.)

———, "Egyptian elements in the *Christus Patiens*," *BSAC* 27 (1985) 45–51.

———, "Three cultures under Arab rule: The fate of Coptic," *BSAC* 27 (1985) 61–70.

———, "The isopsephistic poem on St. Senas by Dioscorus of Aphrodito," *ZPE* 62 (1986) 51–53.

———, "The first appearance of Aphrodito in the papyri," *ZPE* 62 (1986) 54.

———, "Dioscorus of Aphrodito and John Philoponus," *Studia Patristica* 18 (Kalamazoo 1987) I.163–168.

———, "Further notes on the Greek-Coptic glossary of Dioscorus of Aphrodito," *Glotta* 64 (1986) 253–257.

———, "*P.Cair.Masp.* II 67188ᵛ 1–5: Dioscorus' 'gnostica,'" *Tyche* 2 (Vienna 1987), 95–97.

Malz, G., "Papyri of Dioscorus: Publications and emendations," *Studi Calderini-Paribeni* 2 (Milan 1957) 345–356.

Martin, V., "A letter from Constantinople," *JEA* 15 (1929) 96–102.

Maspero, J., "Etudes sur les papyrus d'Aphrodité," *BIFAO* 6 (1908) 75–120, 7 (1909) 47–102, 8 (1910) 97–152.

———, "Un dernier poète grec de l'Egypte, Dioscore, fils d'Apollos," *REG* 24 (1911) 426–481.

———, *Organisation militaire de l'Egypte byzantine* (Paris 1912).

———, "Horapollon et la fin du paganisme égyptien," *BIFAO* 11 (1914) 163–195.

Papini, L., "Notes on the formulary of some Coptic documentary papyri from Middle Egypt," *BSAC* 25 (1983) 83–89.

———, "Due biglietti oracolari cristiani," in *Trenta testi greci,* ed. M. Manfredi (Florence 1983) 68–70.

———, "Annotazioni sul formulario giuridico di documenti copti del VI secolo," *XVII Congresso internazionale di papirologia* III (Naples 1984) 767–776.

———, "Biglietti oracolari in copto dalla Necropoli Nord di Antinoe," *II International Congress of Coptic Studies* (Rome 1985) 245–256.

Pedersen, F. S., "On professional qualifications for public posts in late antiquity," *Class.etMed.* 31 (1975) 161–213.

Poethke, G., "Metrocomiae und Autopragie in Ägypten," in *Graeco-Coptica,* ed. P. Nagel (Halle 1984) 37–44.

Quibell, J., "Kom Ishgaw," *ASAE* 3 (1902) 85–88.

Remondon, R., "*P.Hamb.* 56 et *P.Lond.* 1419: notes sur les finances d'Aphrodito du viᵉ siècle au viiiᵉ," *Cd'E* 40 (1965) 401–430.

Robinson, J. M., "The discovering and marketing of Coptic manuscripts," in *The roots of Egyptian Christianity*, ed. B. Pearson and J. Goehring (Philadelphia 1986) 2–25.

————, "Reconstructing the first Christian monastic library," Smithsonian Institution Libraries lecture, 15 September 1986.

Rouillard, G., *L'administration civile de l'Egypte byzantine*² (Paris 1928).

Saija, A., "La metrica di Dioscoro di Afroditopoli," *Studi A. Ardizzone* 2 (Rome and Messina 1978) 823–849.

Salomon, R. G., "A papyrus from Constantinople," *JEA* 34 (1948) 98–108.

Šanda, A., *Johannis Philoponi opuscula monophysita* (Beirut 1930).

Schiller, A. A., "Interrelation of Coptic and Greek papyri," *Festschrift F. Oertel* (Bonn 1964) 107–119.

————, "The courts are no more," *Studi E. Volterra* (Milan 1969) 469–502.

————, "The fate of imperial legislation in late Byzantine Egypt," in *Legal thought in the USA under contemporaray pressures*, ed. J. N. Hazard and W. J. Wagner (Brussels 1970) 41–60.

Shisha-Halevy, A., *Coptic grammatical categories* (Rome 1986).

Steinwenter, A., *Das Recht der koptischen Urkunden* (Munich 1955).

Timm, S., *Das christlich-koptische Ägypten in arabischer Zeit* III (Wiesbaden 1985) 1438–1461, s.v. 'Kom Išqaw.'

Torp, H., "Leda Christiana," *Acta Inst.Rom.Norv.* 4 (1969) 101–112.

van der Wal, N., "Die Schreibweise der dem lateinischen entlehnten Fachworte in der frühbyzantinischen Juristensprache," *Scriptorium* 37 (1983) 29–53.

van Roey, A., "Les fragments trithéites de Jean Philopon," *OLP* 11 (1980) 135–163.

Vikan, G., "The so-called 'Sheikh Ibada' group of early Coptic sculptures," *Third BSC Abstracts* (New York 1977) 15–16.

Viljamaa, T., *Studies in Greek encomiastic poetry of the early Byzantine period* (Helsinki 1968).

Volbach, W. F., *Elfenbeinarbeiten der Spätantike*³ (Mainz 1976).

Wenger, L., "Ein mündliches Testament in koptischer Sprache (P.Lond. V 1709)," in *Aus Novellenindex und Papyruswörterbuch* (Munich 1928) 45–58.

Winkelmann, F., "Ägypten und Byzanz vor der arabischen Eroberung," *Byzantinoslavica* 40 (1979) 161–182.

————, "Die Stellung Ägyptens im oströmisch-byzantinischen Reich," in *Graeco-Coptica*, ed. P. Nagel (Halle 1984) 11–35.

Wipszycka, E., *Les ressources et les activités économiques des églises en Egypte du IVᵉ au VIIIᵉ siècle* (Brussels 1972).

————, "Le degré d'alphabétisation en Egypte byzantine," *RevEtAug* 30 (1984) 279–296.

Zaloscer, H., *Die Kunst im christlichen Ägypten* (Vienna 1974).

INDEX OF SOURCES

A: GREEK PAPYRI

BGU
VII 1630 64

BKT
V 1 137–146
VI 10677 19

P. Apoll.
69 . . . . 75n.42

P.Berol.
9799 . . . . 75, 131–134
10580 137–146
13894 . . . . 94, 104, 143

P.Cair.Masp.
I 67002   21, 24, 26–29, 96, 114, 143–144
67003 . . . . 24, 26, 29–31
67004 . . . . 75, 115
67005 . . . . 75n.42, 78
67006 85
67009 . . . . 47, 75, 100, 115
67019 . . . . 75n.42
67024r 11
67024v 11
67025 11
67026 11
67027 11
67028 11
67032 . . . . 1, 10–11, 124
67052 122
67055 . . . . 12, 134–136
67087 10

67089 . . . . 115, 117
67095 10
67096 . . . . 6, 29, 134
67097r 112–113
67097v 39, 66, 86, 112–121
67108 10
67109r 12
67109v 10
67116 10
67118 10
67120 96–102
67121 75
II 67126 75
67127 10
67128 . . : 10
67129 10
67130 11
67131 76–81
67134 144
67135 144
67136 136
67151 . . . . . 13, 50–54, 79, 81, 115n.73
67152 13
67153 75
67154 . . . . 75, 133
67155 . . . . 75, 81n.51
67156 . . . . 81n.51
67158 12
67159 . . . . 81n.51
67161 12
67162 12
67163 . . . . 81n.51
67164 13

P.Cair.Masp. (continued)

67166 12
67168 65
67169 13
67169 bis 13
67170 .... 11n.40, 12, 23
67171 .... 11n.40, 12, 23
67172 .... 72, 104
67173 .... 72, 104
67174 .... 72, 104
67175 71
67177 63–66
67178 .... 90, 107, 125–126
67179 .... 12, 78, 88–91, 111
67180 108–111
67181 108–111
67182 121–123
67183 .... 65, 72–76
67184 .... 65, 121–125
67185 .... 75, 105, 107
67187 .... 102–103, 105, 130–131
67188 .... 55n.98, 128–129
67205 100
67251 10
III 67279 .... 13, 100, 106–107
67283 .... 8n.24, 10, 21–22, 144
67289 .... 75n.42
67299 .... 13, 115
67303 11
67309 12
67311 .... 13, 75
67312 .... 13n.43, 107
67314 .... 12, 35–36
67315 91–96
67316 .... 75, 103–104, 129–130
67317 137–146
67319 .... 12, 144
67321 75
67325 .... 14, 55–56
67326 144
67327 144
67330 78
67332 11
67338 127–128
67353v 39–41, 78, 130

P.Eg.Mus.S.R.
3733 A6r 10

P.Flor.
III 280 122
295 79
297 122

377 65
390 130

P.Fouad
87 65

P.Freer
1 .... 30, 70
2 .... 7, 30

P.Grenf.
I 62 .... 35n.55
II 112 19

P.Hamb.
III 231 12

P.Haun.
II 31 .... 49n.85

P.Köln
IV 172 143

P.Lit.Lond.
98 68–72
99 108–111
100C 81–84
100D 86–88
100F 79, 84–85
100G 78, 85–86
101 12
239 .... 79, 80

P.Lond.
V 1660 .... 82, 144
1661 11
1665 144
1666 144
1671 122
1672 78
1674 .... 47–50, 75, 77
1677 .... 24–26, 144
1686 .... 11n.40, 12, 23, 143–144
1689 144
1692 11
1702 144
1708 .... 12, 31–34, 44
1710 12
1712 75
1713 .... 75, 81n.51
1714 .... 81n.51, 107
1761 122
1788 122
1802 122
1821 ...... 54, 90, 120–121, 157n.32
1844 122

P.Mich.
XIII 669 12

P.Michael.
40 .... 29, 143
41 143
42 143

P.Oxy.
I 126 32
XVIII 722 79
XX 2267 44

P.Rein.
II 82 68–72

P.Robinson
29 99

P.Ross.-Georg.
III 48 .... 6n.17

P. Ryl.
I 17 .... 9n.29

PSI
I 76 65
IV 432 112
VII 836 122
845 .... 9n.29

P.Turner
10 .... 79, 106, 143
54 148

P.Walters
517 66–68

SB
I 1896 122
4369 112
4890 107
VI 9453 142

SPP
III 253 64
XV 250 79
XX 248 122

III 321 44
350 75

B.L.Ms.Or.
6202 .... 19n.25
6203 .... 19n.25
6204 .... 19n.25

BM
439 44
449 .... 75n.42
450 .... 75n.42
464 .... 75n.42
514 .... 75n.42

CLT
5 34

CO
189 44

Ep
II 149–152 19
247 68
260 44
272 44
300 68
520 44
575 44

KRU
16 44
44 44
67 44
89 44
100 44

O.Vat.
19901 122

P.Alex.inv.
689 .... 13, 29, 36–39, 44

P.Berol.
11349 .... 11n.40, 22–23, 118n.78

P.Cair.Masp.
II 67176r 13, 29, 36–39, 44, 123
III 67353r 13, 41–45, 85, 123

P.Lond.
V 1709 .... 13, 45–47, 85

P.Vat.Copti Doresse
1 .... 11, 20, 143
5 .... 20, 97, 143

B: COPTIC PAPYRI

Bal
191ff. 75n.42

BKU
I 97 34

P.Yale
  inv. 1862 75

Ryl
  33 104

ST
  172 44

VC
  6 44

WS
  100 44

C: LEGISLATIVE SOURCES

Justinian
  Codex I.33.5 and 34.3 55
      III.1.14.1 119
      VI.23.21 50
  Edict XIII 117
  Novel V 44–45
      VII 30n.45
      LXXIV 34
      CXXVIII 48

Justin II
  Novel II 30n.45, 75

D: BIBLE

Genesis 15:5 119

Exodus 7–11 . . . . 21, 24
       31:18 . . . . 71, 78

Numbers 24:6 72

Deuteronomy 10:19 100

Psalms 1:2 28
     18:6 72
     24:7–10 104
     39:13 50
     44:8 141
     63:11 40

     64:10–12 126
     64:14 126
     84:11 90
     91:13 69
     118(119) 142

Proverbs 23:31 87

Ecclesiastes 4:1 27
      4:2–3 28
      5:18 51

Song of Songs 2:1 . . . . 90, 126
       5:11 84
       5:15 72

Isaiah 1:26 71

Jeremiah 2:23 100

Ezekiel 17:23 72

Jonah 4:11 27

Mark 4:37–41 128

Luke 1:28 99
     1:63 85
     10:29, 36–37 78
     11:4 95

John 3:1–2 109
     4:10–14 106
     14:18 49
     14:27 136
     15:19 136
     17:14–16 136

Acts 12:23 40

Ephesians 4:13 49

1 Timothy 6:14 106

Hebrews 11:12 119
     12:28a 119

James 1:27 106

1 Peter 1:19 78
     5:8 28

2 Peter 3:14 106

GENERAL INDEX

Aelius Aristides, 103
Agathias, 16, 61, 102
Alcaeus, 117
Anacreon, 94, 104, 119–121
Aphrodito, topography of, 5–8
Aphrodito papyri, discovery of, 2–4, 20
Apion family, 1, 15, 33, 150
Apollinarius (pseudo-), *Metaphrasis Psalmorum*, 57–146 *passim*
Apollonius Rhodius, 65
Apollos (father of Dioscorus), 1, 9, 12, 14, 20–22, 29, 38–39, 149
Athanasius, Duke of the Thebaid, 45, 94, 113–114
Athanasius of Alexandria, 61, 65
autopragia (independent tax collection), 1, 10–11, 24, 117, 150

Blemmyes, 115, 145

Callimachus, 90, 94, 104, 127
Callinicus, Duke of the Thebaid, 13, 91–93
Chalcedon, council of, 8, 48n.81, 98, 144, 148, 151
Christodorus of Coptos, 60, 131
Christus Patiens, 60, 78, 96
Chronicon Paschale, 127
Colluthus (poet), 60, 68, 82, 109
Colluthus (saint), 97, 102, 152
Colluthus of Antinoë (official), 60, 68, 82, 96–97, 100–103

Constantine of Lycopolis, 153
Constantinople, 1, 10, 21, 65, 124, 131, 149
Coptic language, 19, 62–63, 154–157
Cosmas Indicopleustes, 75
Cyril of Alexandria, 19, 25, 32, 48–49, 61–62, 65, 95, 116n.74, 151–152; *in Isa.*, 143; *in Jul.*, 106
Cyril of Scythopolis, 34, 40
Cyrus of Panopolis, 59n.6, 60, 66

Damascius of Alexandria, 88n.58, 109, 144n.83
Damian, Patriarch of Alexandria, 9, 19, 62, 153
Dioscorus I, Patriarch of Alexandria, 110, 144, 148
Domninus, *cancellarius*, 103–105
Dorotheos of Antinoë, 24–25, 98–99

Egypt, personification of, 145
Elias of Alexandria, 86
Epiphanius of Salamis, 44n.72
Euphorion, 127

Flavius Strategius (Apion), 150

George Grammaticus, 120, 129
George of Pisidia, 75

Harpocration of Panopolis, 59
Hesychius, 107
Horapollon, 17n.9, 144

Jacob Baradaeus, 9
John, Duke of the Thebaid, 14, 59, 105, 134-146
John Chrysostom, 94, 122
John Lydus, 32, 33n.50, 150
John Moschus, 34
John of Gaza, 61, 83
John of Hermopolis, 153
John of Parallos, 153
John Philoponus, 19, 40, 52, 61, 65, 86, 94, 143, 149-150; *in Anal.*, 55; *in De Gen. et Corr.*, 90, 100; *in De Philos.*, 106
Julian the Egyptian (poet), 61
Justinian I, emperor, 10-11, 22-23, 98, 115, 134; *De recta fide*, 65
Justin II, emperor, 11-12, 39-40, 45, 72-75, 96, 114, 133-134, 141-142

Latinisms, in Dioscorus, 35, 46, 51, 53, 58, 75
Leontius of Neapolis, 34, 40

Macarius of Antaeopolis (Tkow), 62
Malalas, 34, 127, 130, 143-144
Maurice, emperor, 55
Menander, *Sententiae* 71, 79
Menander, Rhetor, 66, 93-94, 98, 104-105, 111, 145
Menas, pagarch of Antaeopolis, 23-28, 40
Musaeus, 60-61, 87, 109

Nestorius, 148
Nonnus of Panopolis, 9, 30, 60-61, 57-146 *passim*, 149

Olympiodorus of Alexandria (biblical commentator), 27
Olympiodorus of Alexandria (philosopher), 80, 98, 141
Olympiodorus of Thebes, 60, 66
Oppian, 72

Palladius, *comes sacri consistorii*, 1, 10
Palladius, *Historia Lausiaca*, 100
Pamprepius of Panopolis, 60, 66, 81, 83, 90, 94, 131
Panolbios (poet), 70

patronage, 58, 117-119
Paul, Saint, 105
Paul of Alexandria, 99n.67
Paul the Silentiary, 61
Pbow (monastery of Pachomius), 6
Pindar, 70, 136
Plotinus, 27, 90
Plutarch, 127
Proclus, 102
Procopius, 58n.3, 102
Psimanobet (great-grandfather of Dioscorus), 6, 9, 149

Quintus Smyrnaeus, 70, 130

Romanos Melodes, 67, 116
Rufus of Hypselis, 5, 62

Senas (saint), 11, 40, 61, 152
Serapion of Thmuis, 117
Severus of Antioch, 9, 48, 65, 148
Shenoute, 2, 5-6, 9, 62, 95, 110, 128, 153, 158
Sinouthios (brother of Dioscorus), 1, 10, 12, 149
Sophia, empress, 114, 134
Sophronius of Jerusalem, 120
Stephen of Heracleopolis, 153

taxiarch, 33-34
Theodora, empress, 10, 21-22, 144
Theodore, bishop of the Pentapolis, 65, 67-68, 72
Theodoret, 119
Theodosius, emperor, 74
Theodosius, Patriarch of Alexandria, 9
Theophylact Simocatta, 94
Thucydides, 21, 27, 34, 133
Tribonian, 16
Triphiodorus of Atripe, 59, 90, 109, 130

Victor (cousin of Dioscorus), 10
Victor, prefect, 76-77
Vision of Dorotheos, 6, 60

Zosimus (historian), 122

PLATES

1. The region of Aphrodito

2. Aphrodito (Kom Ishgaw) in 1980

3. Canal outside Aphrodito

4. The Coptic church at Kom Ishgaw

5. Detail of *P. Cair. Masp.* III 67353r (Coptic)

6. *P. Cair. Masp.* II 67177

7. *P. Cair. Masp.* III 67315

8. *P. Cair. Masp.* I 67120

9. *P. Cair. Masp.* I 67097, top

10. *P. Cair. Masp.* I 67097, below

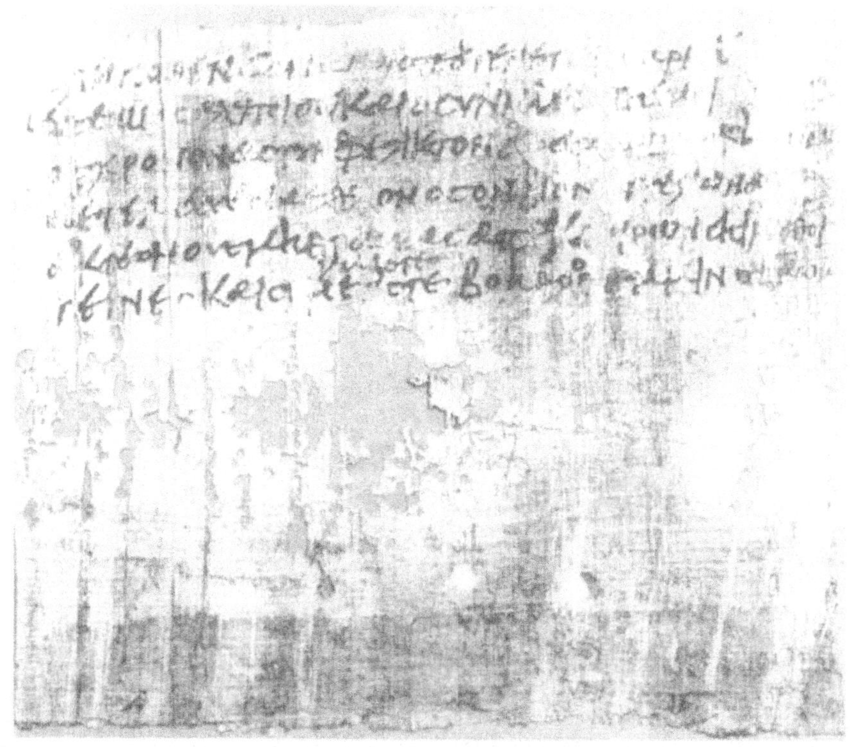

11. *P. Cair. Masp.* II 67182

Printed in Dunstable, United Kingdom

85050413R00119